READING DERRIDA / THINKING PAUL

Cultural Memory
in
the
Present

Mieke Bal and Hent de Vries, Editors

READING DERRIDA / THINKING PAUL

On Justice

Theodore W. Jennings, Jr.

STANFORD UNIVERSITY PRESS

STANFORD, CALIFORNIA

2006

Stanford University Press
Stanford, California

Printed in the United States of America
on acid-free, archival-quality paper

Library of Congress Cataloging-in-Publication Data

Jennings, Theodore W.
    Reading Derrida / thinking Paul : on justice / Theodore W. Jennings, Jr.
      p.   cm. — (Cultural memory in the present)
    Includes bibliographical references and index.
    ISBN 0-8047-5267-2 (cloth : alk. paper)
    ISBN 0-8047-5268-0 (pbk. : alk. paper)
      1. Bible. N.T. Romans—Philosophy.   2. Justice—Biblical teaching.
    3. Derrida, Jacques.   4. Justice (Philosophy)   I. Title.   II. Series.

BS2665.6.J8J46   2005
227'.106—DC22
                                                                    2005013562

Original Printing 2006

Last figure below indicates year of this printing:
15   14   13   12   11   10   09   08   07   06

For
Hendrikus Boers

Contents

This essay, or thought experiment, is an effort to suggest a certain relationship between the attempt to understand Paul's texts (most especially Romans) and the ways in which Derrida pursues certain themes integral to what I take to be some of Paul's central concerns.

The essay has a particular precipitating occasion—the announcement of a discussion with Derrida organized in connection with the Society of Biblical Literature. This announcement and the ensuing call for papers served as the catalyst for my attempt to put down on paper ideas that have occurred to me as I have taught a seminar on Romans over the last several years, a time when, for reasons unrelated to that seminar, I have also taken up, as a kind of hobby, the reading of Derrida. What I have found again and again is that the latter pastime has shed unexpected light on, as well as confirmation of, some of the things I have been trying to clarify with my students as we have read Romans together. This has been especially true of ideas about justice and law, gift and exchange, duty and debt.

In attempting to think through some of these connections in a more deliberate way, I have not sought to produce a treatise (still less a commentary) on Romans nor an independent treatise on the thought of Derrida. I do not have the competence for the latter, and the former (a rereading of Romans) is a quite different project that this one both interrupts and complements. Instead, I have sought to indicate some of those issues in the attempt to think Paul's argument where a reading of Derrida seems to me to be most helpful. I hope that what I write will be an incitement (and an invitation) to others to take up the question of the relation of deconstruction to the themes and issues of biblical theology generally and to Pauline theology more particularly. At the same time, I hope to offer a case for repositioning the reading of Paul within the context of philosophical rather than exclusively theological (or "historical" or even ecclesial) reflection.

I am not unaware that the procedure here adopted entails a certain violence to the texts both of Derrida and of Paul, for it requires extracting bits and pieces of their respective arguments in order to show points of convergence and illumination. In the case of Derrida, that means that the reader of this text does not have a sense of the extreme care and precaution often taken by Derrida in the patient work of deconstruction. In the case of Paul, this means that the forward movement of his overall argument is regularly halted or even reversed in order to make the point that his concern is precisely with the question of justice. I hope, however, that the violence of this reading is to a certain degree mitigated by its attempt to undo the greater violence that has come from the supposition that neither author is really concerned with the question of justice.

Because this work would not have been undertaken at this point without the catalyst of SBL discussions, I must express my gratitude to those who organized these sessions concerned with deconstruction and biblical interpretation, especially Yvonne Sherwood. An early version of Chapter 4 of this book was published in the volume that resulted from those discussions, *Derrida's Bible*, edited by Yvonne Sherwood (London: Palgrave Press, 2004).

Of course I could not have thought of pursuing this project had I not already been engaged in the reading of Romans. That I have wrestled with Paul fruitfully (and otherwise) for many years I owe to the tutelage and friendship of Hendrik Boers. For more than a third of a century, our friendship has been mediated by way of conversations about Paul. The reading of Paul requires a context, and this has been provided first by the Seminario Metodista de Mexico, where I first ventured to teach Romans, and then, for the last several years, by the Chicago Theological Seminary. I am grateful to the friends and students who have been a constant source of inspiration and admonition in this task.

The reading of Derrida also began in the context of friendship, first many years ago with Jim Creech and Peggy Kamuf. It resumed after a too-long hiatus under the prodding of my colleagues at the Chicago Theological Seminary, especially BoMyung Seo, Benny Tat-siong Liew, Kunitoshi Sakai, and Virgil (Bill) Brower. I am especially grateful to those who were able to read the manuscript at early stages of its preparation and made important encouraging as well as cautionary interventions. Hendrikus Boers and Peggy Kamuf read the first chapters, and Benny Tat-siong Liew and Virgil Brower read an early version of the entire book. Their insightful comments have provoked me to greater clarity. Norris Pope, Angie Michaelis, and Tim Roberts of Stanford University Press have been unfailingly helpful and cheerful in the long process of seeing this project through to publication. I am also grateful to Wil Brant and Adam Kotsko for their assistance in the preparation of the manuscript for publication. Without the generous assistance of Kunitoshi Sakai it would have been impossible to keep track of the many projects in which I am involved, and this work would have been greatly delayed. And without the forbearance of Ronna Case, the obsessional neurosis that any book project involves would have been unthinkable.

READING DERRIDA / THINKING PAUL

1

Introduction

    The reading of Paul's letter to the Romans has largely been restricted to a confessional/ecclesiastical ghetto of doctrinal interest. As a consequence, Paul's concern for the question of justice has been transformed into a question of interior or private righteousness. This has been accompanied, especially in the Protestant era of exegesis, by a "forensic" view of justification that has severed justification from justice and turned "salvation" into a private affair between the believer and God. As a result, Levinas can suppose that the complex of doctrines thus derived make explicable the history of Christian/western atrocity, including the Holocaust.[1] The God of this reading cares for belief instead of justice, and remedy for crime is found not in restitution and transformation on the plane of the ethical or political, but in the virtuality of an imagined relation to an indulgent divine.

    Until recently the thought of Derrida has been associated in the minds of its critics with a nihilistic evisceration of ethical and sociopolitical "norms" that make it also irrelevant for issues of ethics and justice. More recently, it has become less easy to ignore the ethical and political significance of deconstruction. In a sense, Derrida has been more fortunate than Paul in that he has been able to fight back against his interpreters.

    In this chapter, I wish to demonstrate several ways that a reading of Derrida may help to rethink some of the issues with which Paul was concerned, especially in his letter to those who were then living in the capital of the empire, Rome. The task, then, of this essay, or thought experiment, is to determine how some of the issues with which Paul is wrestling in Romans are illuminated by a reading of Derrida. I will maintain that Derrida's reflections on justice, law, gift, duty, debt, welcome, and cosmopolitanism, among others, provide clarification of key issues in Paul's letter to the Romans and, moreover, help to make intelligible some of the tensions, ambiguities, or ambivalences in Paul's thought that have often puzzled interpreters of Romans.

I will begin with indicating some of the ways in which Paul may be rescued from the dogmatic confinement in which his theological "friends" have imprisoned him. This prepares the way for opening this text through an engagement with the thought of a contemporary philosopher whose concerns, I will argue, often intersect those of Paul. In order to set the stage for this reflection, it will be necessary to show that both Paul and Derrida are concerned with the question of justice. Because each has been interpreted in ways that either deny or conceal this concern, it will be important to suggest at least the initial plausibility of focusing on this theme in their respective work. In addition, I will also point to some of the ways in which Derrida's writings do at least occasionally make explicit reference to Paul, even though these references do not generally touch on the themes of most importance for this essay.

Having thus prepared the ground for a substantive discussion, I will turn to what seems to me to be the crux of the issue to which both Paul and Derrida respond: the relation and tension between the claim of justice and the demands of the law. I will show that some of the distinctions and reflections introduced by Derrida help to clarify the problem with which Paul is wrestling, namely the possibility and necessity of justice "outside the law."

But on what basis is a distinction possible between justice and law? In particular, what is it about law, law as such or in general, positive law or moral law, that makes it both necessary to justice and yet fundamentally at odds with the claim for justice? For Paul, this issue seems to come to a head with the condemnation and execution of God's messiah, that is, with the one who is the bearer of the divine justice. For Derrida, following Benjamin, the interior deconstruction of law relative to justice comes to a head in that which exposes the violence inherent in the foundation and perpetuation of law. This enables us to think the cross in relation to the problematic of justice and law.

But if law does not itself serve as the basis of justice, how then does justice come to be in some sense thinkable? For Paul, the contrary of law (but not of justice), I will argue, is grace. In the contemporary world no one has done as much to clarify the meaning of grace/gift as Derrida. Accordingly, I will suggest that the impossible possibility of grace/gift as this has been reflected on by Derrida helps again to think what it is that Paul is struggling to say.

The problem with gift, however, as Derrida has shown, is that it falls inexorably back into a logic of exchange that abolishes or threatens to abolish its character as gift. Ineluctably, our thinking of gift returns us to the sphere of debt in which no gift is possible. This insight helps at least to make clear certain tensions in Paul's thought as he struggles to go beyond debt and work and exchange in a thinking of the gift and of a response adequate or appropriate to the gift (beyond what he calls "works"). It is precisely in this context that Derrida has dealt often with the question of a duty beyond debt, a theme that Paul also engages in his reference to a love of the neighbor that "owes no one anything" and which "fulfils the law."

It is within this same context of explicating the significance of gift for justice that Paul is also drawn to the theme of a welcoming of the other, a theme much more exhaustively explored by Derrida in his many reflections on hospitality. In this connection, the more recent work of Derrida has focused on the question of a certain cosmopolitanism that he identifies as basic to the question of international politics today and that he also finds to be rooted in the reflections of a certain Paul, the Paul of Ephesians. We will see to what extent this theme itself is also based in some of Paul's reflections in Romans.

Toward the end of these reflections, we will turn to a theme that has increasingly occupied the attention of Derrida, that of forgiveness. This will enable us once again to address the problem that justification in Paul has often been understood as merely forgiveness and so has been severed from the question of justice. Derrida's reflections on forgiveness may help us get a fix on the limits of this notion in Paul and on its subordination to, or facilitation of, the question of justice.

Throughout his reflections on these matters, Derrida has insisted on the importance of a certain eschatological reserve relative to justice, the gift, and so on. Throughout these reflections, I will be wondering whether the thought of Paul may be deficiently eschatological owing to the presupposition that the messiah has already come or whether, even here, Paul has been significantly misinterpreted by his ecclesiastical friends who seek to defuse the eschatological situation in favor of an institutional or doctrinal foundation. However, to a significant degree, the present study will only prepare the ground for a more sustained treatment of this question.

In thus trying to think Paul in relation to a reading of Derrida, it is not the case that I will seek to show all in Paul, or even in Romans, that can be illuminated by a reading of Derrida. Rather, my focus is on the question of justice and how precisely this question as it is addressed by Derrida helps to illumine that in Paul which also may be concerned with this question. Many issues that may also be clarified in Paul's argument through a reading of Derrida will be barely touched on here.[2] Moreover, I do not suppose that Derrida is the only philosopher who may be of assistance in rethinking Paul today. Indeed, I hope that the rereading I propose will encourage others to undertake readings of Paul in relation to other forms of contemporary philosophy.[3] Precisely by extricating Paul from the clutches of his ecclesiastical defenders and expropriators as well as the stifling embrace of his theological friends, it may be possible to engage in multiple "philosophical readings" of Paul. But for that to be possible, it may be helpful to suggest how Paul may be understood by reading one especially important "example" of philosophical discourse today. I leave aside for now the question of whether deconstruction is simply one example among other philosophical discourses that may illumine what Paul is up to or, on the contrary, is exemplary—that is, more than an example, but somehow resonant with Paul in ways that, for example, liberal or conservative political philosophy are not.

Paul in Public

In order to approach the question of a reading together of Derrida and Paul, it will be necessary to take out a certain line of credit in the form of a set of hypotheses that cannot be verified in the space that is available for this task. The collateral for this line of credit is simply the work I have attempted to do over the last several years in my seminars on Romans, where I have sought to develop a theopolitical reading of that document. I will therefore simply identify certain theses or hypotheses in order to facilitate the more limited treatment of certain Pauline themes in this essay.

Humanistic Reading

Paul is all too often approached by the interpreter as if he were the private possession of Christendom, as if his concerns and interests were reducible to the dogmatic interests and concerns of an institutionally segregated mentality. On the contrary, I believe that Paul may be read as an intellectual who is struggling with issues that may be of concern to anyone who thinks seriously and deeply about the human situation. In supposing this, I align myself with the project of Hendrik Boers announced in *Theology out of the Ghetto*.[4] What this basically supposes is that Paul may be read also as a "philosopher" who is concerned with issues that may reasonably be thought to concern philosophy, then and now. Moreover, this means that the cogency of his treatment of these themes must be assessed in the same way that the cogency of other philosophical contributions are to be assessed; that is, without appeal to his presumed authority either as a vehicle of revelation or as a founder of an institution.[5]

Justice (Not Righteousness)

But with what questions or issues of this type is Paul concerned? With respect to a reading of Romans, it has regularly been supposed that Paul is concerned with issues of grace and law insofar as these bear on the question of the justice of God and the act of justifying human beings. This set of issues, which has an undoubted significance in this text (as well as Galatians), have, however, been sealed off from critical appreciation by the tactic of supposing them to deal with something that in English has been called "righteousness," a term that has been given a restricted religious meaning—a meaning, moreover, reduced to the interiority of the individual.[6] The thesis I propose is that the common distinction between, and differential deployment of, the terms *righteousness* and *justice* have served to obscure Paul's meaning and the significance of what he is up to. Although there have been occasional protests against this semantic and theological (and ideological) distinction and hierarchialization, the first to make clear the falsity and ideological functioning of this operation was José Porfirio Miranda, a Mexican biblicist and leftist intellectual and activist (and student of Levinas).[7] The first upshot of this proposal is that Paul's use of the terms based on the root *dik-* should always be translated as justice and never as righteousness in order to make clear, in a preliminary way, the problematic with which we are to deal here.[8] The second is that this entails that Paul is to be understood as seeking to make a contribution to the question of justice, a question that is of undoubted philosophical concern and lineage.

Sociopolitical Rather than Interior/Individual

A further hypothesis that will be developed in this discussion is that Paul's concern for justice is a concern for what might be termed the social or political question of justice. In philosophical terms, it seems clear that the question of justice has often been taken to have at least two sides: that of the just society, and that of the just person. The interplay between these questions is found in Plato and Aristotle, although there is a tendency in the period more contemporary to Paul to reduce the social to the individual dimension, as the question of a just constitution appropriate to the context of the city-state receded under the press of empire to be replaced with a concentration on the justice of the individual (Seneca, Epictetus, Marcus Aurelius, and so on). In contrast to this reduction, I suppose that Paul may be read as seeking to reinstate the question of justice at the level of something like civilization (or the empire) as a whole.

In order to make this clear, it may be helpful to return to some of the theses of José Porfirio Miranda who, like Derrida, was an assiduous reader of Levinas.[9] Porfirio Miranda maintains that "Paul's gospel has nothing to do with the interpretation, which for centuries has been given to it in terms of individual salvation. It deals with the justice which the world and peoples and society, implicitly but anxiously, have been awaiting" (179). But if this is true, then this throws into question the way in which Paul has generally been interpreted: "If the problem with which Paul is dealing is that of human civilization and not that of individuals as such, if what distresses Paul has dimensions much broader than those of the anthropological human subject, then the word 'justice' has acquired a meaning completely different from the one that customarily has been supposed" (176).

It is precisely in this way that Miranda already anticipates the form of the question of the relation of law and justice to which we will be directing our attention in the following chapters: "Paul's revolutionary and absolutely central message, that justice has been achieved without the law, would lack all force if this were not precisely the same justice that the law hoped to realize; this is the revolutionary and unprecedented core of his message" (152). Latin American liberation theology is not alone in attending to the political character of Paul's various concerns. North American and (some) European scholarship has begun to emphasize the political and imperial context of Paul's concerns. Dieter Georgi had already signaled the fruitfulness of such an approach as early as 1987. Two important collections of essays edited by Richard Horsley have subsequently emphasized the importance of this approach. However, unlike the Latin American contributions to which I have referred, these essays do not take up the question of the political or social meaning of Paul's concerns in Romans with justice and law, with grace and works.[10]

Jew and Gentile

Although it is often the case that Paul's reflections on the law are restricted in application to something like Jewish law or the law of Moses, I take it as axiomatic that Paul is concerned with law as such, with justice as such, with gift or grace as such. The Christian exegetical tradition that restricts the significance of what Paul says about the law to the law of Moses is complicit in a long history of Christian anti-Judaism and is unfounded in the texts of Paul. In this connection also Miranda has anticipated the direction of our argument. Thus he refers to Otto Michel's comment on Romans 7:1: "Paul is referring not only to the knowledge of the Mosaic law but also to the juridical thinking of antiquity" (183). In one of his relatively rare discussions of the Paul of Romans, Derrida too insists that the question here is not simply that of a particular kind of law but perhaps, of law as such.[11]

In general, then, the background to the readings I will propose of Paul in relation to Derrida is the supposition that Paul may be read outside the confessional ghetto to which he has been confined by his theological "friends" and that if this is done in relation to Romans, it will entail coming to terms with the theme of justice, not as confined to the private sphere and virtual realm of a pretended relation to the divine, but as opening to the philosophical and political sphere that both in antiquity and today concerns itself with the hope for a justice that goes beyond whatever has been codified by law as the instantiation of justice.

In general, then, the background to the reading together of Paul and Derrida that I embark upon is this: that in Romans (as well as Galatians) Paul is concerned to develop the thesis that justice is not and cannot be established through the law, but rather is in some way the consequence of grace or gift. The latter does not abolish the necessity of justice but on the contrary somehow is the inception of the very same justice that has also been the subject, aim, or legitimation of the law.

Why Derrida?

Derrida and the Question of Justice

That Derrida is concerned with the question of justice and its relation to the political, ethical, and indeed geopolitical sphere has been something not always obvious either to his critics or to his "friends." In particular in the United States, Derrida's thought has most often been influential in departments of literature, where the question of justice is less obviously thematized as such in academic publications. From the time of Derrida's address to the Cardozo School of Law first published in 1990,[12] however, this representation of Derrida and of what is called "deconstruction" has become less and less tenable.[13]

The relation of deconstruction to a concern for justice has been the theme of a number of texts to which I will be turning my attention in this essay. But it has also come to expression in "practical" terms in Derrida's own engagements with human rights activists in Prague, in the struggle against apartheid, in the "Algerian question," in the controversies swirling about immigration and amnesty in contemporary France, and so on. Somewhere "in between" the theoretical reflections of the texts that we will treat and the practical engagement to which I have alluded, there are also a series of references to the context of global injustice that have the quality of quasi-prophetic or oracular jeremiads that have come to pepper some of his more theoretical texts and that establish a kind of horizon of concern within which the theoretical and practical interventions take their bearings.

For example, in a text that we will have to consider later because of the way in which it develops the question of justice and law, Derrida reminds his readers/hearers as he writes/speaks of deconstruction "(and let us not forget, if we do not want to sink into ridicule or indecency, that we are comfortably installed here on Fifth Avenue—only a few blocks from the inferno of injustice)" (*Religion*, 272). The reference here is enclosed in the marks of parenthesis, as indicated, but we are entitled to ask, as Derrida does in many contexts, about which is the enclosed and which the enclosing. Does the context adverted to here (Fifth Avenue, the adjacent inferno of injustice) not enclose within parentheses the reflection on law and justice that textually encloses the reference to context?

We may also ask whether the reference to the context is not itself in a certain way exemplary. Of course the context is, one may say, geographically specific (New York, Fifth Avenue, Harlem), but in another way, it stands for features of a wider context, the so-called gap between rich and poor so much greater today than when Derrida spoke/read these words—not only in New York but also globally. As the event(s) of September 11, 2001, also make clear, New York remains the epicenter of this conflict that pits the cry for justice against and within the capital of commerce and of globalization.

A further example: Derrida's discussions of the other and of welcome to the stranger are situated within a concern for the plight of a world of refugees. In his "Word of Welcome" (*Adieu to Emmanuel Levinas*), there are references to this plight that serve to situate his own reading of Levinas (71, 101). Again, the "center" of this concern has a quite definite location: the church of St. Bernard, in which African immigrants huddled in sanctuary from the application of French government restrictions on the right of refuge, and where citizens of France sought to protect them from the force of the law in the name of justice.

Another example: the text *The Other Heading*—which treats essentially of the question of Europe—is regularly and insistently situated within the context of the Gulf war. In the introduction "Today," Derrida notes that the concern expressed in this essay (originally written for a newspaper) with Europe, with democracy, and the right to think and speak, was written "in the midst of what is called the 'Gulf' war" (3). One of his endnotes calls attention to "the today of this note, on the third day of what is called 'the Gulf War'" (116). And this is how it will also be referred to years after in the text of *Aporias* (16). In the latter text, there is a similar situating or contextualizing in relation, for example, to AIDS and to the bombardment (in 1993) of Sarajevo and Iraq (60).

In *The Gift of Death*, these examples abound, now under the heading of sacrifice, where the mere decision to do something or care for someone entails sacrificing the no less legitimate claim of a multitude of others. Thus in simply doing his work he is (I am) "sacrificing and betraying at every moment . . . my fellows who are dying of starvation or sickness . . . every one being sacrificed to every one else in this land of Moriah that is our habitat every second of every day" (69).

Similarly speaking of a civilized society and its presumed judgment on the crime or would-be crime of Abraham, he notes:

On the other hand, the smooth functioning of such a society, the monotonous complacency of its discourses on morality, politics and the law, and the exercise of its rights . . . are in no way impaired by the fact that because of the structure of the laws of the market that society has instituted and controls, because of the mechanisms of external debt and similar inequities, that same society *puts to* death or [. . .] *allows* to die of hunger and disease tens of millions of children [. . .] without any moral or legal tribunal ever being considered competent to judge such a sacrifice, the sacrifice of others to avoid being sacrificed oneself. Not only is it true that society participates in this incalculable sacrifice, it actually organizes it. The smooth functioning of its economic, political, and legal affairs, the smooth functioning of its moral discourse and good conscience presupposes the permanent operation of this sacrifice. (86)

These few examples, chosen almost at random from Derrida's texts, suggest what may be described as a sort of penumbra of serious ethical concern that surrounds the theoretical discussions with which, as a philosopher, Derrida is preoccupied. As we shall see, the sensitivity to the urgent ethical quandaries of our time goes beyond this peripheral awareness to animate a sophisticated and highly original grappling with the theoretical questions of justice that is both political and international or cosmopolitan in character.[14]

Derrida and the Question of Paul

But how is any of this related to a concern for Paul? Here I will only point to some of the direct references to Paul in some of the texts of Derrida. These references to Paul are usually made in passing. They may not constitute the most important contribution of Derrida to the understanding of Paul. Indeed, these references may sometimes seem to lead us into blind alleys of Pauline interpretation. Yet some attention to them is necessary if we are to see how the central concerns of Derrida do make contact with themes of Paul that are normally not referred to in Derrida's allusions, even or especially when what is in view is the Paul of Romans.

As we approach this issue, however, we may first note what Derrida says in his "The Force of Law" (in *Acts of Religion*) concerning deconstruction and its relation to both law and theology. "If it [deconstruction] had a proper place, such a deconstructive questioning or metaquestioning would be more 'at home' in law schools, perhaps, as it does happen, in theology or architecture departments, than in philosophy or literature departments" (236). As is well known, deconstruction, at least by that name, has made itself at home in literature departments in the United States and has even been known to be discussed in departments of philosophy both here and in France. But that deconstruction is or should be at home in departments of law and theology at the time this was first said could really be taken as a provocation. It is a provocation that is taken up from the side of law by Druscilla Cornell in *Philosophy of the Limit* but is only now beginning to find a voice in schools of theology, most especially in the reflections on biblical theology. Although there has been attention to deconstruction and its relation to talk of God, this has yet to move into the discussion of themes like justice and justification, gift and grace, faith and faithfulness.

In order to get some sense of the kind of references to Paul that we may find in Derrida's writing, I will offer a survey of some that I find most suggestive. Others will appear in my discussion later, when I come to specific questions (like that of cosmopolitanism) where Derrida makes use of Paul.

It should be noted that Derrida does mention Paul, and even Romans, in his "A Silkworm of One's Own." The principal discussion of Paul is reserved for the section "Sao Paulo, 4 December–8 December, 1995" (344–47). The references identify Paul with the problematic of circumcision and with that of veils. Romans is mentioned but not discussed, save for the odd and unsustainable suggestion that Paul thought that he was the first to distinguish between a circumcision of flesh and heart: "How to avoid hearing even here, in the name of this city, the *Epistle to the Romans*? Its author thought that he knew the literality of the letter. He prided himself on being able to distinguish, for the first time, he no doubt thought, wrongly, the circumcision of the heart, according to the breath and the spirit, from the circumcision of body or flesh, circumcision 'according to the letter'" (344). The note refers to Romans 2:25–29 but actually provides us with texts from Galatians 6:11–17. We then move to discussion of 1 Corinthians 11:2–16 and the question of veils. Romans, although mentioned, is not, it seems, even read in this connection. It is, of course true that the law and the prophets make this distinction between the circumcision of the heart and that of the flesh. But Paul can scarcely be ignorant of this; his argument in fact depends on this distinction concerning circumcision not being an innovation (see Deuteronomy 10:16; Jeremiah 4:4,

9:26; Ezekiel 44:9). After all, at this point Paul has explicitly addressed the one who knows the law (Romans 2:17) and so cannot be presumed to be ignorant of Deuteronomy 10:16, nor even of Jeremiah or Ezekiel. The very plausibility of Paul's argument relies on this not being something that he is the first to discover, but rather on its being a distinction well known to the interlocutor. It is therefore not clear, at least to this reader, how we are to understand Derrida's characterization of Paul.[15]

Derrida also refers, briefly, to Paul in *The Gift of Death*, where he is concerned with the phrase "fear and trembling" that has played such an important role in Kierkegaard's text of that name. Thus Derrida refers to Philippians 2:12, where Paul exhorts his readers to "work out your own salvation with fear and trembling," and then to Philippians 2:13: "For it is God who works in you both to will and to do of his good pleasure." In connection with the last passage, Derrida notes that "the text doesn't name God's pleasure but his will . . . not just in the sense of desiring the good, but as the will that judges well" (57). Here Derrida's reference to the text and to the words of the text serve to suggest the origin of the phrase "fear and trembling," which is the title of Kierkegaard's book on which he intends to comment. It may be noted, however, that Paul is concerned with the result, if we may put it like that, of a sacrifice not of the other but of the self, of self-interest ("have this mind which was in Messiah Jesus"). But it is not Derrida's intent here to read Paul, but to read Kierkegaard.

Paul also puts in an appearance in *Of Spirit: Heidegger and the Question*. Derrida has been commenting on Heidegger's closure of the "historical triangle" of language within which "spirit" is to be thought in Greek, Latin, and German and wondering about the foreclosure from this triangle of Hebrew—the Hebrew that shapes or reshapes the thinking of spirit in Greek and Latin at least. Indeed, he suggests that it is precisely this Hebrew thought of spirit that seems to oddly parallel what it is that Heidegger thinks can be thought, really thought, within the privileged domain of German, perhaps especially "old high German." It is in this context that Derrida writes:

without citing the evidence from the Gospels of a pneumatology which has the ineradicable relationship of translation with *ruah*, I will refer only to one distinction made by Paul in the First Epistle to the Corinthians [2:14] between *pneuma* and *psyche*. Corresponding to the distinction between *rauh* and *nephech*, it belongs— if it is not its opening—to the theologico-philosophical tradition in which Heidegger continues to interpret the relationship between *Geist* and *Seele*. (101)

And in the note that explicates this reference Derrida continues, "Let us make clear however that Paul distinguishes between the 'psychic man' [*psychikos anthropos*]—also translated as '*animalis homo*' or 'natural man'— and 'spiritual man' (*pneumatikos*) (*spiritualis*). The former does not accept what comes from the spirit of God [*ta tou pneumatos tou theou*]. Holy spirit which can also, as *pneuma*, be a *parole soufflée*" (137–38). The reference is to what Paul says here concerning the souled human who is incapable of understanding what the spirited human, the one who has been in a certain way invaded or taken over by divine spirit, is enabled to understand. That the distinction is comprehensible only starting from Hebrew (rather than Greek) seems quite correct.[16]

Paul also makes an appearance, indeed a spectral appearance, in an essay written many years earlier in Derrida's discussion of Kafka: "Before the Law" in *Acts of Literature*. This essay, based on a lecture of 1982, thus precedes by several years the discussion of the Law and Justice to which we will be turning. Although there is a great deal here that rewards attention, and to which I hope to return below, I wish at this point only to observe how it is that Paul comes into the discussion of Kafka's story.

The discussion of the decision, if it is that, of the man from the country to wait rather than enter into the place of the law produces this reflection from Derrida:

For the law is prohibition/prohibited [*interdit*]. Noun and attribute. Such would be the terrifying double bind of its own taking place. It is prohibition: this does not mean that it prohibits, but that it is itself prohibited, a prohibited place. It forbids itself and contradicts itself by placing the man in its own contradiction: one cannot reach the law, and in order to have a rapport of respect with it, one must not have a rapport with the law, one must interrupt the relation. One must enter into relation only with the law's representatives, its examples, its guardians. (203–4)

This wonderfully rich observation suggests that the representatives of the law, including positive laws (examples) are somehow distant from the law. What is critical for our limited purposes here in the reflection on Derrida and Paul, specifically the Paul of Romans, is that in the midst of the cited text, Derrida, in a footnote, cites Paul, the Paul of Romans, as follows:

This contradiction probably is not simply that of a law, which in itself supposes and therefore produces transgression, the active or actual relation to sin, to the fault. *Before the Law* perhaps gives rise to, in a kind of movement or trembling between the Old and the New Testament, a text which is both archived and altered, such as the Epistle to the Romans 7. More time needs to be devoted to the relationship between these two texts. Paul reminds his brothers, "people who know the law" that "the law exercises its power over man as long as he lives." And the death of Christ would be the death of this old law by which we "know" sin: dead along with Christ, we are released, absolved from this law, we are dead to this law, to the great age of its "letter," in any case, and we serve it in a new "spirit." And Paul adds that when he was without law, he lived; and when, along came the law, the commandment came, he died. (203)

This encrypted reference, encrypted in a note within the middle of a sentence, is remarkable. What seems to draw Derrida to think of Paul is precisely the situation of a contradiction with oneself into which one is thrust by a relation to the law. It is this coming into conflict with oneself that brings Derrida to think of Romans 7 with its all too well known articulation of what seems to be an internal conflict: "in my flesh I can will what is right, but I cannot do it. For I do not do the good I want, but the evil I do not want is what I do" (7:19). From the time of Augustine to that of Bultmann and even Altizer, this text has served to exemplify the situation of one caught in the double bind of the law. I am not of the view that what Paul writes here should be read (only) within the Augustinian tradition of reading, which makes of it a kind of autobiographical notice, nor even as referring to an interior drama that is somehow supposed to be universalizable.[17] I am far more inclined to see here an exposition of the situation of the one who seeks to be just but is thereby made complicitous in injustice. This is the very sort of bind that Derrida will discuss in *The Gift of Death*, when he reflects on the way in which the response to the claim of another entails the sacrifice of the claim of any other and all others who have as rightful a claim on my response. That this situation of conflicting and even opposing responsibilities exists is what makes clear that justice has not been actualized, that it remains distant, and that in any case, the good conscience is impossible. For even or precisely where one responds to the call or claim of justice, one is implicated in injustice all the more. That is, I incline to read even this text of Romans within the larger social or political context of the question of justice and responsibility rather than the autobiographical or interior conflict (invented by Augustine, I believe), which has served to render Paul safe for the imperial guardians of a certain Christianity.

In the text of Derrida that we have been referring to, there is a further reference to Paul in which he says that his own reading could have had "metonymical hand to hand engagements" with *The Problem of Our Laws* or with Paul's Epistle to the Romans 7" (217), and then shows what he calls "a prodigious scene of Talmudic exegesis" in chapter 9 of *The Trial*, within which is found the parable also known as "Before the Law."

An account of this Talmudic exegesis is interrupted by an account of his own Kafkaesque adventure with the Prague police (218). But in returning to the priest who is interpreting the story within the trial, Derrida remarks,

So we get a second exegetico-Talmudic wave from the priest, who is both, in some way, an abbot and a rabbi, a kind of Saint Paul, the Paul of the Epistle to the Romans who speaks according to the law, of the law and against the law, "whose letter has aged"; he is also the one who says that "apart from the law sin lies dead"; "I was once alive apart from the law, but when the commandment came, sin revived and I died." (Romans 7) [219]

That Derrida sees the combination of abbot and rabbi that he ascribes to the priest as a Paullike figure certainly is suggestive of the figure of Paul that has emerged in more recent biblical scholarship of a Paul who is decidedly Jewish and so, if this were not too anachronistic, also rabbinical, not only as regards Paul's biography, but also as regards his style of argumentation and frame of reference. The manner in which Paul may be properly read as one who speaks according to the law and against the law when speaking of the law will be the subject of our attention in the next chapter.

The passages I have cited from Derrida are at best representative of the kinds of references he makes to Paul and to the Paul of Romans. As I have indicated, it is not in these references that I find the greatest help in interpreting Paul. Indeed, there seems to be something of a tendency to read Paul through the concerns of the theologian who has transmitted a certain paulinism to the West, namely Augustine. This results, to my mind, in a certain traditionalism in some of Derrida's readings of Paul. Toward the end of the present essay, we will discover a rather more daring reading of a certain Paul in connection with the question of cosmopolitanism and international law.

At the end of his reading of Kafka's "Before the Law," Derrida remarks on the narrated glimpse of "the silver image of some saint" in the gloom of the corridor and suggests, "Saint Paul perhaps" (220). Whether or not the ghost of Paul may be said to haunt Kafka's pages, we will certainly have occasion in the reading of several of Derrida's texts to wonder to what extent they are haunted by the ghost of Paul, and of a Paul who wrote far more than the seventh chapter of Romans.

Nietzsche, Derrida, and Paul

In the text that I initially cited in this regard, "A Silkworm of One's Own," there is another reference, almost, to Paul that I will take to be an invitation to open a rather different discussion of Derrida in relation to Paul. In this text, Derrida says, "what I admire most in Nietzsche is his lucidity about Paul" (325). This a remarkable assertion for one well known for his admiration for Nietzsche, for his reading of Nietzsche.[18] The most admirable thing of this admirable thinker is his lucidity about Paul.[19]

But what is this lucidity? The text does not tell us. No note sends the curious reader unerringly to the inscription of this remarkable lucidity. It appears, however, that Derrida is referring to Nietzsche's *Daybreak* (paragraph 68), where we find his discussion of the one he calls "the first Christian," apart from whom, he supposes, Christianity would have been a quickly forgotten "little Jewish sect." But he says this in a very odd way, for he also maintains that had Paul ever been really read, then the fate of Christianity would have been the same: it would have been forgotten. "If the writings of Paul had been read . . . *really read* . . . Christianity would have long since ceased to exist" (39).[20] An odd foundation indeed: one that founds, and at the same time, one that, if it had been read, would have unfounded what is known as Christianity.

At first this may be supposed to be because of what Nietzsche identifies as Paul's very unpleasant personality: "one of the most ambitious and importunate souls, of a mind as superstitious as it was cunning" (39). That is how Paul had been described. And a subsequent description is, perhaps, even more pointed: "a very tormented, very pitiable, very unpleasant man who also found himself unpleasant" (40). Of course there is more than a grain of truth in this characterization of Paul's personality insofar as we can get at this at all from a reading of his letters. But Nietzsche has far bigger fish to fry here, for the foundation/antifoundation of Christianity has a more significant source than a possibly unpleasant personality. It is to this that Nietzsche turns: "He suffered from a fixed idea—or even more clearly, from a fixed question which was always present to him and would never rest: what is the Jewish law really concerned with? And in particular, what is the fulfillment of this law?" (40). I leave aside now the reconstructed biography of Paul, which is more than a bit maudlin and which reads Paul through the conflicted experience of Luther (Nietzsche's father was, after all, a Lutheran pastor), not to mention Augustine. Nietzsche describes a soul in torment, in conflict about the law. And he shows his hand, that he is thinking of Luther here, and so of a Paul perhaps first read by Luther (he has said there were no real readers of Paul for 1,500 years), when he adverts to what he sees as a parallel between Luther and Paul: "Luther may have felt a similar thing" and, a few lines later: "a similar thing happened to Paul" (40). (The reversal of this similitude, from Paul to Luther, from Luther to Paul, suggests the substitutability of these names, at least in certain respects.)

In this, and in the somewhat melodramatic depiction of Paul's struggle, Nietzsche may perhaps be somewhat less than lucid. For Paul, despite what his interpreters from the time of a certain Augustine have alleged, shows no such anterior or interior conflict about the law.[21] He can even describe himself in rather self-satisfied terms: in Philippians, he even says he was both a Pharisee and also blameless with respect to the law (3:6). What does seem to be the case, however, is that Paul, as Nietzsche says, "had become at once the fanatical defender and chaperone of this God and his law, and was constantly combating and on the watch for transgressors and doubters . . . and with the extremest inclination for punishment" (40). This much at least seems warranted by the texts. Paul himself can say of himself that he had been: "as to zeal, a persecutor of the church" (Philippians 3:6), and Acts 9:1 describes our hero as "Saul, still breathing threats and murder."

Then Nietzsche writes of a great reversal to which we shall return in a moment. But this reversal has as its consequence that "from now on he is the teacher of the destruction of the law" (40). And Nietzsche concludes: "This is the first Christian, the inventor of christianness. Before him there were only a few Jewish sectarians" (42). It is this critique of the law that Nietzsche identifies, it seems to me, as the (anti)foundation of Christianity.[22] And it is this that we will be concerned with in the next chapter: how is the law to be understood? But, as we shall see, the critique of the law is by no means a simple matter, not even as simple as Nietzsche thought. As both the reading of Derrida and that of Paul will show, this really depends on the placing in relation to one another the question of justice and the critique of the law. And it is the perdurance of the question and the priority

of justice that Nietzsche's Lutheran forebears had prevented him from seeing in Paul.

But Nietzsche does provide a telling identification of the crisis of law
beyond the psychologizing of an alleged inner torment or conflict in Paul
relative to the law. It has to do with the cross: "Hitherto that shameful
death had counted with him as the principal argument against the 'Messi-
ahdom' of which the followers of the new teaching spoke: but what if it
were necessary for the abolition of the law!" (41). For Nietzsche, the execution of Jesus through crucifixion somehow brings the law as law into question; indeed, he thinks it serves somehow to destroy the law. He attributes
this insight to Paul's encounter with Jesus (Acts 9:3–9)—explained natura-
listically as an effect of epilepsy—and links it to his identification with the
one of whom he had had the vision. "To become one with Christ—that
means also to become with him the destroyer of the law; to have died with
him—that means also to have died to the law" (41).

That the violence and violation of the cross somehow brings into
question the law, renders it profoundly questionable as the basis of something like "morality," is something also to which we will have to attend. Altogether apart from the melodramatic way in which this depiction of Paul
is presented, it seems to me to connect precisely with the lucidity about
Paul mentioned by Derrida and that will illumine our reflections. The theses we will appropriate from Nietzsche are, first, that the overriding question is that of the law, and second, that the reversal of the law somehow has
to do with the "ignominious death."

What does not seem to be thought by Nietzsche here is that the passion for justice has not gone the way of the passion for the law in the
thought of Paul. Justice remains the passion, a justice outside or even
against the law: outlaw justice. But that is precisely what the reading of
Derrida will enable us to think.

Justice Beyond the Law

In this chapter, I turn to the question of the relation between justice and law. In general, I will be arguing that Paul's critique of the law does not mean the abrogation of the claim of justice. In order to clarify this contention, it will be helpful to attend to the way in which Derrida works out the relation between justice and law. As we shall, see this may be characterized as a relation without relation, in which justice may be characterized as indeconstructible, whereas law is always deconstructible. Put differently, justice necessarily exceeds, questions, or even destabilizes law even though justice also is the provocation of law and its (provisional) legitimation. Thus it will be necessary to think of justice outside, beyond, and even against law without depriving justice of the impetus to instantiate itself in and as law. Considering how this is worked out by Derrida will help us to understand what sometimes seems to be an ambivalent attitude of Paul with respect to law that he can claim is "holy, just, and good" while at the same time speaking of a justice (divine, he will say) that is outside the law. The apparent ambivalence of Paul relative to the law will be explicable in terms of his concern for justice—the very justice that the law aims at while nevertheless betraying.

Narration as Delegitimation of Law

The question of the relationship to the law is first thematized by Paul in Galatians. There he produces what seems to be a critique of the law as understood, above all, as the law of Israel, the very law of which he, as a Pharisee, had been a defender. In Galatians, his view of the law comes close to being one of outright rejection and the means by which this undermining of the law is undertaken is a strategy on which some of Derrida's early reflections on law shed light, as we shall see.

However, the discussion of the law in the text of Romans is considerably more complex. Some have even seen here Paul responding to criticisms of his rather one-sided view of the law in Galatians. For in Romans he will speak of law both as that which is somehow opposed and overcome and of the law as "holy, just, and good." It is this far more paradoxical, dialectical (in a Barthian rather than Hegelian sense), or aporetic view of the law for which Derrida's reflections provide invaluable illumination.

Accordingly, in this discussion, I will first juxtapose Derrida's earlier reflections on the law with Paul's delegitimating strategy in Galatians. This is a sort of prelude to the main discussion of Derrida's subsequent reflections on the law and justice that will serve to clarify what Paul is driving at in his more balanced and complex discussion in Romans.

"Before the Law"

In the text "Before the Law," to which I have already referred, Derrida explores the relation between literature and law, in particular as this is exposed in the story of Kafka. The problem is posed in the following way: "There is a singularity about relationship to the law, a law of singularity, which must come into contact with the general or universal essence of the law without ever being able to do so." Kafka's story, then, "names or relates in its way this conflict without encounter between law and singularity" (187). This conflict between law (as universal) and the singularity of the one who waits on the law will then be transposed into the question of the temporalization or narrativizing of law.[1]

Derrida notes that his discussion of Kafka occurs within a seminar devoted to Kant on the moral law and to Freud and Heidegger on this question as well (190). Concerning Kant, he notes the "as if," of which he says, "it almost introduces narrativity and fiction into the very core of legal thought. . . . Though the authority of the law seems to exclude all historicity and empirical narrativity" (190). This is further explained: "To be invested with its categorical authority, the law must be without history, genesis, or any possible derivation. That would be the *law of the law*. Pure morality has no history: as Kant seems at first to remind us, no intrinsic history" (191).

The very attempt to inscribe law within a narrative brings law into question. As law it can have no origin, that is, no temporal origin. For in that case what is threatened is the "law of law," its being universal and thus timeless. At this point, we are referred to the attempt of Freud to narrativize law in his tale of the brothers who murder the father and then, in remorse, institute law. As Derrida remarks, however, this narrativization of law fails, for everything hinges on the brothers feeling remorse for their deed. But if they feel remorse, this can only be because they are already aware of a prohibition of patricide. Such an interdiction is law whether or not formulated as statute.

In spite of the failure of Freud's attempt to think the origin of law and so to put it into a narrative, this very failure does suggest that there is a contradiction between the being-law of law and the attempt to place it into a narration. In this sense, then, there is a kind of opposition of literature and law, of narrative and the being-law of law (216).

Relativizing the Law

It is in this connection that the strategy of Paul in Galatians, with respect to an undermining of the absoluteness of law by way of providing it with a narrative of origin, may be understood.

The argument, or rather that fragment of it which interests us here, is composed of a double gesture. First Paul maintains the priority of promise to law by temporalizing the law relative to promise: "Now the promises were made to Abraham and his seed . . . the Law which came four hundred thirty years later does not annul a covenant [promise] previously ratified by God" (3:16, 17). The space of 430 years serves to make law secondary relative to promise. Moreover, it is secondary not only temporally but also "legally" because the law does not supersede the promissory contract that precedes it, but rather is to be understood as a kind of codicil that is governed by the antecedent contract implied in the promise.

This strategy is complemented by a related one of mediation: "[the law] was ordained through angels by a mediator" (3:20). This reference to a sort of double mediation of law (angels and a mediator) also serves to distance it from that which is absolute: "Now a mediator involves more than one party; but God is one" (3:21). This dual strategy of Paul in relation to law does not seem to aim at the destruction of law but rather at relativizing it. At least Paul will want to maintain that the law is not negated by being made posterior to the promise: "Is the law then opposed to the promises of God? Certainly not" (3:21); but its "writ" is limited to the period of tutelage that has an origin and also, now, an end.

It may, however, be that Paul's attempt to relativize the law goes further than he intends because law as law may be, as Derrida suggests, incompatible with such secondariness. Thus Paul's argument seems to lead into a definite sort of antinomianism that may be quite far from his intention. Although he writes, "if you are led by the Spirit, you are not subject to the law" (5:18), Paul still wants to maintain the incompatibility of this spirited freedom from the law with a series of behaviors interdicted by the law—"fornication, impurity, licentiousness, idolatry, sorcery" (5:19–21)—and will want to enjoin upon his readers certain behaviors against which "there is no law," like love and generosity (5:22–24). Thus something like law makes its appearance beyond the law. And this is presumably not law as relative but as absolute and invariable: a different law of law.

It is not my attempt to explicate the argument of Galatians as a whole, even with respect to this thorny question of the law, but to show that Derrida's reflections on law and literature help to illuminate what Paul is up to here. Of course this is not Paul's last word on the subject. It may be that things have gone too far in this way of opposing law to spirit and to faith. In any case, his discussion of this theme in Romans seems far more nuanced, or at least more complex. Gone will be the attempts to undermine law through a narrative of origin, a periodization, a multiple mediation. Instead, Paul will maintain that justice is in some way absolute, and that although compliance with law cannot make us just, still we must become just, and a way has been given by which this is to be made effective. This way, far from contradicting what law intends or wants, is instead the fulfillment of the law by other means or otherwise.

Derrida on Law and Justice

In order to get at this more subtle argument, I will first try to represent something of the subtlety of Derrida's discussion of law and justice. This will prepare the way for an indication of the way this discussion illuminates what Paul seems to be up to in Romans. It will be necessary to proceed step by step in this discussion because it serves to orient all that follows.

As Derrida will note in subsequent discussions, he first explicitly announces the preoccupation of deconstruction with justice in the essay *The Force of Law: The "Mystical Foundation of Authority."* This text was first published in 1990 (as "Deconstruction and the Possibility of Justice") and then revised and published, in French, in 1994 and finally, in English in 2001 in *Acts of Religion*. This essay is in two parts, of which the second consists of a close reading of Benjamin's *Critique of Violence*. The first half concerns the problem we are dealing with in this chapter. We will turn to the main argument of the second half of Derrida's essay in the next chapter.

Deconstruction and/as Justice

An initial argument in this essay concerns the linkage of the question of deconstruction with the problem of justice and law. As we have seen, the earlier essay of Derrida on Kafka's "Before the Law" had already gone some distance in working on the relation between law and deconstruction, in the form of the question of the deconstructibility of law. And we have seen how this echoes an argument of Paul in Galatians that also seems to subvert the law by a series of gestures designed to indicate its secondariness.

Now in this essay, which also deals with Kafka, Derrida turns to the question of the possibility of a distinction between justice and law: "The suffering of deconstruction, what makes it suffer and what makes suffer those who suffer from it, is perhaps the absence of rules, of norms, and definitive criteria to distinguish in an unequivocal manner between law and justice" (231). One might suppose that the essay will set out to provide just such "definitive criteria to distinguish in an unequivocal way." But such a move would be impossible because it would invoke the competence of a law (rule) to unequivocally distinguish law and justice. The result would be a law that governs justice (in its relation to law) and thus ensures the hegemony of law relative to justice. That is precisely what Derrida will not do here. Instead, there will be an attempt to distinguish these terms (but if not by rule, norm, or what have you, then how?) in such a way that justice will be a kind of limit, or "beyond," of law.

THE OBLIQUE

In order to prepare the ground for this move, Derrida claims that a number of themes to which he had earlier turned his attention are in fact already oblique discourses on this relation of justice and law:

That is how I would like to employ myself here: to show why and how what one currently calls deconstruction, while seeming not to "address" the problem of justice, has done nothing else while unable to do so directly but only in an oblique fashion. I say *oblique*, since at this very moment I am preparing to demonstrate that one cannot speak *directly* about justice, thematize or objectivize justice, say "this is just," and even less "I am just," without immediately betraying justice, if not law. (237)

Here Derrida seems to be responding to his critics, who have often enough accused "deconstruction" of being morally frivolous, of in fact undermining any possible ethical seriousness. At least in certain respects, Derrida is prepared to agree that, on the surface level, there is some justification for such a view, because the question of justice has been only obliquely raised, even if in certain of his essays, like the one we have already mentioned and his much earlier discussion of Levinas ("Metaphysics and Violence"),[2] the ground has already been prepared for the rendering of this question and concern more explicit.

Even though Derrida will now turn to a somewhat more explicit thematization of the *question* of justice, this will still, as he says, be oblique, and necessarily so because one cannot speak of justice otherwise than obliquely; that is, one cannot speak directly, for direct speech would again be to subordinate justice to the law, that is, to a norm by means of which to unequivocally distinguish it from law. At a minimum, this means that we will not speak of justice as a *theme* but rather as a *question*, for to make justice a theme would be to aim at producing a set of statements of the form, "justice is *x*." But this is precisely not the way Derrida will be deploying the term *justice* insofar as it is used to indicate that which stands outside law.

This already has certain consequences here briefly alluded to, namely that no actual state of affairs, no actual comportment in which I am or have been engaged, can claim for itself the mantle of justice and so the complacency of a social or personal "good conscience."

This is, it seems to me, one of the most telling insights of Derrida concerning justice. We have only to think of the ways in which, from Aristotle to Kant and beyond, the question of ethics has been concerned above all to discover how or in what way we may in fact acquire a good conscience. It is the abiding significance of Levinas to have made the good conscience untenable.[3] And the relation of this to the good conscience of those, who from Auschwitz to Afghanistan, have prided themselves on the lawful and or dutiful character of their actions, indicates the political radicality of this insight. In terms of the disjuncture that we will be considering between justice and law, good conscience always belongs on the side of the law rather than justice. But for this to become clear, we must continue with the question of the relation between deconstruction and justice.

DECONSTRUCTION AS JUSTICE

That the question of justice has been already at work in what is called "deconstruction" is substantiated in a next gesture by invoking themes that have been more explicitly treated up to now in the course of Derrida's own work: "It goes without saying that discourses on double affirmation, the gift beyond exchange and distribution, the undecidable, the incommensurable and incalculable, on singularity, difference and heterogeneity are also, through and through, at least oblique discourses on justice" (235).

This claim that the question of justice relative to law has already been prefigured in earlier discussions is further substantiated (244) in terms of the "theme" of aporia, the impossible, and so on. That Derrida's reflections characteristically lead to an aporia, to the impossibility of what is necessarily possible, is true in many texts. That justice is here linked to this condition suggests that justice has obliquely been discussed wherever the aporetic has opened up. Thus here too Derrida can say of justice that it requires "the experience of aporia"; and thus that "justice would be the experience of what we are unable to experience." Moreover and in sum, "I believe that there is no justice without this experience, however impossible it may be, of aporia. Justice is an experience of the impossible" (244).

Although this may seem to the unwary reader to be unnecessarily difficult, it is another way of saying that if justice is the "beyond" of law, then it is not directly graspable. We could say that it may only be glimpsed on the periphery of vision. We are not able to experience it directly because it is not present, and certainly not present in or as a given set of laws. The whole point of this indirect discourse, however, is to provoke some kind of indirect experience of what justice might be like. In this sense, the discussion is "performative": it seeks to produce in the reader what it indirectly aims at, much as wedding vows produce a marriage or a declaration of war produces a war, to use the most familiar examples of performative speech. Thus talk of the "impossibility" of justice aims at provoking a disquieting thinking of that which law both aims at and betrays. We shall see this at work here in the discussion of justice and law and again in the discussion of gift and duty and so on. What is important to note at this point is a certain parallelism between this discussion of justice (as aporia, as impossible, and so on) with the procedure of deconstruction in other contexts and relative to other questions.

This may also be the point at which it would be salutary to ask the reader to be patient with the possibility that difficulty and perplexity are not at all unnecessary or frivolous but may be required by fidelity to that which one is trying to think about. Since the time of Socrates, the role of a questioning that leaves us perplexed about what we had thought before to be a relatively simple matter as the very task of thought that is or seeks to be "intelligent" has been made evident.[4] I intend to show that both Derrida and Paul belong within that tradition and that it is fruitful for theology.

The thinking of a distinction between law and justice involves Derrida in a discussion of law and force or enforceability, to which we will return in the next chapter. But it is in connection with this discussion that we get, by way of a discussion of Montaigne, the preliminary indication of the distinction: in this discussion, he says that Montaigne "is here distinguishing laws [*lois*], that is to say law [*droit*] from justice. The justice of law, justice as law is not justice" (240).

It is this discussion that will have served to substantiate what Derrida has already said that he intends: "I want to insist at once to reserve the possibility of a justice, indeed of a law that not only exceeds or contradicts law but also, perhaps, has no relation to law, or maintains such a strange relation to it that it may just as well demand law as exclude it" (233). The formulation of this distinction in relation to the project or process of deconstruction is as follows: "The paradox that I would like to submit for discussion is the following: it is this deconstructible structure of law, or, if you prefer, of justice as law, that also ensures the possibility of deconstruction. Justice in itself, if such a thing exist, outside or beyond law, is not deconstructible. No more than deconstruction itself, if such a thing exist. Deconstruction is justice" (243).

It is the affirmation in the form of a negation, "justice . . . is not deconstructible," to which Derrida will continue to refer in subsequent texts.[5] It is this formulation, then, that serves as a kind of motto.[6]

A couple of observations may be in order. We note the parallel between deconstruction and justice: "If such a thing exist." This parallel will also be found in formulations about the gift "if such a thing exist," or "if there is any" in texts to be discussed below.

It is important that it be said with respect to justice, at any rate, "if such a thing exist" because we have already been warned against expecting any sort of statement (constative) that would have the form of "this is just" or "I am just" or "justice is this." The reason for this reserve is precisely that such a statement subordinates justice to (a) law or norm. But what is at stake here is a thinking of justice outside or beyond law, in terms of which law or norm may be interrogated.

"Deconstruction takes place in the interval that separates the undeconstructibility of justice from the deconstructibility of law" (243). On the basis of the formulation "deconstruction is justice," we might have expected deconstruction to be found on the far side of the distinction between justice and law, that is, as justice. But here it is located in the between, a "between" that happens only insofar as the distinction is thought and so justice thought of as beyond law.[7] Accordingly, Derrida can even suggest inverting the title that he had been given for the talk that serves as the basis for this essay ("Deconstruction and the Possibility of Justice") to "Justice as the Possibility of Deconstruction" (243).

Unstable Distinction Between Justice and Law

Derrida proposes to offer examples that "will make explicit or perhaps produce a difficult and unstable distinction between justice and law, between justice (infinite, incalculable, rebellious to rule and foreign to symmetry, heterogeneous and heterotopic) on the one hand, and on the other, the exercise of justice as law, legitimacy or legality, a stabilizable, statutory and calculable apparatus" (250). Let us look at the provisional distinctions suggested here. In order to think of the distinction between justice and law, a set of oppositions is introduced. As we shall recall, such a set of oppositions will not remain "stable," for that would vitiate the kind of distinction being thought here. But as a kind of preliminary pointer in the direction of the kind of distinction being thought, we get the contrast between that which is calculable (law) and that which is incalculable (justice); between what is legitimate or legal (law) and what is "rebellious to rule" (justice); between what is heterogeneous/heterotopic (justice) and that which is or that which aims at stable, fixable (statutory) law.

Derrida further underlines this distinction as follows: "Law is not justice. Law is the element of calculation, and it is just that there be law; but justice is incalculable" (244). He goes on to wonder: "How to reconcile the act of justice that must always concern singularity, individuals, groups, irreplaceable existences, the other or myself as other, in a unique situation, with rule, norm, value, or the imperative of justice that necessarily have a general form?" (245). These last reflections pick up some of the concerns expressed in the earlier essay on "Before the Law" about the relation between singularity and the universal. But it is crucial to note here that it is the singular act that is associated with justice, whereas it is the general rule or norm that is associated with law. Thus the claim or provocation of justice stands outside or beyond the universalizable and calculable form of law.[8]

Now the theologian would be tempted here to say that justice names a transcendent category in terms of which immanent formulations (laws or the law) can be tested. And this would not be far from the truth at this point.[9] But we could not rest here, for all such formulations remain here, on this side of the distinction to which they seek to point. We may get a sense for this if we ask what it would mean to stabilize a distinction between what is stable and what destabilizes. If such a distinction could be carried out in a direct way, then the very stability thereby produced would ensure that we have not yet succeeded in indicating that which destabilizes as exceeding the stable. The stable or universalizable or what have you (law) would have succeeded in eliminating, or at least subordinating, the destabilizing (justice). In that case, the immobility of law would have triumphed, and what is involved in deconstruction would have proven to be a mistake. I trust that this may become clearer as we go. But for now, what is important is to see the necessary but provisional character of the distinctions here deployed. They are necessary if we are to be helped to see what might be involved in a distinction between law and justice, but they are provisional, and necessarily so, if we are to prevent this distinction from returning without remainder to the triumph of law, to its swallowing up of justice, to its elimination of any question that would really destabilize it, set it in motion, keep it open to its (the) other.[10]

In order to get some sense of what may be at stake in the distinction between justice and law, it is important to relate it to, and distinguish it from, the kinds of questions that arise at various points about the injustice of the law as a concrete system of legality and legitimacy. Derrida provides us with a way of formulating this in relation to his discussion of Pascal and Montaigne, of whom he says, "then one can find in it the premises of a modern critical philosophy, even a critique of juridical ideology, a desedimentation of the superstructures of law that both hide and reflect the economic and political interests of the dominant forces of society. This would always be possible and sometimes useful" (241). The reason that this is only "sometimes useful" is that it still does not go to the radical heart of the problem. It would leave one with the impression that the disjunction between law and justice is such as to be remediable by a simple reform of the law. In this case, the disjunction between law and justice would be only a temporary one. The difficulty with supposing this is that it could be the case that having instituted a reform of the laws one would then suppose a coincidence of law and justice such that justice as a question would have been dissolved. The history of reform movements relative to the law suggests that it is precisely in this way that any existing legal order seeks to silence the question of justice. The law has been reformed (we have abolished the monarchy, the aristocracy, Jim Crow legislation), and therefore, the existing order is "just" and so unquestionable from the side of justice.

There is, however, a danger involved in the way of limiting the pertinence of the question of reform (that existing law is the sedimentation of the political and economic interests of the powerful). For this is, in fact, always an urgent issue.[11] Moreover, it is precisely by way of noticing this subservience of the law to the interests of the powerful that an initial opening onto the question of justice relative to law can often be made. If we notice that the legal order regularly winds up protecting the interests of the powerful, this may serve to make the question of justice acute. In the next chapter, we will see that Derrida has a more basic or radical way of exposing this heterogeneity of justice to law. However, it is this apparently dismissive gesture toward this sort of critique of law ("sometimes useful") that will cause the unwary to suppose that deconstruction has not taken history, politics, or the concrete question of justice seriously. Would it have been better to have said: almost always useful and generally quite urgent save for when it is a question, as it must always be if we are not to fall into irresponsible naïveté, of asking about what is fundamentally at stake in this relation for which historical and concrete situations are but instances?[12]

Interaction of Justice and Law

That it is not possible to keep law and justice neatly separated in airtight containers (according to some fixed or stable norm) is made clear by identifying the complexity of the relation between them. "But it turns out that law claims to exercise itself in the name of justice and that justice demands for itself that it be established in the name of a law that must be put to work (constituted and applied) by force 'enforced.' Deconstruction always finds itself and moves itself between these two poles" (251). We may formulate this in the following way. Law, whenever it is articulated or enforced, has recourse to the notion of justice. Any law or body of laws is constituted precisely by reference to justice. Concretely this takes the form of placing the administration of the law within "departments" or "ministries" of justice. It is the task of such offices to administer or make effective the law or laws. Law always is law only by reference to justice, and without such reference, it could not maintain itself as law or be administered or enforced as law.

On the other hand, a commitment to justice inevitably takes the form of making the call or claim of justice effective, intelligible, applicable to the social order. If it does not do this, the commitment to justice remains a purely speculative, a merely utopian, view. But this would contradict the very idea or claim of justice, which is always a demand that it be made effective, that it become practicable, that its claims be recognized as binding on human sociality.[13] Thus law and justice, however sharply we may need to draw a distinction between them, nevertheless require one another—indeed, are embedded in one another.

To this point in the argument, then, we have the need to make a distinction between justice and law. Without such a distinction, we cannot really think law; that is, thought is immobilized before the adequacy of law, whether as positive law or as the moral law. That thought ought not to be so immobilized here or elsewhere is the very heart of deconstruction, which seeks to set everything in motion, that is, to open the space for thought, to think the spacing necessary to thought.

These reflections on law and justice will return again, but first it is important to look at three subsequent texts in which Derrida takes up the distinction he has suggested here and develops that distinction in important ways.

Law(s) and Right(s)

In a later text, *Specters of Marx*, Derrida returns to this question of the relation between justice and law. Here he builds from the discussion that we have already considered: "A deconstructive thinking, the one that matters to me here has always pointed out . . . the undeconstructibility of a certain idea of justice (dissociated here from the law)" (91).[14] But we shall attend here to certain more or less tentative amplifications of the distinction already proposed.

In the preface, he writes, "If I am getting ready to speak at length of ghosts . . . it is in the name of *justice*. Of justice where it is not yet, not yet *there*, where it is no longer, let us understand where it is no longer *present*, and where it will never be, no more than the law, reducible to laws or rights" (xix). The relation of the talk of justice to that of "ghosts," that is, to the odd mode of bearing upon the present of those who have died (and, indeed, as Derrida also suggests, of those yet to be born),[15] and bearing on the present in such a way as to provoke a certain responsibility to and before them, is a theme that we will have to postpone.[16] The important thing for our purposes here is the way in which two additional categories seem to be put into play.

On the one hand, we have the association of law as such with justice insofar as a distinction from laws and rights in the plural are concerned. That is, there is a way in which we are invited to think of *the* law in the singular or of law as such, as distinct from laws. At this point, we may simply wonder whether here law or the law is another word for justice or if we are being invited to think a double distinction: one between justice and the law, and one between justice/the law and laws/rights in the plural. If we are to think a double distinction here, then "the law" is not only placed between laws and justice but is also somehow unstable in that it may be thought as on the side of justice in the distinction between justice and the laws and on the side of laws in the distinction between justice and law(s).

At this stage of wondering, we may say that "the law"—let us say something like the Kantian categorical imperative, the moral law—cannot be reduced to statutory formulation; it always exceeds that formulation. Thinking of the Kantian imperative also helps us to see how laws and rights are concretely associated here; for the imperative, "deal with other persons as ends rather than as means," suggests that respect for the law is to be understood as respect for the other person. Such a respect is formulizable as a set of rights (what does it mean to be the object/subject of such respect?) or of laws (what does it entail that I must respect the rights of the other and that the other must respect my rights?)

Thus the second thing that seems to be in play here is the relation of law and right to laws and rights. This association is crucial for the modernity in which the question of right and rights becomes the characteristic way of asking the question of justice and of the foundation of law. That we are to think of a double distinction is clarified in a later passage in which Derrida says, "an idea of justice—which we distinguish from law or right and even from human rights" (59). What is crucial here is that even modernity's fascination with right and rights is distinguished from, and subordinated to, justice. We are returned to the kind of distinction we had noted before when he writes: "One must constantly remember that it is even on the basis of the terrible possibility of this impossible that justice is desirable *through* but also *beyond* right and law" (175). Here I want only to observe again that we have in play a double distinction of justice relative to law/right and of law/right relative to laws/rights.[17]

We may tentatively summarize the conceptual apparatus that seems to be emerging here. Justice stands in a somewhat oppositional relation to law (and right) that in turn stands in a somewhat oppositional relation to laws/rights. We thus have right (as in, for example, the "rights of man") related to our earlier problematic of law and legality relative to justice. In addition, we have the double distinction that we might provisionally represent to ourselves in terms of levels or dimensions: justice—law/right (as such)—laws/rights. So long as we keep in mind the necessary instability of these distinctions, we may also say that this instability may be most in evidence at the point of the middle term, that is, law as such. For this may on the one hand designate that by virtue of which any body of laws may be regarded as deficient (and to that extent law as such will seem to function as justice vis-à-vis laws); and on the other hand still remain problematic from the side of justice regarded as indeconstructible relative to the deconstructibility of law, including law as such.

This last point will be made especially clear, I think, in the discussion of Kierkegaard in *The Gift of Death*, for there it will be clear that what is claimed by justice may also contravene law as such in the sense of universalizable responsibility. We will return to this question below.

Beyond Retributive and Distributive Justice

But first it is important that Derrida offers us another way of thinking of justice as the beyond of what is sometimes even called "justice," as when we speak of retributive and even distributive justice. "If right or law stems from vengeance, as Hamlet seems to complain that it does—before Nietzsche, before Heidegger, before Benjamin—can one not yearn for a justice that one day, a day belonging no longer to history, a quasi-messianic day, would finally be removed from the fatality of vengeance? Better than removed: infinitely foreign, heterogeneous at its source?" (*Specters of Marx*, 21). Of course, this notion of a justice utterly beyond revenge and thus beyond repayment is what stirs the question of gift or, as Christians say, of grace. The notion of justice Derrida is concerned with here is one that escapes from retribution and so from a revenge that runs into the endlessness (a bad infinite) of the cycle of vengeance from which there seems no escape. It is this task of vengeance that so wearies Hamlet, which so makes him wonder about another way, another justice, a different kind of time.

One of the issues that so perplexes Derrida is the endless cycle of revenge, calling itself justice, that spirals on and on in the fratricidal struggle whose capital seems to be Jerusalem but which endlessly threatens to engulf us all. Yet the cry that so often reignites this spiral is precisely the cry for justice, for justice as revenge, as payback, that will somehow settle accounts. But is this endless cycle of grievance-vengeance-grievance what is really called for when the call for justice, or rather the call of justice, is heard?

The law is or seems to be a way of limiting this endless cycle, of formalizing, calculating, and displacing this endless accumulation of grievance, this endless incitement to settle accounts. The justice that is a beyond of law cannot be a return to the bad infinite of revenge. But if not that, what? "How to distinguish between two disadjusments, between the disjuncture of the unjust and the one that opens up the infinite symmetry of the relation to the others, that is to say, the place for justice?" (*Specters of Marx*, 22). The question of disadjustment in relation to justice is related to Heidegger's thinking of *dike* as gathering or joining or perhaps "adjusting." The *adikia*, then, would be injustice as disadjustment, which disrupts what is commonly called justice (to which retribution or even distribution would correspond). But there is also here the thought of a disadjustment (*adikia*) between justice and law that opens the space for a relation to others. In "Nietzsche and the Machine" Derrida explains,

The concept of justice that I am elaborating is opposed to the Heideggerian one of *dike* as joining, as *Fug*, as bringing together; it suggests that justice is, and must be a discordance. As soon as justice implies a relation to another, it supposes an interruption, a dis-joining, a disjunction or being-out-of-joint; which is not negative; an out-of-jointness that is not deconstructible, that is justice as deconstruction, as the possible deconstruction of any determined law [*droit*]. (*Negotiations*, 230)[18]

The discordance of justice as regards law is not only an interruption of the (endless) cycle of the law of retributive justice, it is also an interruption of the proper calculation of what is due in the sense of a law of distributive justice. "Not for calculable equality, therefore, not for the symmetrizing and synchronic accountability or imputability of subjects and objects, not for a *rendering justice* that would be limited to sanctioning, to restituting, and to *doing right*, but for justice as incalculability of the gift and singularity of the an-economic ex-position to others. 'The relation to others—that is to say, justice,' writes Levinas" (*Specters of Marx*, 22/23). As is almost always the case, a number of issues are compacted in this sentence. We will postpone the discussion of gift to a later chapter and attend here to what is said concerning restitution and calculation. An important way of accounting for or calculating justice has to do with distribution: to each his due; a rendering of accounts whereby rewards and punishments seek to match virtue and vice. This is justice as a kind of Santa Claus who carefully totes up who's been naughty and nice in order to appropriately distribute the benefits that are within his gift. But Derrida wants us also to think of justice beyond this second way of settling accounts, of calculating. We have seen that law may be understood precisely as this sort of calculation. Hence Derrida challenges us to think of a justice that is beyond calculation.[19]

In "The Deconstruction of Actuality," Derrida writes, "Justice is not the same as rights; it exceeds and founds the rights of man; nor is it distributive justice. It is not even, in the traditional sense *respect* for the other as a human subject" (*Negotiations*, 105).[20] Here, Derrida again notes the distinction between justice and rights (even the basis of rights in respect for the other person), as well as the distinction with which we are concerned at this point between justice and what is called "distributive justice." In *Specters of Marx*, Derrida again makes clear that whatever it is that justice as the beyond of law is to mean, it must not be reducible to what can simply be calculated as the retributive or even distributive rule of "to each what is due." "Does it come simply to render justice or, on the contrary to give *beyond* the due, the debt, the crime, or the fault?" (25). Here again, we abut the discussion of gift that will return in a later chapter.

The Law(s) of Hospitality

Many of these reflections are brought together and given sharper expression in *Of Hospitality*. Here the question of the relation between justice/law/laws is worked out in connection with the question of the welcome to be given to the stranger, a theme already much worked over by Levinas but that is here situated in relation to the specific case of the opening of the national territory and space to refugees, a question of consider-

able moment at the time of writing for the case to which I have already referred in Chapter 1, the collision between the state's limitation of the right
to refuge and the claim of the refugee for shelter. Characteristically for Derrida, this becomes an occasion to think through what it might mean to
take seriously the claim to hospitality of the stranger in relation, for example, to certain texts of Kant; that is, to ask, what gives itself to be thought
in this conflict, and how may this thinking avail itself of the (philosophical and literary) canon?

We shall have to return to the question of the welcome to the other as
the exemplary question of a politics or ethics of justice later. Here I will only
point to the discussion, sharpened in relation to this question, of the relation of justice to law and of law (or justice) to laws. Derrida writes, "justice
is heterogeneous to the law to which it is yet so close, from which it is in
truth indissociable" (27).[21] This formulation of heterogeneity and indissociability is one that will appear in many connections in our reflections. It
serves here to specify the way in which justice is both other than (heterogeneity) while also necessarily implicated in (indissociable from) law.

But here also we get a formulation concerning the relation of law to
laws: "The antinomy of hospitality irreconcilably opposes *The* law, in its
universal singularity, to a plurality that is not only a dispersal (laws in the
plural), but a structured multiplicity" (79). This then sets up a rather extraordinary passage in which Derrida comes close, I will subsequently argue, to a paraphrase of Paul's argument in Romans.

The tragedy, for it is a tragedy of destiny, is that the two antagonistic terms of this
antinomy are not symmetrical. There is a strange hierarchy in this. *The* law is
above the laws. It is thus illegal, transgressive, outside the law, like a lawless law,
nomos anomos, law above the laws, and law outside the law. . . . But even while
keeping itself above the laws of hospitality, *the* unconditional law of hospitality
needs the laws, it *requires* them. This demand is constitutive. It wouldn't be effectively unconditional, the law, if it didn't *have to become* effective, concrete, determined, if that were not its being as having-to-be. It would risk becoming abstract,
utopian, illusory, and so turning over into its opposite. In order to be what it is,
the law thus needs the laws, which however deny it, or at any rate threaten it,
sometimes corrupt or pervert it. And it must always be able to do this. For this
pervertibility is essential, irreducible, necessary too (79).[22]

These two regimes of law, of *the* law and the laws, are thus both contradictory, antinomic, *and* inseparable. They both imply and exclude one another simultaneously (79–81).

The law, in the absolute singular, contradicts laws in the plural, but on each occasion it is the law *within* the law, and on each occasion *outside the law* within the law. (81)

I have reproduced this rather long, if fragmentary, excerpt from Derrida's argument because it so closely approximates what I want to say concerning Paul's argument. There is, however, also this that must be noted: Derrida here does not speak of justice relative to law, the law, but of law or the law relative to laws. Here is a good example of what I wanted to get at in the discussion of the texts from *Specters of Marx*, namely that law may stand in relation to laws in much the same way that justice seems to stand in relation to law, at least in terms of the formulations here of a law outside of or even against law. Here it is a matter of the law of hospitality that is transgressive with respect to any given law that always inscribes hospitality within bounds or limits that violate the unrestricted claim of the law of hospitality.

In the United States, for example, as the government waged war in Central America, many of the citizens of the countries subjected to this (low intensity) war sought safety, refuge, in the United States. Several groups sought to give them refuge, even though doing so placed them in opposition to the law(s) governing asylum or refuge. The "law" of welcome and sanctuary stood over and contradicted the laws concerning refuge, even if the laws were themselves produced to offer refuge and so were an articulation of the claim to asylum and refuge. Altogether apart from the ideological distortions of the actual laws (yes to those escaping communism, no to those escaping right-wing death squads funded by the U.S. government), there would still be a problem even if the ideological bias were corrected, for an unrestricted opening would seem to abolish the very identity of a nation granting such hospitality. Here it is not a question of taking sides in a debate about immigration policy, or even of seeking to clarify what is at stake in the very notion of hospitality (the theme of this essay and of several others both by Derrida and by Levinas), but of seeing how the notion of law and laws comes to expression here also. At a later point, we will have to ask whether this question of "welcome" is simply one example among others of the relation of justice and law or is instead a "privileged" example, a necessary paradigm, exemplary of the question of justice as such.

Several other points call for some comment. First is the point that there is a hierarchy, even a "strange" hierarchy in that law is always above laws. Yet as we saw earlier in the case of justice that claims that it be done, the law must be instantiated in laws. Just as much as the claim of justice brings any given law into question, so also it still requires instantiation in laws, in concrete forms of legality that prescribe rights and responsibilities while still limiting these. It is in this way that what we earlier saw under the heading of the interaction of justice and law (now in terms of the interaction of law and laws) is developed in this text.

Eschatological Justice

These reflections are, it seems to me, taken a step further in the discussions published as *A Taste for the Secret*, by Jacques Derrida and Maurizio Ferraris. We note first that here Derrida gives yet another formulation of the distinction between law and justice: speaking of Giovanni Falcone, a just man, he writes, "And what I have called 'justice,' which is not the same as right or 'law' [*droit*], is a relation to the unconditional that, once all the conditional givens have been taken into account, bears witness to that which will not allow itself to be enclosed within a context" (17). This formulation of the unconditional in contrast to the conditioned (context) owes something to Kierkegaard, who has been spoken of earlier in this same text. In a certain way it elaborates the distinction we have seen developed in *Of Hospitality*, between Law and laws. But yet another distinction we have tried to think is also invoked: "Justice is not right [*droit*]; it is that which attempts, nonetheless to produce a new right" (17). Here Derrida seems to return to a formulation we had encountered in *Specters of Marx*: the relation of right and rights and the way in which justice stands in an oblique relation to both right (law) and rights (laws).

Beyond these echoes of earlier discussions, Derrida will also develop what I call the eschatological character of justice as a way, perhaps the best way, of distinguishing it from law and laws. The eschatological character of justice will be announced here. But it seems already in a certain way to be present in *Specters of Marx*, where Derrida makes the following observations: "the injunction of a justice which, beyond right or law rises up in the respect owed to whoever *is not*, no longer or not yet living, living, presently living" (97). This iterates what had already been said in the preface to *Specters of Marx*: "No justice—let us not say no law and once again we are not speaking here of laws—seems possible or thinkable without the principle of some responsibility . . . before the ghosts of those who are not yet born or who are already dead" (xix).[23]

I place these reflections here because the question of justice as it relates to the dead, to a responsibility to, for, or even of the dead (and to those as yet unborn) belongs to the question of justice as "to come," at least in a theology that has any interest in the themes of the resurrection of the dead or the judgment of "the quick and the dead." In *A Taste for the Secret*, he makes this reference more explicit: "Justice—or justice as it promises to be, beyond what it actually is—always has an eschatological dimension" (20). The direction, then, in which justice is to be looked for is not in some founding event of the past (as in the founding of a legal order), nor in the dimension of a timeless transcendence somehow "above," but in that to which promise orients us, the future or the advent of that which is to come.

This eschatological dimension has a certain relation to what may be termed ontology: "Justice has always to be thought of as that which overflows law [*droit*], which is always an ensemble of determinable norms, positively incarnated and positive. But justice has to be distinguished not only from law, but also from what *is* in general" (21). That justice must be distinguished from what is means at least that that which is to come is not yet present and so does not belong to the order of what is "in general." The connection between the question of "what is" and the question of responsibility in relation to the dead brings Derrida, in a word play that is an extraordinary incitement to further reflection, to speak of hauntology in place of ontology (*Specters of Marx*, 161).

Until now, we have seemed to have justice as the beyond or above of law. But here (and already in several of the formulations in *Specters of Marx*), it becomes clear that the way in which justice is beyond law is that it is ahead of law, that is, that the excess of justice relative to law is conceived of as the excess of the future relative to the present. "I think that the instant one loses sight of the *excess* of justice, or of the future, in that very moment the conditions of totalization would, undoubtedly be fulfilled—but so would the conditions of the *totalitarianism* of a right [*droit*] without justice, of a good moral conscience and a good juridical conscience, which all adds up to a present without a future [*sans avenir*]" (*Taste for the Secret*, 22). The reference to the future as the utopic "site" of that which exceeds any given present serves to keep open the space for a critique of what is and so to prevent its stabilization in any regime or order that would claim for itself an adequation to justice.

It is precisely this insistence on the "to-come" as the way of orienting ourselves toward justice that leads Derrida to wonder about messianism, especially that messianism (Christian, for example) that claims that the divine justice has in some sense already come: "I do not want to take sides in a war of religions, but the religions for which the Messiah has arrived, where the messianic vocation has already been accomplished, always run the risk of lacking this transcendence of justice and the to-come with respect to totality" (*Taste for the Secret*, 22). In reflecting on this warning one wants to ask whether Paul, or at least a Christianized Paul, has fallen into the possible trap of suspending the eschatological horizon in terms of an already. I doubt that this suspension of the eschatological actually occurs in Paul, but I do believe it essential to take this warning with the utmost seriousness. We shall have to ask, therefore, not only whether Paul understands justice to be in some sense eschatological (this is the easy part), but also whether this is undermined by his belief that in some sense the messiah has already come. In order to see more clearly whether this is the case, we will first have to attend carefully to what Paul has to say about justice and the law.

Paul and Outlaw Justice

Let us see how the reading of fragments of Derrida may help us to think the problem of law and justice in Paul. I will first indicate that Paul is concerned with the question of justice, and that for him this remains paramount. I will then turn to the problem with the law. Here it will be necessary to indicate that the law here is not only the Mosaic law, but also Roman law and so, perhaps, law as such. But then it will be necessary to show that for Paul, the law or the body of laws is in contrast to justice; that justice as such or the justice of God stands in fundamental tension with the law or body of laws. This will not mean that a stable distinction is made here any more than in Derrida. This very instability is what the reading of Derrida helps us to think. I will then show how questions of retributive and distributive justice are also present in Paul and that he struggles to distinguish this from the justice of God or "true justice." Remarks on the eschatological character of divine justice will conclude this part of my engagement with Romans on the basis of a reading of Derrida.

Divine Justice

The question for Paul, let us suppose, is that of justice. To what extent can this be verified? In English, this concern is concealed by introducing "righteousness" to translate terms that have *dik-* as their root without the slightest lexical justification. A first step toward the recognition of the place of justice in Paul's thought therefore comes in eliminating "righteousness" from the Englishing of the Greek and replacing it with justice. This alone will produce a compelling transformation in perception.

Thus, for example when at 1:16–17, where Paul states what has been supposed to be his thesis, he writes, "I am not ashamed of the gospel" and explains, "For in it the justice of God is revealed." In the decisive clarification of the divine aim which he believes to be disclosed in the "good news" (chapter 3), he will again speak of divine justice. First he says that justice is somehow confirmed by our injustice (3:5); that it is precisely the failure of human justice that brings divine justice—let us say, true justice—into focus.

In 3:21–26, a passage we will have to read with some care in a moment, this divine or true or absolute justice is mentioned four times (3:21, 22, 25, 26). At no point is the claim or call of justice undermined or relativized. On the contrary, what is at stake is the insistence on justice, the claim of justice, true justice; what is called therefore the justice of God. It is precisely this that Paul wants to maintain is to be distinguished from law, as we shall see. But whatever may be said about law, whatever may be claimed about the effect of the gospel or the transformation of which he wants to speak, it in no way "deconstructs" justice. Justice is God's justice and in this way stands as the goal, the aim, of whatever it is that may be thought to disturb our relation to law, *the* law, or laws.

Thus in some way the message with which Paul believes himself to be entrusted concerns the having been disclosed of divine justice (3:21). This justice of God is to be related to that which has happened through the faithfulness of the messiah of God (3:22). Whatever this is that has happened to and through this messiah demonstrates the justice of God (3:25) and was done so as to show that the divine is just; that the divine is just in such a way as to actually somehow produce justice (3:26).

For our purposes, it is well, I think, to bear in mind the question raised by Caputo: "is justice another name for God, or is God another name for justice?"[24] In any case, it is clear that for Paul, there is this complete intertwining of justice and the divine such that his thesis may be represented as divine = justice. This equation is, or seems to be, reversible. The burden of his argument, then, will be to show that it is precisely justice whose claim and call is validated through what he has to say, even when what he has to say brings the law as expression of the claim of this justice into question.[25]

This justice is at first contrasted with injustice, human injustice, which in Paul's view is always to be measured by divine justice. Thus his indictment of gentile and, subsequently, Judean society is an indictment precisely of their injustice. In a kind of programmatic statement that anticipates the indictments to follow, Paul says, "The wrath of God is revealed from heaven against all human impiety and injustice that imprisons the truth in injustice." Of course one might never know that Paul is speaking about injustice here because English translations substitute "wickedness" and "unrighteousness" for the single term *adikia*, "injustice." But clearly human injustice seems to call forth the justice of God, and to call it forth precisely as wrath. And it is precisely this human injustice (1:29) that leads off his summary indictment of gentile civilization. Moreover, at the conclusion of his indictment of Israel, he can even say that "our injustice serves to confirm the justice of God" (3:5). Whether in the indictment of gentile or of Judaic injustice, that which seems to be brought into ever sharper relief, and so in a certain sense revealed, is precisely divine justice. If the sphere of the human is characterized by injustice, this only serves to make all the more clear the association of the divine with justice itself.

Justice vs. the Law

It is precisely on the basis of this indissociability of justice and the divine that Paul will seek to raise questions about the law or laws. Justice is somehow unconditional; the same is not true of law. For what is of utmost importance for Paul is that justice (divine, we recall) is "apart from the law" (3:21). Justice, real justice, stands outside of, beyond, and in a certain way, against law.

This is substantiated in a number of ways. If Abraham may be said to have been just, then it is clear, at least to Paul, that this is "before" the law (4:1–5, 13). To be before, to be outside or beyond the law—these prepositional positions have been associated for us by Derrida's reflections on Kafka's "Before the Law," which played on some of the senses of "before" (German *vor*), which include the relation of anteriority as a form of exteriority with respect to the law. Here Paul is claiming Abraham's justice "before" the law in the sense of anteriority to the command concerning circumcision (4:10) in order to generalize toward other forms of exteriority, including both the uncircumcised, who are "outside" the sphere of this command (4:11), and even the circumcised, whose justice is or should be one that is not restricted to circumcision but actually imitates the justice of the one who was faithful prior to that command (4:12).[26]

It is a staple of biblical exegesis that Paul is concerned with what is in some way outside the law, beyond the competence of the law to judge or condemn. But what this traditional and conventional exegesis has often or regularly failed to recognize is that what is to come to expression "outside" the law or "apart from" the law is precisely justice. And that calling this the justice of God or divine justice is so far from being a way of neutralizing the claim and call of justice that it actually underlines and emphasizes precisely this as justice.

It is precisely in relation to the call of justice, to its claim and indeed promise, that Paul can proceed to relativize law. Thus, for example, the promise (to Abraham) does not come from or on account of the law (4:13) but through a different kind of justice—namely, that which has to do with faith. Again, as we shall see, it is not the case that the "justice of faith" is somehow to be understood as abrogating justice, as muting or eliminating its claim, but precisely as instantiating that claim, as corresponding in a way that adherence to the law cannot, to that justice which is divine (or, as Derrida would say, indeconstructible).[27]

Thus the becoming of justice—the corresponding to the call or claim of justice—is dissociated from compliance with law: "a person is made [or becomes] just, . . . apart from works of [or in compliance with] the law" (3:27). The point here seems to be that no one may assure oneself of being or becoming just by way of doing what the law requires. But as we have seen, this is generally the function of law: to provide that set of rules and norms through compliance with which one may assure oneself of a good conscience, that is, of being just. That justice cannot be actualized through compliance with (works of) the law therefore already "deconstructs" law, and in this case seems to offer a fundamental critique of law.[28]

Already we may see that a certain advance has been made over the discussion in Galatians. For it is becoming clear that the critique of the competence of the law is based on the prior, or basic, or unconditional claim of justice. It is by way of thinking of justice or the justice of God that the law may be regarded as in some way secondary, even suspended, as some of these formulations might suggest.

One of the formulations that seems most explicit in terms of a suspension of the law is what Paul says in chapter 10: "Messiah is the end of the law" (10:4). But what Paul explicitly then adds is "so that there may be justice." That is, the suspension of the law has no other aim than, precisely, justice. And this justice is unrestricted in its effect, for he says "for everyone." Thus the ending of law aims at the realization or actualization of justice for everyone. The "everyone" here indicated is precisely inclusive of both Jews and gentiles and thus all of humanity (there is no third form of humanity alongside Jew and gentile for Paul). To be sure, he then also adds, "for everyone who has faith." However this is to be understood, it cannot be taken in the sense of setting up a new division of the same kind as that between Jew and gentile.[29] Rather, it aims at saying that faith or faithfulness is something like that which responds or corresponds to what it is that makes justice possible and even actual. We will not be able to clarify that until we have dealt with the question of gift or grace. At this point, however, we should be clear that the suspension or even apparent abolition of law through the messiah has as its goal the realization, or the making effective, of the call and claim of justice.

Moses and Rome

We saw in our discussion of Derrida that it was important to make clear that the discussion of justice relative to law also applied to the preoccupation of modernity with the language of right and rights. In a somewhat similar way, the argument of Paul with respect to law and justice needs to take account of two ways of speaking of law, of instantiating law. In Galatians, it seems Paul was primarily concerned with the Law of Moses—that is, with that law or body of laws that was the possession and pride of Israel, of which he himself had been an ardent defender. In Romans, however, Paul is concerned to think the relation of law and justice more amply. Thus while a certain privilege is still accorded the biblical law, the law of Moses or the Torah, Paul is here concerned with a critique that also and necessarily implicates Roman law.

It is no innovation of Paul to suppose that in some way Roman (gentile) and Israelite law may be compared with one another. There appears to have been something of a genre of this sort of comparative law or comparative polity or politics.[30] The self-promotion of Rome entailed reference to its law as the bearer of justice for humanity. Over against this imperial propaganda certain Jewish thinkers argued for the superiority of Mosaic law to Roman law. In his argument Paul never contests that superiority. Indeed, much of his argument depends on this perception of the superiority of Mosaic law to Roman law. Hence a critique of the former would apply a fortiori to the latter.

Within this framework, Paul makes clear that he intends to address both polities, just as he intends to address the gentile/Jewish realities designated by these polities. Hence a refrain throughout the letter is "to the Jew first and then to the gentile" (1:16; 2:9; 2:10), which is supplemented by "both Jews and gentiles/Greeks" (3:9, 29; 4:11–12; 9:24; 10:12). There is, as the first slogan indicates, always a certain priority within this both/and. But it is really always both who are addressed.

And even though the surface level of his rhetoric most often suggests Jew, the basic address suggests gentile or Roman. How so? The letter, as we know but generally forget, is addressed to people in Rome: "to all God's beloved in Rome" he says (Romans 1:7). It has as its aim that people in Rome will be persuaded that Paul has something important to say to them, precisely as those who live in Rome: "I long to see you that I might impart some spiritual [spirited] gift to you" (Romans 1:11; compare 15:23, 28, 32). They are addressed above all, therefore, as Romans.

Now the working out of this relationship takes us into some of the most contested areas of Pauline interpretation. I will have occasion to explore this at greater length in the next chapter, when it will be possible to focus more sharply on how it is that the critique of law comes into focus. Here, all I want to suggest is that this double concern of Paul, with Jew and gentile, also applies to his critique of the law. When he speaks of justice outside or apart from the law, we must bear in mind this double referent of law, both gentile (Roman) and Judean (the law of Moses). It is undeniably true that he seems more explicit here with respect to Jewish law, but to read this as his exclusive concern when he speaks of law would be to make a mockery of his basic procedure throughout this letter. A failure to recognize this double reference of the critique of law has made it possible for subsequent Christian theologians to characterize Judaism as a religion of the Law and so to propose an absolute contrast between it and Christianity.

The Necessity of the Law

In spite of the fact that Paul brings to bear a fundamental critique of the law in relation to justice, he is at considerable pains to insist that this does not mean the destruction of the law. (Deconstruction is not destruction.[31]) We have seen that his earlier argument in Galatians may have taken Paul further than he intended to go in critiquing the competence of the law to produce salvation (or justice, as he now says). One of the ways that critique had taken effect was through the claim of a double mediation of the law that separates it from the divine (by angels, through a mediator, and therefore not God). But in Romans, he wants to clarify that "the law is holy, and the commandment is holy and just and good" (7:12). That something is "holy" or even "holy, just, and good" seems to associate it with the divine in unmistakable ways. What besides God is good (as another rabbi asked), or holy, or, as the argument we have already read suggests, just?[32]

The law, although unable to produce justice (which remains outside the law) nevertheless is necessarily implicated in justice, in the project and promise of justice. We may briefly note other declarations of Paul to similar effect: "Do we then overthrow the law. . . . By no means! On the contrary we uphold the law" (3:31). Or he again suggests that that which has been identified as outside or apart from the law nevertheless has the aim, "that the just requirement of the law might be fulfilled in us" (8:4), even though it seems to remain the case that "you are not under the law" (7:14). What Paul seems to be aiming at here is something like what Derrida helps us to think, namely that although there is a necessary (but, we remember, unstable) distinction between justice and law, nevertheless, justice requires law. Its very insistence that it be done (the call or claim of justice) and that this take effect in our social reality entails its articulation in/as law.

Paul's reflections on the law are exceedingly complex, as are those of Derrida, but we should, before moving further, pay attention to Paul's principal argument concerning what may be termed the use of the law. Already in Galatians Paul had given thought to the proper or even necessary function of the law, and he concluded that it served as a kind of guardian and disciplinarian in the interim marked by a number of years following the promise and by the coming of that which goes beyond law.

In Romans, Paul offers a positive argument for the necessity of law, for its necessity relative to justice. The argument is that without law, there is no recognition of injustice, of violation, or, as this is often understood, sin. Let us for the moment simply suppose that sin names injustice—that is, the wronging of the other person. The point then would be that law is indispensable to the goal of justice because it is precisely as law that we are awakened to the seriousness of the violation of the other—that is, to injustice (or sin). What Paul says, then, is, "If it had not been for the law, I would not have known sin. I would not have known what it is to covet if the law had not said, 'you shall not covet'" (7:7). This is, on one level, an affirmation of what he had said earlier: "through the law comes knowledge of sin" (3:20). Thus, in Romans, Paul argues that the law belongs to the order of knowledge, that it functions in order that one may know "injustice." Nor does Paul shrink from asserting of those who know the law that they have in the law "the embodiment of knowledge and truth" (2:20).

One of the ways in which the relation between law and justice comes to expression is through the use of law as a way of measuring the justice of the peoples or nations. In relation to the gentiles, he provides a catalog meant to demonstrate what he terms their "injustice" (1:18, 29), which then subjects them to the "just judgment" (1:32; 2:5) of God or what we might term the judgment of justice itself. The way that this is initially formulated has to do with the law. Thus Paul can argue that those who do the law or what the law requires, whether or not they have the law, will be safe from the wrath of God, and those who do not do what the law requires will perish. Here it is quite clear that the doing of the law and the doing of justice are (provisionally) identified (2:12–14). This argument is basically repeated a few sentences later (2:25–27). However, this provisional identification of law and justice is immediately problematized: "Therefore by the deeds of the law no flesh will be made just before Him for through the law is the knowledge of sin" (3:20). Here, that which makes sin or injustice evident is regarded as insufficient to produce justice itself. We may say that law has a different, and perhaps incompatible, function.

However, there is an even more compelling way to distinguish justice from law while still relating them. "But now, apart from the law, [the] justice of God [divine or undeconstructible justice] has been revealed, the justice testified to by the law and the prophets" (3:21). Here we may attend not only to the fact that justice stands outside or apart from the law, but that this same justice is what is testified to and through the law. The law, then, is not identical to justice but is that which points to or testifies to justice. Indeed, we may suppose that apart from the law (from laws), justice is not testified to, pointed to, or indicated. At any rate, this would be consistent with what we have seen about law throughout this discussion—namely, that it points to justice, that it is inscribed in the name of justice, and so it is that by which the claim of justice is instantiated, even where it itself may be seen to be not just or as actually producing injustice.

I have spoken of the intention of the law as justice. This is confirmed by an expression that Paul uses when speaking of the gentiles: "They show that what the law requires is written on their hearts" (3:15). This they do by doing "instinctively what the law requires" (2:14); moreover, he later speaks of those who are of the uncircumcision who "keep the requirements of the law" (2:25). Obviously, this cannot mean doing all that the law concretely specifies; they are, after all, uncircumcised. But it does mean doing what at heart or essentially the law aims at, namely justice. But once again, justice is testified to outside the law. Yet does this "outside the law" entail the nullification of the law? Paul responds, "may it not be, on the contrary we establish the law" (4:31). Although law and justice are certainly heterogeneous, as Derrida has taught us to say, they are certainly not dissociable.

One of the most striking ways this "instability" of law comes to expression is in the paradoxical formulation "law of the messiah." In this case, law is used as a name for what must be supposed to be ultimate justice, that justice which goes beyond law or is the beyond of law. But in our reading of Derrida, we noted that this use of law (distinguished then from laws) was used precisely in the context of a discussion of "hospitality." As it happens, that is also the case with Paul. The phrase "law of Christ [or the messiah]" appears in the call for responsibility to and for the other: "Bear one another's burdens and so, thereby, fulfil the law of the messiah" (Galatians 6:2)—messianic law, if we can say such a thing.

The Instability of Law

We saw in reference to Derrida that the place of law relative to justice on the one hand, and to laws on the other hand, is necessarily unstable. And we find something like that also in Paul's argument. Thus for Paul the law may be spoken of as justice itself, while on the other hand it is deconstructed as laws or bodies of law. Although some may think this to be a lack of clarity in Paul, it should also be wondered whether what Paul's argument reflects is an incorrigible ambiguity in law itself or, as one might now say, "as such."

Paul's argument that the law cannot produce justice but rather that it produces injustice leads him to ask, "What then shall we say, is the law sin?" (7:7), to which he replies, "God forbid, I would not have known sin but for the law," by which he wants to say that the law, in forbidding "sin," or let us say injustice, the harming of the other, makes us see the seriousness of this harm, produces a consciousness, a public monument, to the unacceptability of this damage to, or violation of, the other. (The illustration used is precisely the most general form of this damage, namely the coveting of what is the other's; that is, the will to appropriate the other for one's own purposes.) The difficulty, then, is that the commandment "which was to bring life, I found to bring death" (7:10). That is, the law or commandment aims at life—that is, justice—but in fact, it brings death. In terms of its orientation toward justice, then, "The law is holy and the commandment is holy and just and good" (7:12). That is to say, the law as the law of justice comes to expression in the law and the laws. But it is this same law, not a different one, that operates to bring not justice but injustice, not life but death. Of the law in the first sense, Paul can say, "I delight in the law of God according to the inward man" (7:22), but the same law under the aspect of what Paul calls flesh is that which becomes death and death dealing.

This ambiguity at the heart of the idea of law comes to sharpest focus in Paul's juxtaposition of law in these two senses in Romans 8:2: "For the law of the spirit of life in messiah Jesus has set you free from the law of sin and death." Thus "law" may express two quite different realities: that which is messianic and so associated with life and justice; and that which is associated with death and so with "sin" (or injustice). What is perhaps most surprising given his argument about law is that the messianic spirit also may be expressed as "law," and precisely as that law which overcomes law in the sense of that which deals death and is imprisoned in injustice. We could scarcely expect to find a closer parallel to Derrida's assertions concerning a law outside or against law. And as we saw in that connection, the ambiguity of law is precisely the ambiguity of its relation to justice: that which both articulates and betrays the call and claim of justice. But these notions do not stand simply alongside one another for Paul. Rather, it is his claim that law in the sense associated with justice (life) has overcome law in the sense of that which is associated with death and so with sin or injustice.

Law and Flesh

That the law is distinct from justice even though it exposes injustice comes to expression through the relation between law and its inevitable corruption. As we shall see, this is related to the question of the violence of the law. But there is another way in which this comes to expression in Paul, through his meditation on flesh. Flesh (*sarx*), at least in Hebrew (*basar*), indicates, above all, the weakness of the human: human vulnerability and mortality. This weakness and vulnerability provokes or may provoke the sort of self-protective concern that seeks its own advantage, even, perhaps especially, at the expense of the other.[33] In this way, it is precisely as flesh that injustice as the violation of the other is incited. At least a part of Paul's argument is that it is precisely "flesh" understood in something like this way that has seized control of the law and which does so always and everywhere. This is the essential corruptibility of the law, the always already having been corrupted of the law.[34]

To this seems to be added, however, a different but related insight, namely that as soon as justice is articulated as law, then injustice is awakened as well. That is, law is always already captured by its own opposite, injustice, or by that which opposes its aim or intention in producing justice. What Paul says is, "But sin seizing an opportunity in the commandment, produced in me all kinds of covetousness" (7:8). Here I would be inclined to say that the expropriation of law for the purposes of the interests of the strong against the weak is not simply an accidental feature of law but its inevitable concomitant. This means that I take this question more seriously than it seemed to me that Derrida did in his reference to Pascal et al. But this does not diminish the importance of Derrida's basic point: that the difference between law and justice is by no means remediable through a mere reform of the law as useful as that ("sometimes") is. Rather, this difference is a permanent, an irreducible one. Paul's initial way of thinking that irreducibility is through what he says about flesh. In a certain way, we may even suppose that the law, precisely as that which awakens us to our mortality (if you do these things you will die) is therefore in its own way an incitement to injustice because it is an incitement to take control of the law to make the law subservient to our interest, our survival, and so on. Under these conditions, the law as instrument of flesh serves to apportion blame, but most especially to deflect or to displace it.

A fine illustration of this is found in Derrida's discussion of Kierkegaard's reflections on Abraham's willingness to sacrifice Isaac.[35] Our laws—and indeed any civilized law—would and must condemn such an act. Yet it is the same law, let us say the law on which we now so much pride ourselves, the law of western (capitalist) democracy, that makes invisible the sacrifice of millions of children to hunger and disease, and which not only deflects attention from this "sacrifice" but also actually requires it, because this law is above all the law of property, and so the law in the name of which the very forces of capital expansion are protected at all costs.

Indeed, this becomes even more visible (and so invisible) when we take into account the energy today expended in combating the evil of terrorism, this utter disregard for the law for what is called civilized law. For instead of this leading to an attempt to address the causes of the fear and resentment and hopelessness and desperation that are the breeding ground of these acts, instead of restraining the violence of which terrorism is a kind of counterviolence; instead, in the name of the law of civilization itself, almost unimaginable terror is wreaked upon the weak and vulnerable. Indeed, there is little attempt to mask the direct mimicry of terror that this implies: surrender to us Osama bin Laden or we will bomb your towns and villages; surrender to us Saddam Hussein or we will make sure your children die of hunger and disease. The law becomes the mechanism for the deflection and displacement of blame. And it does this not simply now and again but at heart, always and everywhere.

At least this is what it might mean to speak, as Paul does, of "sinful passions" being "aroused by the law" (Romans 7:5). Or how it is that "sin" may be said to seize or grasp "an opportunity in the commandment" (7:7, 11). Or even that sin (and again let us think of injustice) "through the commandment might become sinful beyond measure" (7:13).[36] And indeed, the coming of the law may even be understood as that "the law came in, with the result that the trespass [violation] multiplied" (5:20).

In these formulations, Paul is pointing to the inevitability of the corruption of law, any law. It is this inevitable corruption or pervertibility that distinguishes law from the justice to which it nevertheless bears witness. In the next chapter, we will see that for Paul, this corruption of the law comes to a focus in the fate of the messiah at the hands of the guardians of law (both forms of law, as we shall see). But Paul, through his reflections on what he calls "flesh," has also provided a kind of middle axiom between the occasional or empirical failure of the law to instantiate justice (the question that provokes reform) and the violence that serves to definitively mark the heterogeneity of law and justice.

Justice and Distributive/Retributive Justice

We have seen that Derrida's consideration of justice leads him to distinguish true justice from the terms of retributive and distributive justice. This can also be seen to be at work in Paul.

With respect to retribution, Paul can certainly invoke this—especially, it would seem, in relation to the gentiles, to gentile injustice. Thus he writes, "For the wrath of God is revealed from heaven against all ungodliness and wickedness of those who by their wickedness suppress the truth"

(1:18). So reads the New Revised Standard Version, but Paul does not here speak of wickedness but of *adikia*, that is, injustice. Thus the wrath (*orgai*) of the divine—the fury of the gods, let us say—is disclosed in a way that the pagans can understand (celestial signs, let us suppose), and this fury is directed against, precisely, injustice, an injustice that takes the form of the suppression or even imprisonment and so oppression of truth. That divine retribution is in order here is the basis of Paul's argument. And the argument ends with the ominous warning that these same pagans or gentiles already know that in accordance with divine justice, those who practice this injustice and spread this injustice "deserve death" (1:32).

Thus an initial argument of Paul seems to presuppose that justice— here, divine justice—may take the form of vengeance, of retribution, of payback. But Paul's argument as a whole has the aim of disassociating this divine justice or true justice from retribution. How so? For one thing, Paul is concerned to eliminate payback from the sphere of interhuman justice. This is the meaning of his reservation of vengeance to the divine as a way of excluding it from the sphere of the interhuman practice of justice: "Never avenge yourselves but leave space for the wrath of God" (12:19). The association of the divine with vengeance serves to eliminate it from our relationships to one another.

But beyond this, it is clear that the whole tenor of Paul's argument is to maintain that divine justice consists in the abolition of payback, of vengeance, of punishment. For the act of the divine that instantiates or initiates true justice, justice outside the law, is precisely a justice which does not, or does no longer, "calculate offenses," and is to that extent associated with the idea and act of "pardon" (see Chapter 7 below).

Similarly, with the closely related notion of justice as the measured distribution of rewards and of penalties, justice is dissociated from a measuring of merit. But first they seem to be associated. Thus, again speaking of divine justice, Paul can write, "For [the divine as the agent of just judgment, or of judgment as justice, *dikaiokrisis*] will repay according to each one's deeds; to those who by patiently doing good seek for glory and honor and immortality, he will give eternal life, while for those who are self-seeking, and who obey not truth but injustice, there will be wrath and fury" (2:6–8). In this case—again addressing gentiles or pagans on their own terms as those who seek honor and glory through good deeds—Paul deploys the notion of justice as giving what is due.

Yet this also will be placed in question in Paul's subsequent argument.

For as much as justice regularly means this giving in accordance with what is due, it is also (and even more) a giving beyond what is due, an exceeding of what may be counted or counted on by maintaining something like the unmerited and unmeritable character of the divine gift of justice. The clarification of the suspension of this calculation and settling of accounts as expressions of justice (on account of grace) must await my discussion of gift/grace in Chapter 4. At this point, it is enough to see that Paul is not unaware of the philosophical positions that identify justice with retribution and distribution and is intent on going beyond them. It is thus appropriate at this point to remind ourselves of what Derrida has written concerning this: "Does it come [the gift of *dike*] simply to render justice or, on the contrary to give *beyond* the due, the debt, the crime or the fault?" (25).

The Future of Justice

Although I will not be able to deal fully with the question of the eschatological character of justice relative to law in the current context, I may at least identify some of the ways in which for Paul the distinction between law and justice entails a reference to the coming of a future that is other than the prolongation, or expansion, of the present. That the thought of Paul must be situated within a horizon variously described as apocalyptic or eschatological has been expressly asserted by Kasemann,[37] and then elaborated forcefully and extensively by J. Christiaan Beker.[38] This holds for the whole of Paul's work and for the letter to Romans as well. But to what extent may and must we relate this "eschatological" perspective to the question of justice and of law? Certainly in connection with the notion of judgment—that is, the coming into being of divine justice—Paul has made use of eschatological perspectives. Thus the coming wrath of God, the coming judgment of God, and so on have been already cited.

But even with respect to what for Paul will be the beginning of the actualization of justice beyond law among those who adhere to the justice of God manifest in the Messiah, there remains the importance of living in anticipation of the accomplishment of that justice. Thus Paul can write, "For by hope we were saved. Now hope that is seen is not hope. For who hopes for what is seen? But if we hope for what we do not see, we wait for it with patience" (8:25). The theme of hope displaces the new justice from that which is present, from that which is "seen." Hope is possible only on the basis of the nonpresence of what is hoped for. But what is hoped for here is the accomplishment of that justice that has already been glimpsed beyond the law. Accordingly, even those who have somehow become participants in this project of making justice beyond the law are encouraged: "you know what time it is, how now is the moment for you to wake from sleep. For salvation is nearer to us than when we became believers; the night is far gone, the day is near" (13:11–12a).

These assertions do not yet establish that Paul's concern for justice—for the justice beyond the law—is "safe" from the potential problem indicated by Derrida about the way in which an already accomplished messianism may be destructive of the very idea of justice. But they do indicate that for Paul, that which is announced as justice remains to a certain extent within the horizon or dimension of hope, of waiting, for that which is yet to come and so for that which "we do not see."

Force, Violence, and the Cross

How does the rupture between justice and law come into being or into consciousness? How does it come to be thematized as an opposition, as justice against law, law against justice? We have seen that this is by no means the only way in which we have to think the relation between justice and law. But it is indispensable that an opposition be thinkable in order that the problem of a relationship between them come into focus. In the case of Derrida, this question seems to be most vigorously put in his reflections on Walter Benjamin's essay "Critique of Violence"[1] (or "Critique of Force"—*Gewalt*) that is the counterpart to the reflections we have already considered in the first half of "The Force of Law" (otherwise known as "Deconstruction and the Possibility of Justice"). I will first identify some of the features of that reading of Benjamin and then indicate how those reflections help to identify the occasion of Paul's own recognition of the problem of law with respect to justice. I will suggest that this has to do with the question of the cross.

If the law intends justice and so is intimately connected with that question, then there is no doubt as well that for Paul there is something like a crisis of the law. We may suppose that the crisis of the law has to do with the way in which Jesus had been condemned by both instances of law, namely the law(s) of Moses and the law(s) of Rome. In some way, Paul's reassessment of Jesus as innocent seems to bring law into question (perhaps law as such) because it shows that the two instances of law come into opposition to justice and thus delegitimate themselves. The law then subverts justice and produces injustice instead of justice.

Derrida

Although the issue is most directly discussed in the second part of Derrida's essay on the "Force of Law," it is already prefigured in the discussion of the first half of the essay. In reference to Kant's *Theory of Right*, Derrida writes: "There are to be sure laws that are not enforced, but there is no law without enforceability and no applicability or enforceability of the law without force" (233). This is further substantiated by reference to a remark of Pascal's, about which Derrida says, "Justice without force is powerless—in other words, justice is not justice, it is not achieved if it does not have the force to be 'enforced'; a powerless justice is not justice, in the sense of law" (238). What I focus on here first is that a powerless justice is not justice *in the sense of law*. That is, it is not justice as such, if one could say such a thing, but justice as law, as effectively law, that requires force. The question of the power of a powerless justice will return below.

The question then seems to be of a law that is outside of justice, or at least of the founding of law in a manner that stands outside of justice. Precisely at the point of violence or force, we encounter the exteriority of law and justice. "Yet the operation that amounts to founding, inaugurating, justifying law, to *making* law, would consist of a *coup de force*, of a performative and therefore interpretive violence that in itself is neither just nor unjust" (241). This formulation of a foundation of law that is neither just nor unjust corresponds well to what Derrida had maintained already in 1976 in his "Declarations of Independence" (*Negotiations*, 46–54) in which he reads the U.S. Declaration of Independence as an "interpretive 'coup de force'" (51).[2]

It is, however, in grappling directly with Benjamin's critique of force or violence that the relation between violence and law is deepened. First Derrida maintains that in thinking violence and its critique we are "in the sphere of law and justice" (265). "The concept of violence belongs in the symbolic order of law, politics and morals" (265). And this is quickly related to the specific order of law itself. Derrida cites Benjamin to the effect that law has an "interest in a monopoly of violence. This monopoly does not strive to protect any given just and legal ends but law itself" (267; see Benjamin's "Critique," 281). Derrida comments, "This seems like a tautological triviality. Yet is not tautology the phenomenal structure of a certain violence of the law that lays itself down, by decreeing to be violent, this time in the sense of outlaw [*hors-la-loi*], anything that doesn't recognize it?" (267). This rests upon the complexity of the relation between violence and the law. On the one hand, the law offers itself as a substitute for, or a sublimation of, violence. It thus decrees that violence is to be superseded by the law. Benjamin writes, "the legal system tries to erect, in all areas where individual ends could be usefully pursued by violence, legal ends that can only be realized by legal power" (280). But this substitution of law for violence occurs by way of taking the outside or exteriority of law and legality to be violent. This outcome is readily apparent. Even today, those who refuse to accept the right of a certain legal authority are called "terrorists," even if what they do has nothing in it of the use or threat of death-dealing force.[3] Because the law offers itself, advertises itself, as the substitute for violence, then whatever is outside is necessarily violent. But as we shall see, this is because that which is somehow outside the law reveals, precisely, the violence of the law itself.

Thus Derrida cites Benjamin's example of the "great criminal": "The admiring fascination exerted on the people by 'the figure of the "great" criminal . . . ' " (183/E281), can be explained as follows: it is not someone who has committed this or that crime for which one feels a secret admiration; it is someone who, in defying the law [*loi*], lays bare the violence of the juridical order itself" (267). It is noteworthy that it is not the particular crime that is important here but rather the apparent defiance of law as such which may be said to excite a certain admiration.[4] And this admiration has as its basis what has been exposed as the violence of the law. Anyone who has read Paul will be reminded of the way in which he designates the messiah Jesus as something like "the great criminal," that is as one who is "sin itself" (2 Corinthians 5:21) or as one who is accursed (Galatians 3:31). Thus it seems to me that this very nicely identifies the position of Jesus in the thought of Paul—more precisely, the figure of the crucified, one who is identified thereby as something like a great criminal, or, as Paul will also say, one who is made to be sin (or crime) itself. Jesus is, of course, made to be precisely this as one who is executed not as just any criminal, but as one who is somehow a threat to the order, let us recall not only or even primarily the Judean order, but precisely the gentile order, the Roman order, the order that radiates from the place to which Paul is writing in the text we are to read.

Derrida goes on to extend the suggestion of Benjamin concerning the great criminal to include also a certain legal strategy pursued by the lawyer who contests the competence of the law to judge through the "strategy of rupture," which contests "the order of the law" (267), and adds "But what order of law? The order of law in general, or this order of law instituted and set to work ('enforced') by the power of this state? Or order as inextricably mixed with the state in general?" (267).[5] Thus we have the same effect seemingly produced both by the great criminal and the great lawyer who from different positions—one inside, the other outside, the law—expose the arbitrariness and so the violence of the law.

Derrida then goes on to cite what he takes to be Benjamin's "discriminating example" of the right to strike, but then, most directly the general strike, which in going beyond specific demands to resisting the order of law itself, results in a violent response on the part of the defenders of the legal order. Of this situation, Derrida writes, "Such a situation is in fact *the only one* that allows us to conceive the homogeneity of law and violence, violence as the exercise of law and law as the exercise of violence. Violence is not exterior to the order of law. It threatens law from within law" (268).

This, it seems to me, goes somewhat beyond, at least in terms of clarity or lucidity of formulation, what one may read in Benjamin's essay. However, in Benjamin's essay, there is reference to another phenomenon that allows one to see the relation of violence and law: "Benjamin distinguishes between two sorts of general strikes, some destined to replace the order of one state with another (general *political* strike), the other to abolish the state (general *proletarian* strike)" (271), to which Derrida immediately adds: "In sum, the two temptations of deconstruction" (271). That is, deconstruction as a way of thinking critically about law may be said to face the temptation either of replacing one order with another through a kind of founding violence, the violence of a deconstructive interpretation; or deconstruction is tempted to abolish the very idea or reality of an existing order. In the first case, there is a kind of philosophical Jacobinism, in the second a philosophical anarchism. But note that these are *temptations* that beset deconstruction. And as we have seen, the deconstructibility of law does not serve and must not serve either to erect or found another law (institution even), nor does it seek to abolish law as such, for it insists on the necessity of law, however deconstructed, as the way in which justice must come to expression.

We should not overlook the fact that these "temptations" may also be seen in the reading of Paul who may be read either as abolishing the law, destroying law as such (recall Nietzsche's reading), or as instituting a new law that is all the more inexorable in its demand and its capacity to judge, especially as this is institutionalized in a church law that seeks to impose itself even in the most interior recesses of the human will.

We have seen that there appears to be an alternative between a general strike and a general proletarian strike in the thought of Benjamin. But Derrida goes on to "deconstruct" this opposition or alternative: "there is never a pure opposition between the general political strike looking to refound another state and the general proletarian strike looking to destroy the state" (272). Deconstruction in some sense is this general strike, political/proletarian, in that it in one way or another is an undermining of the law or the force of law (of language, of genre, of the moral or juridical law). At the same time, the deconstruction of law aims not at its annihilation but at demonstrating that it is exterior to, while required by, the claim of justice.

Much the same happens to the proffered distinction between founding and preserving the law, between the violence that does the one and the violence that does the other. Derrida notes that Benjamin offers an important "distinction between two kinds of violence of law, in relation to law: the founding violence, the one that institutes and posits law and the violence that preserves, the one that maintains, confirms, insures the permanence and enforceability of Law" (264). Derrida notes that the opposition of founding and preserving violence is at best unstable because the founding violence supposes its own "iterability" and thus preservation (272), while preservation again and again refounds what it "preserves."

The relation of law and violence seems especially exposed in what Benjamin suggests regarding the strict coimplication of law with the death penalty. Here Benjamin speaks of what is "rotten in law" as the way in which law is contaminated by violence: it focuses precisely on the death penalty. Derrida maintains, "Law is condemned, ruined, in ruins, ruinous, if one can risk a sentence of death on the subject of law, especially when it is a question of the death penalty. And it is in a passage on the death penalty that Benjamin speaks of what is 'rotten' in law" (273). This is played out again in a subsequent passage. In Derrida's reading of Benjamin, the critique of the death penalty is not superficial because "when one tackles the death penalty, one does not tackle one penalty among others but law itself in its origin, its very order" (276). This is explained as follows: "The legal system [*l'ordre du droit*] fully manifests itself in the possibility of the death penalty. By abolishing it, one would not be touching upon one *dispotif* among others. Rather one would be disavowing the very principle of law" (276).

Although this is not explicitly said by Derrida, it would seem that here we have the very heart of (legal) violence. Violence is violence when it entails the violation of another's very life, that is, when it is able to deal, or threaten to deal, death to the other. Thus when we are involved in a critique of violence, we are involved in a critique of the license to kill, the legitimation of murder. And this comes to expression most basically, as Benjamin notes, in war and in the death penalty. Until now, these are licensed forms of death dealing in which the law or the state as bearer of law comes to expression, comes into existence. And in our own time, as nations seek to abolish the death penalty, what remains to be thought is to what extent this means the abolition of law, the enforceability of law. What remains when law in this sense is decidedly transformed?[6] At a minimum, the transformation of law that comes about through the abolition of the death penalty would be the recognition of the subordination of law, always and everywhere, to justice and thus a permanent relativizing of the law relative to justice.

In the last pages of this essay, there is also a reflection on sacrifice and life and life even beyond death that bears as well on our theme, where it seems to me we move to the difference between sacrificing the living being (of another) to the acceptance or assumption of sacrifice (of one's own life) for the sake of the living. Here it may be we open into a new set of issues, also to be brought to bear on the scene and symbol of the cross, but we shall not (yet) tarry here. I will, however, tarry over this: the confluence of so many ways in which the very order of law, of state, is brought into question. They are, so far, the great criminal, the lawyer who contests the order of law, the general strike, the opposition to the death penalty, and deconstruction. In each of these instances, what happens is that the difference between law and justice comes to expression. And in each case (save that of deconstruction?), we have the appearance of a certain violence as that which exposes the noncoincidence of justice and law and so that which makes thinkable both the deconstructibility of law and the indeconstructibility of justice.

The Last Name of Walter

The second part of Derrida's essay "The Force of Law" is entitled "The First Name of Benjamin" and was actually offered as a reflection for a conference entitled "Nazism and the Final Solution: Probing the Limits of Representation," held at the University of California at Los Angeles in 1990. Benjamin's first name is of course Walter, and this is played in relation to *Gewalt* or "force" or "violence."

Let us take the reflection on the first name of Benjamin as an oblique invitation to also think of the last name, the family name of Walter (or even of violence). For the name of Benjamin has its own resonance with the theme of violence both outside and in the name of the law. The name is, of course, the name of a tribe of Israel named for the youngest son of Israel/Jacob. But it is a name often enough associated with a strange violence. Perhaps a violence already inscribed in the violence of his birth that causes the death of his mother, Rachel, the beloved of Jacob/Israel (Genesis 35:16–20).

The violence of this name appears again in the story of the "outrage of Gibeah," in which a Levite is received with hospitality by one who lives among the Benjaminites but who is himself of another tribe. Thus he, like Lot in Sodom, is a stranger who offers hospitality to a stranger. But the Benjaminites, like the Sodomites of Genesis, demand that the stranger be offered as a sacrifice to their violence. In this case, the concubine of the Levite becomes the victim, and when her violated body is returned to the doorstep, the outraged (but still safe and secure Levite) dismembers her corpse to call the other tribes to holy war against the Benjaminites.

Of course, the Levite is by no means a sympathetic character in this narrative. He has not only willingly sacrificed his concubine to the violence of the Benjaminites, he has also sliced her up (living or dead, we are not explicitly told) in order to call for a fratricidal war of extermination. In this he reminds us of the Levites that Moses commanded to launch a "cultural revolution" against his own people by running through the camp killing sons and brothers in order to establish their credentials as holy warriors against the alleged corruption of his own people (Exodus 32:26–29). The violence has the function, precisely, to establish the law, the force of law.

The tale of the outrage at Gibeah (Judges 19) and of the fratricidal war of extermination that comes in its wake (Judges 20 and 21) is contextualized by the narrator as a time "before the law," that is, as a time when there was no king in Israel (Judges 19:1, 21:25), so "all the people did what was right in their own eyes" (21:25). In this way, the narrator invites us to view the coming of a king as the triumph of law and order against the backdrop of the violence before the law. But the irony is that the king who is called is himself a Benjaminite—a certain Saul—who institutes the kingship and so the force of law, and whose murderous rage is first directed against his own son and then to a lifelong attempt to assassinate the one who had been his beloved boy toy but who is also the designated king-to-be.

Nor is this the last of the last name of Benjamin. For we also know of another Saul of the tribe of Benjamin (he says so in Philippians 3:5 and again in Romans 11:1) whose murderous rage against the "Christians"—licensed, as he believed, by the law—is somehow at last transformed into a critique of law and especially the force of law. As much as the first name of Benjamin (Walter), the last name of Walter (Benjamin) invites us to a reflection on the violence of the law and so the disjuncture between the law and justice.

This midrashic reflection on a name may serve as a segue into a consideration of the thought of the Benjaminite (Saul/Paul) who is most concerned with the disjuncture of justice and law.

Paul and the Cross

At the end of our introductory reflections on the relation of Derrida to the question of justice and then to the work of Paul, I noted the "lucidity" that Derrida attributes to Nietzsche's view of Paul. In the section from *Daybreak* that I cited, Nietzsche pointed to the question or problem of the law, a question that we have now explored with the help of Derrida and found that for Paul, the question of the law is central, though not exactly in the way supposed by Nietzsche. For Paul, I have argued, still holds to the question of justice relative to the law. But in those same reflections, Nietzsche had pointed to the crucifixion of the messiah as that which seemed to deconstruct (as we would now say) the law. In the meantime, we have seen that for Derrida, the question of the violence or force of the law, both with respect to its inception or founding and to its enforcement, is that which exposes the unfounded foundation of law and thus renders it deconstructible. What remains, then, is to show that in his characterization of Paul, Nietzsche was right in pointing to the event of the crucifixion of the messiah, or of one who is seen or claimed to be the justice of God, as the point at which for Paul the law becomes fundamentally problematic.

In our discussion of the law in Paul, we noted that his critique appears to apply equally to Mosaic and to Roman law, and that to the extent to which there is a disproportion between these, it is because for Paul, the Mosaic law has precedence over the Roman law. In any case, the problem of law as Paul wrestles with it in Romans is applicable both to Roman and to Mosaic law, and this is a significant part of the advance of the discussion in Romans over that in Galatians.

One of the intriguing and at first perplexing features of Paul's argument in Romans is that it takes him so long to get to an explicit mention of the cross, or otherwise refer to the fate of the one he takes to be the messiah of God and so the embodiment of the justice of God. It is really not until chapter 5 that this seems to come to expression somewhat directly.[7] And this will be perplexing precisely because Paul has elsewhere indicated that his theme is always precisely the cross, that is, the execution of Jesus. He had already maintained this in 1 Corinthians, when he asserted that "I decided to know nothing among you but Jesus messiah and him crucified" (1 Corinthians 2:2), after having maintained that "we proclaim messiah crucified" (1:23). Subsequently, in Galatians, he had reminded his readers that "It was before your eyes that Jesus messiah was publicly exhibited as crucified" (Galatians 3:2).[8] What is the meaning of this reticence in Romans to directly mention the theme of the execution of the messiah at the hands of the imperial authorities?

The answer would seem to be that this letter is by no means a general discussion that is addressed to no one in particular at no particular time, but is addressed precisely to certain people in Rome. Rome was the capitol of the empire. The empire maintained its authority through the violence of the cross. Rebellion against Rome, or what was taken to be rebellion against Rome, was to be punished by this particularly grisly form of execution. And this policy of enforcement through crucifixion was, as we know, remarkably effective.

Now the problem of a letter addressed to people in Rome, to the heart of the empire maintained through the penalty of crucifixion, is precisely that the messiah was crucified. That is, the messiah was subjected to the penalty that enabled the empire as empire to maintain itself. In overturning the verdict of the empire, one comes perilously close to overturning the empire itself.[9] Certain tact therefore seems to be called for.

For Paul, let us suppose, the question of law has been raised in such a way as to make law questionable in relation to justice. We have seen from Derrida that this questioning of law, of the justice of law, has to do with the exposure of the violent foundation and enforcement of law. For Derrida, this is a question that can be discovered always and everywhere in relation to law. For Paul, it seems to have been precisely in relation to the specific "example" of a certain violence (execution, the death penalty, crucifixion) that is imposed upon one whom he subsequently comes to recognize as the messiah of God and so as the bringer of the divine justice.[10]

Now, of course, this verdict could be understood as a simple miscarriage of justice; that is, that the officers of the law acted illegally. In that case, the law would not be in question but rather its servants or its instrumentalities in particular cases. And this is precisely what has often been attempted, beginning in the first century, with respect to the execution of Jesus. The attempt to lay the blame for the execution of Jesus at the feet of the Judean leadership, for example, has too often served as a legitimation for Christian anti-Judaism. It has also served as a way of exculpating Roman or imperial law as the apparent attempts to mitigate the guilt even of Pilate may show. The attempts to deflect blame from Rome to "the Jews" for the execution of Jesus have always had as their problem that Jesus was crucified rather than stoned; that is, that it was the empire that killed him.

In any case, all this seems quite contrary to Paul's own view concerning the cross. In 1 Corinthians 2:8, he makes clear that the agents of the crucifixion were "the rulers of this age." Now the rulers of this age cannot mean something like the Jews or even the Judean officialdom. They are by no stretch of the imagination the rulers of this age. But the emperor and his agents, the apparatus of Roman power and rule, not only could be perceived to be the rulers of this age, but this was also what they claimed for themselves. It is they who, according to Paul, "have crucified the Lord of glory"; that is, subjected the glorious one to the ignominy and humiliation of this particular form of execution. Whatever Paul may have to say about the repudiation of the messiah by the officials of Judea, he is quite clear that the executioners of Jesus were the rulers of this age, the imperial rulers; that is, Rome.[11] And this gets us pretty near understanding why, as I mentioned before, a certain tact may be called for in writing to readers who are in Rome. (As Derrida has made clear, one can never count on who one's readers will really be.[12])

We have seen that Paul does not suppose that the law has simply been subjected to a mistake but that it has been exposed as deeply illegitimate, or at least as incapable of producing justice. For this to be so, it must be the case that the messiah was condemned and executed not through a miscarriage of law but through a fundamental opposition between law and justice. That is, the condemnation of Jesus was not wrong in terms of law, nor was his execution wrong in terms of legality. On the contrary, the condemnation and execution were right in terms of law.[13] It is only then that it could follow that there is a problem with law as law. It was legal but unjust, in collision or fundamental opposition to justice. And this is so because the one legally condemned and executed is the justice of God, the messiah of God.

We should note that there is another way of verifying that the verdict against Jesus was correct from the standpoint of law. It is not necessary to verify the fulfillment of legal niceties in order to make this claim, and indeed we have no way of knowing what sort of information Paul may have had about the legal forms involved in this particular case. But as we have seen, from the standpoint of law, anyone who stands outside the law is deemed "violent" by definition. That is, the calling into question of the legal order is from the standpoint of that legal order, a threat to the very being of law. For it seems to open the floodgates to that very violence that the law claims to keep at bay. If one claims to represent justice (the will of God, let us say) and yet brings the law into question, then that one constitutes a threat, a decisive threat, to the order of law.[14] In such a case, that person may be seen to be an agent of violence, even though he or she may threaten bodily harm to no one. The response of the law to eliminate this threat to what it supposes to be the general welfare is then "justified" if law or the force of law is ever justified.

This, it seems to me, is the only explanation for the fundamental critique of law that we get in Romans: a critique of law, in the name of justice. That the wedge driven between justice and the law is precisely the execution of the messiah is, of course explicitly affirmed in Galatians: "if justification [becoming or being enabled to be just] were through the law then messiah died to no purpose" (2:21). That is, it is precisely the death of messiah that has the purpose or meaning that justice is seen to be heterogeneous with respect to the law.

This is not "the same thing" as we find in Derrida. Paul's perception that the law is incapable of producing justice depends on the recognition that the messiah of God has been legally condemned and executed by the law. Derrida's argument does not rest on the claim about the having come of the messiah but on the thinking through of the claim of law and justice. Derrida asks what is always ("phenomenologically," let us say) the case, whereas Paul thinks in terms of an event, of the having come to pass of this contradiction in the cross of the messiah.

There is, then, another issue that must be at least broached here. It is the relation between event, example, and exemplarity. The question is this: How does the verdict against the messiah of God raise the possibility of a general critique of law relative to justice? The difficulty that we may en-

counter here is that if the uniqueness of this event is too strongly emphasized, then no consequences would follow with respect to law as such. On
the other hand, if this is but one among many possible examples of a general rule, it would not have the elucidatory power to expose a structural issue: we would be back to the problem of a mere miscarriage of justice.
Paul's mode of discourse has the tendency to so underline the unique significance of the cross as to make it sui generis. It is the death of the "Son of
God." If this is too heavily stressed, then we get consequences for God, let
us say, but none on the plane of human history. And this is precisely what
has often happened in the theological interpretation of Paul and of the
cross generally. It becomes a peculiar transaction between God and his son.
And when this happens, the law is simply left in place and often indeed
bolstered in its hegemony.

At this point we may simply offer the hypothesis that Paul be read as
using what are subsequently called christological claims, to stress the elucidatory power of this event (the verdict against the messiah). That is, the
execution of the messiah is "exemplary." It brings to expression in a definitive way the opposition between law and justice. So definitively does this
illumine the situation that a general crisis regarding law relative to justice
becomes thinkable. But we must admit that the very terms that underline
the exemplarity of this event (christological claims, for example) also
threaten to undermine the significance of the event. If the event is regarded
as too singular, then it will have no implications for a critique of law. The
very terms that underline its significance may also undermine it, and,
moreover, actually do so in the history of the theological appropriation of
these claims.[15]

Having suggested that what is at work in Paul's critique of the law
may be the cross as the fate of the messiah, we may now note how this con-
nects us to the discussion we have had earlier of Derrida's reading of Walter Benjamin. First we recall the role of the figure of the "great criminal"
that is one whose fascination lies in the way in which this criminal exposes
or "lays bare the violence of the juridical order itself" (267). This is or
seems to be precisely the role that the "messiah Jesus" plays in Paul's
thought, for he is identified as one who is the very embodiment of violation of crime, that is, of sin. In Galatians, the execution of the messiah is
what places him irrevocably outside the law in the strong sense of accursed
by the law: "Messiah redeemed us from the curse of the law having become
a curse for us, for it is written, 'cursed be everyone who hangs on a tree'"

(Galatians 3:13; see Deuteronomy 21:22–23). Here Paul supposes that the messiah is one cursed by the law, made forever and finally outside and against the law. In some way this will also entail that the law itself is rendered impotent with respect to cursing, as we shall see. In another argument, this time in 2 Corinthians, Paul has maintained, "For our sake [God] made [messiah] to be sin who knew no sin so that we might become the justice of God" (5:21). Once again, Jesus as messiah is made into the very figure of the lawbreaker, sin itself, despite being, in quite another way (one yet to be clarified) the source and impetus of justice itself. In both cases, what is in view is the position of the messiah as bearer of justice, as one whose exteriority with respect to the law is made dramatically evident in his being condemned and executed by the force of the law. The convergence of Roman and Mosaic law in his condemnation and execution places him in the position of being something very like "the great criminal" referred to by Benjamin.

In the discussion of Benjamin, Derrida had pointed to the way in which the death penalty exposes the violence of the law in such a way as to "deconstruct" the force of law. Thus the very point at which the force of law, and the possibility of the enforcement of law, comes into being is precisely in and through the death penalty: "when one tackles the death penalty, one does not tackle one penalty among others but law itself in its origin, its very order" (276). In addition to the way in which the death penalty stands for law as such, its enforceability, it is also and therefore the case that to question this penalty is to bring into question the absoluteness of law itself and as such. "The legal system [*l'ordre du droit*] fully manifests itself in the possibility of the death penalty. By abolishing it, one would not be touching upon one *dispotif* among others. Rather one would be disavowing the very principle of law" (276). Insofar as the law does not have the right to exercise this sovereign judgment, it loses its foundational or absolute character.

It is manifest that the cross is nothing if not this death penalty, and although it cannot be said that Paul is raising the question of the death penalty as a general political issue, what he is doing is perhaps rather more radical in that he is taking the one who has been the object of the penalty of death and making him into the source of life (Romans 5:17–18). The death penalty is thus overturned in the most thorough possible way,[16] for that verdict is overturned by God (Justice itself), not only in the sense of being reversed in a particular case, but also through a "resurrection from the dead" that robs the penalty of death of its power or force quite generally. And if the death penalty has no force, then "there is no condemnation," not only for the messiah, but for all who are in solidarity with that messiah; that is, for all for whom that event is exemplary or who are exemplified by that event. Paul writes of this solidarity, "For if we have been united with him in a death like his, we will certainly be united with him in a resurrection like his" (Romans 6:5). But the logic of his argument has also impelled him to make this an even more universal claim: "One man's act of justice leads to justification and life for all" (5:18). Indeed, Paul regularly is led in his explication of resurrection to suggest the universal significance or effectiveness of the resurrection. Thus the event of the messiah is represented, when resurrection is in view, as exemplary not just for some but for all. In that way, law, the force of law, has been quite thoroughly overturned.

There are a number of consequences that seem to flow from this perspective of the abolition of death and so of the death penalty. First, the competence of those who administer the law to condemn or to judge is abolished. Paul argues this first with respect to the gentile authorities: "Therefore you have no excuse, whoever you are, when you judge others; for in passing judgment on another you condemn yourself" (2:1). Although Paul, for obvious reasons I think, does not here mention the judgment or execution of Jesus, this cannot be far from his mind when he denies the competence of pagan authorities to judge or condemn.

Something similar happens when he turns his attention to the authorities of his own people "But if you call yourself a Jew and rely on the law . . . you then that teach others will you not teach yourself" (2:17, 21). Even here, in this very preliminary delegitimation of the authoritativeness of a certain teaching of the law, what is brought into question is the capacity of its representatives to make the sort of judgments that depend on a certain competence in the law. If Paul himself had been one of these teachers of the law, and if the mode of his teaching had taken the form of a condemnation and even "persecution" of the followers of Jesus as messiah, then this apparently mild rebuke has even greater force.

But this power to condemn or judge is not only revoked for Jew and gentile who had been adherents of a law that was found to be in opposition to the representative of the divine justice. It also applies to the adherent of this messiah, for the adherent is not made into a more competent administrator of divine law and thus placed in a position to judge, but is all the more disqualified from the act of judging. Paul addresses the "believer" as follows: "who are you to pass judgment" (14:4); "Why do you pass judgment on your brother or sister" (14:10); "Let us no longer pass judgment on one another" (14:13). With these admonitions, Paul's exhortation comes into contact with what is also expressed in the Jesus tradition as that has been mediated through the narrative Gospels. There, Jesus is often recalled as opposing himself to judgment and as calling his followers to abandon the habit of judging or condemning one another (Matthew 7:1–6).

The irony is that Christian "morality," as Nietzsche noted, has been characterized by a generalized recrudescence of precisely this judgment, not only in the scenes of a last judgment, which he thought were no longer relevant to Christian moralism, but even more in the tendency to pass judgment on the lives of others and even especially oneself. That Jesus and Paul seem to undermine this possibility makes the invention of a machinery of judging of not only acts but more especially of feelings, desires, and intentions all the more odd. Paul may not be altogether innocent of this tendency, as a reading of 1 Corinthians might demonstrate, despite his later insistence on the abrogation of the law's power to judge. But whatever slippages may be discerned or alleged in his renunciation of the authority to condemn, there can be no doubt that he intends to insist in Romans that this authority is abolished not only for the representatives of Roman and Mosaic law but also for the representatives of what he can call "the law of messiah."

It is not only that Jews, gentiles, and even fellow believers are deprived of the ability to judge, but even God, justice itself, no longer may be said to use the authority to condemn. This at least is what Paul seems to claim: "There is therefore now no condemnation for those who are in messiah Jesus" (8:1); he later insists, "It is God who makes just. Who is to condemn?" (8:33b–34a). What is in view here, I will later argue, is something like a general amnesty.[17] Thus the crisis in the law that comes to a focus in the condemnation and death penalty against the great criminal who is the messiah of God means that the force of law is overturned. Of course this does not mean the overthrow of what the law intends, its goal or telos. God forbid, Paul says. But for an explication of this, we must await more clarification.

In the discussion with Benjamin, Derrida indicated that it was not only the figure of the great criminal and not only the death penalty that in different ways expose the violence of the law and so its exteriority with respect to justice, but there was also the case of a general strike that seems to refuse to cooperate with the order of law itself in the name of justice. That a movement may undermine the "rule of law" is not only the discovery of the anarchists but, in terms of history, may be most importantly seen in movements of civil disobedience or nonviolent resistance. The strategy of such movements is to expose the violence inherent in the system of law.[18] This is the meaning of the provocation of the violence of the British colonial masters by Gandhi or the provocation of the violence of the administrators of Jim Crow legislation in the Southern states of the United States by the civil rights movement, or the velvet revolution in Prague with its counterparts in Germany and even Tianamin Square.

It seems to me that the movement that Paul is here addressing is in certain ways like these more recent ones. It is a kind of general strike in that it is a withdrawal of certain kinds of participation in the sociopolitical order.[19] This comes to expression in Paul only obliquely in his references to the bearing of persecution and to solidarity in the kind of suffering that he understands to have been that of the messiah (precisely opposition, condemnation, imprisonment, execution). Thus Paul can regularly point to his own sufferings at the hands of the authorities, the representatives of law in both its Judean and its Roman instances, as a participation in the sufferings of the messiah, as having a similar origin and effect (2 Corinthians 6:4–10, 11:23–33, 12:10). Moreover, he can do the same with respect to his communities (Philippians 1:28–29). It is not the case that Paul provides his readers with clear indications of how their fate may also serve (like the general strike) to expose the injustice of the law. For that, we must await the work of another creative theologian of the first century, the author of the Gospel of Mark.[20] The greatest obstacle to recognizing the way in which the Pauline communities are to be regarded as subversive communities is precisely something he argues in Romans concerning obedience to the authorities, and we will have to attend to that text soon. But first other aspects of the congruence between what Paul is arguing and the rupture suggested by Derrida between justice and law will have to be noticed.

Weak and Strong

In a sort of preamble to *The Force of Law*, Derrida notes that he has had recourse before to the term "force" most particularly in the context of reflecting on the force of deconstruction and difference. But he says he has been also worried about this in that it might appear to align his project with a different kind of force, with arbitrary or malevolent force. In this connection, explaining as it were the way in which the "force of deconstruction" differs from the force to be explicated here, Derrida refers to "all the paradoxical situations in which the greatest force and the greatest weakness simply change places" (*Force*, 235). The greatest weakness will remind us of what we will have read later concerning the powerlessness of a certain justice—that is, of a justice that is not armed with the law. A further hint is found in a much later reflection on justice to which I have already referred. In *A Taste for the Secret*, Derrida says, "It is the weak, not the strong, that defies dialectic. Right is dialectical, justice is not dialectical, justice is weak" (33). This at least confirms that we are to think of justice "as such" as weak relative to the apparent strength of law, especially as law is backed with force, or violence—that is, the power to kill.

These hints are not unconnected to our reflections on Paul. As we have seen, Paul is cautious in his explicit references to the execution of Jesus in Romans. But he is not always so reticent, at least not when he has an audience that is farther removed from the center of imperial power—and moreover one that knows him and his preaching better. He can describe his own proclamation in Galatians as publicly portraying the cross (Galatians 3:1). And in 1 Corinthians he can say, "I decided to know nothing among you except Jesus the messiah, the crucified" (2:3). What is of greatest interest at this point is that Paul can characterize his message in a way that seems similar to the description of "deconstruction" (in which weakness and strength change places) and to justice. (Recall that deconstruction in some or other sense *is* justice.) Paul is also concerned with what appears to be weak, in fact exceedingly weak. But this weakness (and foolishness as well) is in fact, or in another way, exceedingly strong, as strong as possible; it is even divine strength: "For the message about the cross is foolishness to those who are perishing, but to us who are being saved it is the power of God" (1 Corinthians 1:18), and even: "For God's foolishness is wiser than human wisdom, and God's weakness is stronger than human strength" (1 Corinthians 1:25).

That the discourse concerning the executed messiah should be a discourse concerning the apparent weakness of God is relatively clear. That this discourse should also ascribe a certain power (that of weakness) to God is also clear here. What is added in Galatians is that this discourse concerning divine powerlessness (the trading places of the greatest weakness and the greatest strength) is also or even primarily a critique of (Mosaic) law. And in Romans, without subtracting from the former perspectives what we have then is that the cross, the message concerning the cross, or what Paul will here call the "Gospel of God," is a crisis not only for the Mosaic law but for law generally or as such, and that it is so on account of the concern—precisely—for justice, justice that, as Derrida has said, "is weak," weak at least as long as it is not armed with law, the force of law.[21]

In this way, the cross or the message concerning the cross must be distinguished from what we have been enabled to see regarding the exposure of the violence of law through the great criminal or the general (proletarian) strike. For in these cases the violence of law seems to be exposed through a counterviolence, or what can at least be readily redescribed as a counterviolence. Thus the situation indicated by these examples may be (mis)read as the countering of one violence by another in which the powerlessness of justice relative to law does not really or clearly come to expression. What Paul is driving at, it seems, is a more clarifying instance in which it is the weakness of the messiah (perhaps of God or the divine as well), in the being overcome by violence—the violence of the law—that exposes the violence of the law and so is more powerful than the law and indeed really overpowers the law (which is also to say, the state, the empire, and so on).

This is certainly what seems to happen, at least some of the time, in the cases that I have mentioned of nonviolent militancy. They "succeed," if and when they do, insofar as they expose the violence of the law (the state) both by provoking the law to act, to overact, and by exposing themselves to the full brunt of the force of the law. There is a name for this in history; it is the name of martyrdom. Although this is a theme that is too large for us at this point, it should at least be noted that the martyrs were those who by their self-exposure to death at the hands of the force of the law testified to a power greater than that of the law. No doubt this often enough has been seen in relation to the attempt to impose a new or higher law and has resulted in the imposition of a new empire or state. In that case, we have to do with the apparent weakness that is but a ruse of the same old (kind of) power. Derrida's reflections help us to see that it is not always easy to tell, either in advance or after the fact, which is the case. But they also help us to see that the connection between a certain weakness and vulnerability and the exposure of the violence of law is by no means fortuitous. And this is precisely what it seems to me that Paul's reflections on the cross also bring to expression in a quite different way.

We should not leave this discussion of the way in which the violence of the law and so its disjuncture from justice is brought to light without noticing that Paul is also aware that a certain paradox (or, as Derrida would say, aporia) is indicated here. For he does not shrink from maintaining that the violation of justice also serves to make even more evident the claim of justice. In a series of provocative paradoxes at the beginning of chapter 3, where he has been demonstrating the injustice of humanity as a whole, he faces the question of the way in which this actually seems to confirm the justice of God. He asks whether the unfaithfulness of God's people serves to disconfirm the faithfulness of God: "will their unfaithfulness nullify the faithfulness of God?" (3:3), and he insists that the answer must be negative. Indeed, he will later argue that it actually serves to reveal the faithfulness of God (in chapters 9–11). Similarly, he suggests that human untruthfulness only serves in a certain way to confirm the truthfulness of God (3:7). But the formulation closest to our own concerns (and to Paul's) has to do with the question of the relation between human injustice and divine justice, for he suggests that "our injustice serves to confirm the justice of God" (3:5).

If violence, the violence of the law, is precisely that which discloses the claim of justice beyond the law, then in a certain way, injustice confirms divine justice. That this is an aporia also for Paul is as much as admitted when in his clarification, which does not take back but insists on this aporia, he warns the reader, not for the last time, that he is "speaking in a human way" (3:5), by which one may suppose he means, in a way that is disproportionate to the truth, to the call or claim of justice. And what is precisely in view here is the apparent consequence of his critique of the law, that it must result in moral nihilism: "let us do evil that good may come" (3:8). So far is this from Paul's position that he will claim that we should do good so that evil may be overcome (12:21).

The Authorities

The important test case for our interpretation of Paul to this point is his discussion of the relation to those he calls "the authorities" in Romans 13:1. This text has often been interpreted as simply a call to submit to any authority whatever, especially what may be termed political or state authority. The most "reactionary" conclusions have been drawn from this text in support of state or imperial power. Such an interpretation, however, is dependent on an elimination of Paul's concern for justice and his critique of law as well. Moreover, it requires an isolation of this text from its context, both in Paul's general argument in Romans or his more specific concerns in the "parenesis" or teaching section within which it occurs.

In order to properly situate this passage, it is important to recall that it immediately follows on the discussion of the appropriate response to "persecution." Taken together, these instructions (concerning persecution and the "authorities") are bracketed by a discussion of the overriding theme of the way the community is to live "internally" as it were, it terms of love for one another (12:9–10, 13:8–10). Thus relations among those who are Paul's readers bracket reference to the question of relationship to those who are not only outside the group of "faithful" but also set over against that group. Of course, from another point of view, it is clear that the relations to the "outside" bracket the internal relations as well. Thus the question of which is text, which context—which is within and which is without a parenthesis—remains, in a certain way, undecidable.

In any case, the reflections on the relation to persecution and that on the relation to "authorities" clearly belong together. Persecution is the general context within which Paul writes and is something he knows something about, and that he takes for granted that his readers know something about. This has already been made evident in this text and we know it far more explicitly from other texts (2 Corinthians 1:8–11, 11:23–33; Philippians 1:12–14).

It must also be clear that these concerns are also internally related. Persecution itself requires some relation to what Paul calls "authorities" here. Opposition or criticism may come from any direction, but persecution as such entails the enlistment of authorities to enforce opposition. Without the appearance of "authorities," without their direct involvement, there is no such thing as persecution. Persecution requires that the authorities as agents of the legal order intervene to sanction determined opposition by the force of law.

The reflection on the relation to persecution is clearly linked to our understanding of how it is that the gap between justice and law comes into focus. What follows, however, reminds us that in the discussion of law and justice, the gap between justice and law, their "exteriority," does not result in a simple opposition to law or an abolition of its authority. Whatever may and must be said concerning the heterogeneity of justice and law, it remains the case that justice requires law and that law may be characterized by Paul as "holy, just, and good." It is this side of the relation (without relation) between justice and law that Paul is led to speak of by his discussion of the situation of persecution; that is, the situation in which the hetero-geneity of justice and law comes into focus in the ordinary experience of his readers, who are, we recall, located in the city of Rome.

It is generally assumed that here Paul is dealing with the imperial au-thority, with something like the state at the highest level. This is by no means certain. The fact that he will relate this to the question of paying taxes and customs makes clear that at a minimum, he is dealing with rather low-level functionaries of the administration of the legal order, the very type of "authority" with which his readers might most generally come into daily contact. Moreover, it is also the case that it is possible that Paul has in mind not the functionaries of Roman legal administration, but the administrators of synagogue polity. This at least is the argument put forward by Mark Nanos in *The Mystery of Romans*. It is not my intention to adjudicate this suggestion and the resultant discussion. The point, rather, is that the very possibility of such an interpretation is one that confirms what I have been maintaining all along—namely, that Paul's argument concerning law and justice applies to the two major polities or "politics" he was aware of, that of the Greco-Roman world and that of the synagogue.[22] Both of these at the local level had been involved in what Paul recognizes as persecution, both in his own case and in that of the communities to whom he has written. Thus Paul may indeed be thinking of either in his discussion of persecution and in his discussion of "authorities."[23] This corresponds with our discus-sion of the togetherness of Mosaic and Roman law.

Having maintained that the reader is to "overcome evil with good," Paul then maintains (and here we paraphrase to bring out the point a bit more clearly): "Let every person [soul—*psyche*] be subject to the superior authorities, for there is no authority except by [or through] God and those that are in being are those that have been appointed by God; therefore re-sisting the authorities is opposing the divine ordinance [appointment]." If we were to translate this into the question of justice to which we have been giving attention, we would have something like the following: "acknowl-edge the legitimacy of the administrators of the legal order, for these legal administrators derive their legitimacy from divine justice; thus, they are de-rived from that justice. Resistance to these 'officers of the law' is thus oppo-sition to their divine derivation." We have repeatedly seen that the law and the system of laws (and thus the guardians or administrators of the legal or-der) are derivative from the claim and call of justice. Even if it is necessary to recognize the heterogeneity of law and justice, it is also necessary that jus-tice come to expression, come into being, as law. It is insofar as the claim of justice comes to expression as law, as a concrete form of law or legal order, that this claim or call is made effective or actual in the concrete context of interhumanity. However much we may and must insist on a certain heterogeneity, we must also insist on the becoming law of justice and so the "legitimation" of law relative to justice. Indeed, it is only on account of this double bind, as it were (justice distinct from but requiring law), that we approach the aporia that Derrida has been helping us to think about.

It should also be clear that the insistence on the relation between justice and law (and thus the administration of the system of legality) does not revoke the heterogeneity of justice and law. Although this passage from Paul has often been invoked to justify tyranny, it has also been read as providing the basis for a resistance to tyranny. It is precisely insofar as the governing authorities are linked to the claim of justice that their administration is also subjected to the claims of justice. This perspective determines the orientation, for example of John Calvin, as well as that of Augustine, whose famous saying, "without justice what are kingdoms but great banditries" (*City of God*, 4, 4), is echoed by Calvin in his address to the king of France, with which he prefaces his *Institutes of the Christian Religion*: "That king who in ruling over his realm does not serve God's glory exercises not kingly rule but brigandage" (12). And this position is restated at the conclusion of the *Institutes* with Calvin's reflections not only on the imperative to serve God rather than "man" (by which he means here precisely rulers), but even enjoins the magistrates to oppose and even overthrow the rulers when the latter threaten "the freedom of the people" (4, 20.31). The text from Romans accordingly was used both by those who opposed the American Revolution and by those who supported it, with the latter more often than not influenced by Calvin. The ambiguous role of this text in the civil rights struggle in the U.S. as well as in the struggle against apartheid, provide numerous examples of the way in which Paul's own argument both establishes and undermines legal authority.

Precisely because Paul's argument is in a certain way double-edged, it cannot offer a program that is merely to be put into effect in any and all situations. That is, it is not a text that abrogates the concrete responsibility in any situation to come to terms with a double and contradictory imperative, one that is not accidental or the result of unclear analysis, but one that is ineluctable and thus one that makes possible because necessary the decision that cannot exonerate itself of responsibility by reference to a mechanism that makes decision unnecessary.[24]

The difficulty that confronts what will be called conscience is further highlighted rather than resolved by Paul's insistence that authority does not oppose, still less is a terror or fear (*phobos*) for good conduct, but only for bad behavior. In order not to fear authority, Paul claims it is necessary only to do good, and this will bring about the approval of authority. This is precisely what is the case insofar as authority aims at justice. That the administrator of law aims at justice, at the actualization of justice, is what seems to be in view in Paul's suggestion that this authority is a servant of God and this in a double sense: a servant "for your good" (13:4), as well as a servant to bring wrath upon the unjust. Thus precisely as the one who enforces the protection of the good and the punishment of the unjust, the administrator of justice is a servant of God—that is, of justice. This will only come into question at that point where authority positively opposes the doing of good (justice). Thus the doing of good cannot oppose legitimate authority. On the other hand, the authority that opposes doing good betrays thereby that it is not really authority, not really the administration of justice, even if its agents are paid by a department of justice.

It is again in this context that we hear of the "force of law." As we have seen, the law or legal regime comes into being and maintains itself through the exercise of force. And this is what Paul reminds his readers of in the passage. For he notes precisely that the administrators of the law have the use of force that is brought to bear on the one who does wrong. Moreover, this force, the force of law, is in itself and as such a certain divine violence. Certainly it claims this for itself and in this way invokes the "majesty" of the law. Here we may recall Benjamin's supposition regarding the death penalty, that it is the very foundation of law, of the authority— we may say even the divine authority—of law. We may also note Derrida's destabilizing of the distinction invoked by Benjamin between the force that founds law and the sacred violence that unfounds law. In any case, the threat of death is the way in which the law actually exercises divine authority; it is in this way that it seems to embody the wrath of the divine toward injustice.[25] Paul has already had occasion to speak of this wrath not as mediated by legal authorities but as directed at them in Romans 2:5. For there we have heard of a wrath that is directed to those who judge (2:1), that is, who exercise the power of the law, the force of the law, to condemn. These are warned ("whoever you are," Paul says) that they are but "storing up wrath for yourself on the day of wrath when God's just judgment will be revealed," and thus that "for those who obey not truth but rather injustice: wrath and fury" (2:8). Thus that the administrators of the law do in a certain way serve as instruments of the divine wrath (that is, the wrath of justice toward injustice) is a double-edged sword. For their very exercise of judgment places them in the position of receiving the brunt of that very wrath, the wrath of justice toward injustice.[26]

The response of the reader to legitimate authority—that is, to that authority which embodies the claim of justice (and what authority does not at least in certain respects?)—is to submit not only to avoid the wrath of the authorities (which "figures" the wrath of justice itself) but because of conscience, which here seems to mean because of a clear understanding that authority as authority does have some ineradicable relation to justice, even when it seems also to be a servant, in concrete cases, of injustice.

For we recall the whole discussion has in view the situation of persecution; that is, the situation in which authority is enlisted on the side of injustice and in opposition to what Paul supposes to be the truth. It is precisely in this circumstance that he calls his readers back from the brink of a simple anarchic repudiation of law and of the structures of illegality. It is precisely here where the authorities betray themselves as the servants of injustice rather than justice that it is imperative to recall that nevertheless justice does not stand aloof from law and systems of legality. It is justice itself that comes to expression, however imperfectly and even pervertedly, in and through the force of law. If this were not the case, it would be enough simply to abolish all systems of law—one of the temptations of deconstruction, as Derrida has said, the other temptation being that of founding another law. Is there no other way? In order to think such another way, we turn to the question of justice as gift or grace.

4

Justice as Gift

Our concern is with justice. But we have learned that justice is somehow outside the law, exterior in a certain way to law. This apparent contradiction of law and justice becomes clear when we see the connection between law and violence. It is the violence of law that disassociates it from justice. But we are, it would seem, no nearer our goal, which was to explicate our concern for justice. We have, to be sure, found a certain commonality of interest and procedure in Paul and Derrida. Both seem to think of the tension between justice and law. And neither wants, it would appear, simply to dismiss law. Yet both find a certain violence to be at the heart of law, a violence that means that justice, if it is to be thought, must be thought apart from the law. If this is so, how then is justice to be thought?

For Paul, as we know, the justice that is outside the law is to be somehow expected on the basis of a certain gift or grace. But how is this to be thought, and especially how is this to be thought without relinquishing our interest precisely in justice and thus in accomplishing that which justice promises and calls for? In order to rethink Paul's reflections on grace and the difficulties that this thought entails, I will seek help from the reading of Derrida on gift. It is this that, I will contend, sheds light both on the significance of what Paul is up to and on the difficulties that he runs into as he tries to think justice as, or on the basis of, gift.

Gift and Debt in the Thought of Derrida

Before turning to Paul, it is important to clarify the main contours of Derrida's reflections on the gift and its relation to economy. We will first show that Derrida's thinking of gift is related to his thinking of justice. It will then be necessary to indicate how the impossibility of the gift relative to economy does not mean the end of thinking about gift but is the basis for thinking more clearly about gift. This will provide us with basic tools for attempting to clarify Paul's thought about grace in relation to justice.

Relation to Justice

Derrida has already linked gift and justice in his earliest reflections on justice. Thus in *The Force of Law* he had suggested that deconstruction had already obliquely touched on justice insofar as it had touched upon the question of gift. He had said, "It goes without saying that discourses on . . . the gift beyond exchange and distribution . . . are also, through and through, at least oblique discourses on justice" (235).

But is the relation between justice and gift even more stringent than the impression given through a listing of a discourse on gift as one of the kinds of discourses that are obliquely related to the question (again we do not say theme) of justice? In a later reflection, Derrida will make this connection rather more explicit: "The question of justice, the one that always carries beyond the law, is no longer separated, in its necessity or in its aporias, from that of the gift" (*Specters of Marx*, 26). Here at least we are pointed to what seems an even more stringent relation, in that justice and the gift are said to be somehow inseparable; moreover, to think justice means to think gift. But how can this be so? It would seem that something more is at stake here than a similarity of structure if we may provisionally put it like that, or a similarity of method: we think of gift in the same way that we think of justice—namely, in such a way as to expose or bring to light the aporia, the non-self-evidence of these familiar notions. More than this seems to be claimed: if justice is the question, we can no longer engage in this question without reference to the question of gift.

Derrida does in fact go further in specifying this inseparability: "Once one has recognized the force and the necessity of thinking justice on the basis of the gift," he says in *Specters of Marx* (27). If we are to think justice, we will have to do so "on the basis" of thinking gift. This seems a startling claim, for several reasons. It is startling first because it seems to propose a certain hierarchy[1] in thinking in which the thinking of gift serves as the basis, a sort of ground (groundless itself, as we shall see) for thinking justice. It is startling as well for its invocation of the very term *force* that we have been worrying about in the previous chapter, although we would do well to recall that in the essay that we were reading in that chapter, Derrida writes of a different kind of "force," namely that which he associates with deconstruction and so with justice, rather than the force that betrays the disjuncture between law and justice.[2] It is startling as well because of the way we are immediately put in mind of something Paul says he is concerned with: "being made just as God's gift by grace" (3:24). We seem, then, to be at least on the right track in supposing that the help we need for thinking with Paul about gift as the basis for justice may be forthcoming from reading Derrida.

In "The Deconstruction of Actuality," Derrida again speaks of the heterogeneity of justice relative not only to law but also to rights and even "respect" for the other: "Justice is not the same as rights; it exceeds and founds the rights of man; nor is it distributive justice. It is not even, in the traditional sense respect for the other as a human subject" (*Negotiations*, 105). But this in turn leads him directly to a consideration of gift: "it is the experience of the other as other, the fact that I let the other be other, which presupposes a gift without restitution, without reappropriation and without jurisdiction" (105). Once again we see that there is to be some fundamental connection between justice and gift.

Before we too hastily leap into this last question (gift or grace as the basis of justice), we should retrace our steps to discover more precisely how the question of gift and that of justice bear at least a necessary relation to one another. Toward the beginning of his reflections on the gift in *Given Time*, Derrida points to the relation (in part, one of opposition) between gift and economy and suggests a "sort of tautology [that] already implies the economic within the nomic as such" (6). This is related to the way in which "*Nomos* does not only signify the law in general, but also the law of distribution (*nemein*), the law of sharing or partition" (6). We are thus already put on the track or trace of at least a curious parallel between gift and justice. For both stand in a similar relation to law. And we have already seen as well that Derrida supposes a disjuncture between justice and distribution (or retribution); that is, to what we may now call an economic view of justice, which is still to be understood as on the side of law in the disjunction of law and justice. Here this is anchored in the relation between *nomos* and *nemein*, between law and distribution, as well as that between *nomos* and economy.

That the relation between gift and economy has a certain parallel to the thinking of the relation between justice and law is also indicated in terms of the way in which the opposing terms also seem in a certain way to require one another. For this is what he says about gift in relation to economy: "Now the gift, *if there is any*, would no doubt be related to economy. One cannot treat the gift, this goes without saying, without treating this relation to economy, even to the money economy. But is not the gift, if there is any, also that which interrupts economy? That which, in suspending economic calculation, no longer gives rise to exchange?" (*Given Time*, 7). Certainly this will remind us of what we have read in connection with justice: that it is necessarily related to the law, but that it also is beyond or outside law; or, as here, that it interrupts law. But what is interrupted is law precisely as the law of exchange, the law or "-nomy" of economy. More-over, as that which interrupts economy, "the gift must remain aneconomic" (7), in much the same way that justice remains outside or beyond the law. And here we may recall that he has said a similar thing about law insofar as it is like justice: that it is a *nomos anomos* (*Of Hospitality*, 79).

Thus far we have verified that gift and justice have a remarkable rela-tionship such that both are outside but in necessary relation to law. We have not yet got to the point where we can see clearly how gift will come to serve as the basis of a thinking of justice. We will therefore return to this question.

Impossibility of the Gift

Before we do so we must address another issue: that of the impossi-bility of the gift. This is a much misunderstood view of Derrida. There are those who suppose that Derrida's reflections on gift and the impossibility of gift entail the abolition of the thought of gift, but this is a mistake. Thus first I will try to indicate briefly how the gift is impossible, in what sense this is so, and then indicate how this means precisely that the gift gives it-self to be thought—or, put another way, that the gift is important precisely because it is impossible.

Having just noted that the gift is aneconomic, Derrida says, "it is perhaps in this sense that the gift is the impossible" and clarifies, "Not im-possible but *the* impossible" (*Given Time*, 7). In order to make this clear,

Derrida begins with what would seem to be the structure of the idea of gift: a gives b to c; a subject (giver) a recipient and that which is given. Now this commonsense structure of gift and giving begins to crumble if any sort of intellectual pressure is brought to bear upon it.[3] This becomes clear as soon as we admit that reciprocity destroys gift by making it an item in an economy of exchange: "It is annulled each time there is restitution or countergift. Each time, according to the same circular ring that leads to 'giving back' [*rendre*], there is payment and discharge of a debt" (*Given Time*, 12). The reciprocity of gift giving makes it a trade, or subject to a "market." I give you $50 for that pot. There has been no gift, but rather an exchange. "For there to be a gift, there must be no reciprocity, return, exchange, countergift, or debt. If the other *gives* me *back* or *owes* me or has to give me back what I give him or her, there will not have been a gift, whether this restitution is immediate or whether it is programmed by a complex calculation of a long term deferral or difference" (12).

Let us apply this to the situation of the giver. I give you $50, but I don't want a pot in return. Nor is it a loan that you will someday repay (with or without interest). For this would be a loan rather than a gift; repayment or compensation merely occurs later, is deferred. So I give you $50 without asking anything in return, I say. The problem is that I already may reward myself. What a good chap I am: I gave so-and-so $50. My awareness of my own generosity is itself repayment. Hence I have not given a gift. I have purchased for the mere sum of $50 a sense of myself as a good and generous person. Cheap at the price, a real bargain. Derrida explains:

the gift must not even appear or signify, consciously or unconsciously, *as* gift for the donors, whether individual or collective subjects. From the moment the gift would appear as gift, as such, as what it is, in its phenomenon, its sense and essence, it would be engaged in a symbolic, sacrificial, or economic structure that would annul the gift in the ritual circle of the debt. The simple intention to give, insofar as it carries the intentional meaning of the gift, suffices to make a return payment to oneself. The simple consciousness of the gift right away sends itself back the gratifying image of goodness or generosity, of the giving-being, who, knowing itself to be such, recognizes itself in a circular, specular fashion in a sort of auto-recognition, self-approval, and narcissistic gratitude. (23)

And what of the recipient? Someone gave me $50. I know this and that they have done it. Perhaps they have said that it is a gift. But I am, or sense myself to be, indebted or obliged. "Much obliged," we say in the

South. I may even simply offer my gratitude; it would seem churlish not to. But in that case, have I not returned something for the gift, and so made the aneconomic economic after all?

And finally the gift itself, the "present." (Derrida makes a good deal of this relation between gift as present, presence, the present, and so on—capitalizes on it, we might say.) Insofar as I take possession of the gift (and if I cannot, then has it really been given?), it has already become not gift but possession. I cannot receive what is mine; if and as it becomes mine, it is no longer gift. As soon as it is "present," it disappears as gift.

These reflections have as their goal to make clear that what we take to be the conditions of a gift (that there be a donor, a donee, and a donated or *don*) are at the same time the conditions of the impossibility of the gift as gift. At each point, the gift falls back into exchange, into economy, into the law of exchange, distribution, and so on. Thus it would seem the gift is impossible.[4]

In another text, Derrida reflects somewhat more on this idea of the impossible: "deconstruction has often been defined as the very experience of the (impossible) possibility of the impossible, of the most impossible, a condition that deconstruction shares with the gift" (*On the Name*, 43). This is important first because we have deconstruction associated here with "the gift," something we also have encountered with respect to justice. But it is not only that deconstruction is related to gift and justice, related in such a way that they may actually seem to be much the same thing; it is also that the impossibility of gift is here related to the idea of the possibility of the impossible.[5] The theologian at least will recognize this language. It is the very language in which Barth and Bultmann have spoken of grace and faith.[6] Now whatever may have been said about their use of this vocabulary of impossibility, I do not think that anyone has imagined that because they use this language they simply dismiss faith or grace. That would be absurd, as any reader of their work would know. But Derrida has been accused of rendering the gift, because impossible, also unthinkable.[7] And not only by those who for professional reasons may be supposed to be ignorant of theologians like Barth and Bultmann (for philosophers do not often read theologians—certainly not as often as theologians read philosophers.)

Thus in *God, the Gift and Postmodernism*,[8] Derrida clarifies: "The gift as such cannot be known, but it can be thought of. We can think what we cannot know" (60). Not only can we think what we do not know, but it also seems to be the case that thinking is decisively connected to what we do not know. Thinking requires a certain impossibility even to get under-way precisely as thinking, especially if thinking means something that aims to stay with, rather than liquidate, the question.

The relation between thinking as opposed to knowledge in relation to the gift is amplified—indeed, was already amplified—in *Given Time*: "This gap between, on the one hand, thought, language, and desire and, on the other hand, knowledge, philosophy, science, and the order of presence is also a gap between gift and economy" (29). The thinking of the gift then is in a certain way exterior to "knowledge, philosophy and science" and for that reason is like or associated with "thought, language and desire." It is important to note that the impossibility is again decidedly linked with thinking even if not with knowing: "if the gift is another name for the impossible, we still think it, we name it, we desire it. We intend it" (29).

Accordingly, Derrida has sought to explain, even against his "friends," that the idea of impossibility is not meant to stop but rather to start thought.[9] Thus he maintains in *God, the Gift and Postmodernism*, "I tried to precisely displace the problematic of the gift, to take it out of the circle of economy, of exchange, but *not* to conclude, from the impossibility for the gift to appear as such and to be determined as such, to its absolute impossibility. [. . .] It is impossible for the gift to exist and appear as such. But I never concluded that there is no gift. I went on to say that if there is a gift, through this impossibility, it must be the experience of this impossibility, and it should appear as impossible" (59). In an expression that takes us somewhat further than Derrida seemed prepared to go in *Given Time*, he can even say, "The gift is totally foreign to the horizon of economy, ontology, knowledge, constative statements, and theoretical determination and judgment" (59). It is here that we seem to get a formulation of the exteriority of gift and economy to one another that corresponds to similar statements concerning the heterogeneity of justice and the law.

The Gift "in the Christian Sense"

In *God, the Gift and Postmodernism*, Derrida goes on to say that his attempt to account for or to think the gift has led him precisely to try to think the gift "not only in economy but even in Christian discourse" (59). In discussion with Jean-Luc Marion, Derrida can even affirm that what interests him in thinking the gift is precisely the gift in the sense of a certain Christianity: "I am interested in Christianity and in the gift in the Christian sense" (57). The gift in the Christian sense means here, it seems to me, the understanding of grace that Paul seeks to clarify, especially in Romans. That is, Derrida's reflections on gift are meant to be, intended to be, a reflection also on what Christians, and perhaps especially Paul, call grace.

Just as we have seen that justice is divine as the justice of God, so also, in another text, Derrida takes note of a way in which giving (or gracing) can also be thought as divine. Reflecting on Angelus Silesius, Derrida writes that he "interprets the divinity of God as gift or desire of giving" (*On the Name*, 56). Although it is not my intention here to reflect on the meaning of God under the conditions of deconstruction, a theme that is already being treated by theologians to the exclusion of too much else, this does at least suggest the pertinence of what we have been reading for an attempt to think with Paul about the grace or gift that is divine.

Paul and Grace

In attending to Paul's thought of gift/grace, we will have to notice several things that will connect it to what we have read in Derrida. Among these are the connection of gift and grace, the priority of grace as related to justice, the exteriority of grace and law, the exteriority of grace to debt or work, the instability of grace relative to debt/work, and the grace that surpasses knowledge (but not thought).

Grace and Gift

It is first necessary to indicate the way in which for Paul gift and grace, although semantically different, are nevertheless identified in his thought. The terms *charis* (grace/favor) and *dôrema* (gift) are consistently brought into intimate connection in Paul's thought in Romans—thus already in a text to which we have had occasion to refer: "they are now made just by divine grace [*chariti*] as a gift [*dôrean*]" (3:24). I will return to the question of the relation to justice in a moment. But for now, I simply underline the association of gift and grace. A similar, perhaps even more emphatic, association is discovered when Paul again returns to speak of what may be called the Christ event or, perhaps better, the "messiah-event."[10]

But the free gift [*charisma*] is not like the trespass. For if the many died through one man's trespass, much more surely have the grace [*charis*] of God and the free gift [*dôrea*] in the grace [*chariti*] of the one man, Jesus Christ, abounded for many. And the free gift [*dôrema*] is not like the effect of one man's sin. For the judgment

following one trespass brought condemnation, but the free gift [*charisma*] following many trespasses brings justification. If because of the one man's trespass, death
exercised dominion through that one, much more surely will those who receive the
abundance of grace [*chariots*] and the free gift [*dôreas*] of justice exercise dominion
in life. (5:15–17)

This passage, so rich in provocations to thought, serves at this point to establish the equivalence that Paul articulates between gift and grace, an
equivalence so intricate that the translator is unable to maintain a distinction at all between these terms or the terms developed from these roots.

    This should serve to indicate the pertinence of a reflection on the
problem of gift (as we have it in Derrida) for an attempt to think what
Paul is up to in attempting to think grace.

Grace and Justice

    We have already seen that for Paul, as for Derrida, there is a recogni-
tion that justice cannot be thought simply as a compliance with the law,
that law and justice are disjoined, and that this comes to expression
through the violence of the law. But if law cannot serve as the basis of justice, then perhaps gift can. This at least is what Paul affirms. And he does
so first of all in the very passages where he has associated gift and grace.
Thus in a kind of thesis statement that announces what is to be explicated,
Paul has said, "they are now made just by divine grace [*charis*] as a gift
[*dôrean*]" (3:24). The coming (to be) of justice is precisely what the gift has
in view. It is the gift that serves as the "ground" of justice. And this is also
affirmed in the other passage I have cited where gift and grace are brought
into connection: "but the free gift [*charisma*] . . . brings justification." And
subsequently: "who receive the abundance of grace [*charitos*] and the free
gift [*dôreas*] of justice" (5:16, 17). Again, I am trying to proceed step by
step. And the step here taken is that justice and the becoming or being
made just (justification) are established precisely as gift.[11] Unfortunately,
this connection between justice and grace has not been often seen by the
theological "friends" of Paul, for they have more generally concluded that
because grace is distinct from law, it must also abrogate or suspend the
claim of justice. But at least so far, Paul is maintaining the opposite: that
grace, so far from suspending the claim of justice, actually renders that
claim effective, actually "grounds" that claim in a way that law could not
do. In order for this to be clear, I turn now to how grace suspends law (but
not justice).

Grace vs. Law

That grace serves as the basis of justice would lead us to suspect that grace, like justice, stands in a certain tension with, even exteriority, and perhaps opposition to, law. And this is precisely what we find in certain formulations of Paul. "You are not under law but grace" (6:14). This assertion not only disassociates grace and law, but serves as the basis for Paul's exhortation to his readers to be tools or instruments of justice rather than injustice. That is, they are exhorted to serve justice rather than injustice precisely because they are not under the law (which cannot produce justice, as we have seen) but under grace, which does and must produce justice rather than injustice. The rather odd language in which Paul asserts this claim should not distract us from the fact that it is precisely this claim that is made: "No longer present your members to sin as instruments of injustice . . . [but] present your members to God as instruments of justice . . . since you are not under the law but under grace" (6:13–14).[12] The effect of this passage is regularly mitigated in English by the habit of translating injustice (*adikias*) as "wickedness" as well as that of translating justice (*dikaiousunçs*) as "righteousness." The effect is to abrogate the connection between grace and justice so that the critique or suspension of the law comes to be thought as the suspension of the claim of justice.

Nothing could be further from Paul's language and thought. So little is the claim of justice set aside by grace that it is possible even to describe those who are not under law but under gift as "slaves of justice" (6:18, 19)—that is, as those who are even more than before answerable to justice, captive (we might even say hostage) to its claims and demands. In this way Paul can even say that the ones he is addressing are not only (called to be) slaves of justice but also "slaves of God" (6:22) in an alarming formulation that at least serves to make clear the equivalence we earlier posited between justice and God, justice as divine justice.

Grace as Exterior to Debt/Works

In order to clarify this, it may be helpful to see how the reflections of Paul are related to what we have seen in Derrida's reflections on gift and economy or exchange. In that connection, we noted that economy is to be understood as operating within the domain of law, the "-nomy" of economy. And the law of economy is precisely that of exchange, of debt, of payment, and so on.

Paul also wishes to establish a certain exteriority of grace or gift to the economy of payment and debt. This he does by associating the idea of "works" with that of law. In this case, what seems to be in view is an acting in compliance with the law or in accordance with a certain legality. This compliance with legality is in turn linked with the idea of "boasting," which here seems to function in much the same way as what Derrida has termed a good conscience. That is, boasting is the self-congratulation that satisfies itself that it has complied with the law and therefore is owed some payment or reward. It is not only self-congratulatory in this way but is also able to display itself before others as deserving of praise as a reward or payment that is due.

This is perhaps what Paul is struggling to say when he characterizes those who in his view have sought justice on the basis of law. "But Israel, who did strive for the justice that is based on the law, did not succeed in fulfilling that law. Why not? Because they did not strive for it on the basis of faith, but as if it were based on works" (9:31). In the terms that we have been developing, this would mean that they in fact did succeed in fulfilling the law as written, but that in doing so, they do not fulfill the intent of the law—that is, justice—for this can only be put into effect through that which corresponds to gift (here called faith), and not by an economy or ergonomy of works. Of course what Paul says here concerning his own people is by no means his last word on this subject. Nor is it the case that it can be supposed that it does not accurately characterize many who are called, not without reason, Christians. He further says, "being ignorant of the justice that comes from God, and seeking to establish their own, they have not submitted to God's justice" (10:3), and he goes on to speak again of the end of the law through the messiah, an end that aims at making justice effective for all (10:4) who not only hear and heed the call or claim of justice, but who also respond or correspond to the gift that is the very basis of justice.

I am all too aware of the ways these texts have been used to drive a wedge between Christians and Jews and thus are implicated in the atrocities of Euro-Christianity. But I take it as axiomatic that any interpretation of these texts today must understand this opposition between faith and works, if it is one, to run through all religious traditions, and especially to subvert the claims of any who seek to establish their own place in relation to "God" or "justice" at the expense of others or to satisfy themselves of a good conscience, often enough by perpetrating the most terrible deeds in the name of their own "righteousness," or the "evil" that is attributed to others.

In this concern for a good conscience[13] we encounter an economy—perhaps we might say a symbolic economy—that renders gift impossible. For what one receives in the way of praise or what have you is no more than is already deserved.[14] It is precisely this symbolic economy that Paul wants to overcome by way of his talk about gift or grace. He thus is able to make use of a rather commonsense appeal to what is knowable about economy: "Now to one who works, wages are not reckoned as a gift but as something due" (4:4). Here, works are linked to wages, to what is due or owed, indeed to debt, for that is the word used here. The wage for work is not and cannot be a gift. But gift is the basis, he is arguing, for justice. Here another term is deployed that functions to identify that that corresponds to gift (as work corresponds to the economy of law). That term is *faith*. Whatever this term is used to mean, here it is enough to see that it is that which corresponds to gift (and so to justice) and as such is opposed to work, wages, debt, and so on. Thus boasting, Paul will say, is excluded not by the law of works (economy, or perhaps we should say, ergonomics = *ergon nomou*) but by the "law of faith," that is, by that which corresponds to gift (3:27). It is this that counts as or for or toward justice (4:5). And thus it is that which is, or establishes, or founds, justice—precisely the justice of faith (4:13).

Again the point here is not to give content to the idea of faith but only to notice how it functions. Positively, it is that which corresponds to justice and to gift, or to justice as, or on the basis of, gift. Negatively, it is that which is opposed to a certain economy or ergonomy of works: wages and debt. Hence Paul can say in connection with a later development of his argument, "If it is by grace, it is no longer on the basis of works, otherwise grace would no longer be grace" (11:6). To this some manuscripts add, "But if it is by works, it is no longer by grace, otherwise work would no longer be work." What is at stake here in the shorter or the longer formulation is the exteriority of works (economy) to grace or gift. A gift is not a gift if one is thereby rewarded for doing. And if one is rewarded for doing, then the gift has disappeared into the economy of payment, of exchange, of debt.[15]

Instability of Distinction

And yet. We have already seen in our discussion of Derrida that gift, however it may and must be thought as exterior to economy, nevertheless is always implicated in and by economy. "Now the gift, *if there is any,* would no doubt be related to economy. One cannot treat the gift, this goes without saying, without treating this relation to economy, even to the money economy" (*Given Time*, 7). As we have seen, it is precisely this relation to economy that makes the gift impossible, or rather *the* impossible.

If on this basis we were to suppose that the distinction between gift and economy tends to be rather unstable in Paul's thought, we would not be disappointed. Indeed, the very metaphor of slave (slave of Christ, slave of justice, slave of God) is nothing if not an economic metaphor making use of the very basis of economics in the slave empire, much like "worker" in the case of what is sometimes called "democratic capitalism."

Paul struggles against the tendency of this distinction to collapse. He writes, for example, "For the wages of sin is death, but the free gift of God is eternal life" (6:23). Here Paul places gift and wage into opposition. But to what extent is this "eternal life" really free? Really unconditional? At what point does it get to seem almost as a payment? This is not simply a theoretical question. For Paul can use the vocabulary of economy to speak of that which is presumably beyond economy. He can describe himself as a "debtor" on the basis of the Gospel (1:14). Yet he pulls himself up short when his rhetoric almost leads him to say that those who receive the gift or grace of God are debtors to this gift or the one who gives it. This is noteworthy because he has not shrunk from speaking of these as slaves of justice, or of God. The passage is Romans 8:12, where he begins, "we are debtors, not to the flesh." Here one might expect "but to the Spirit." Instead, what we get is, "But if by the spirit you put to death the deeds of the body, you will live" (8:13). Paul seems to pull back from the brink here, but not without making the work of putting "to death the deeds of the body" seem to have a reward or payment: "you will live."

In order to clarify this problem, I will have to turn to the discussion of duty beyond debt (Derrida) and of the obedience of faith (Paul).

How Much More

Before I do that, however, I pause to ask just how it is that the disjuncture between gift and economy comes to expression in Paul. This is like a question I asked about the disjuncture of justice and law. There, we saw that this disjuncture appears in the recognition of the violence of law. This is not the case, I believe, with the appearance of the disjuncture of gift and economy. That is, what comes into play here is not the violence of economy, although one could certainly make a case for that insofar as what is in question is the "-nomy" of economy, the deployment of law to protect the order of the economy.

Instead, there is another kind of disjuncture here, one that will help us to think how it is that gift is not only like justice in relation to law but also (the question we had earlier suspended) how gift is the basis of justice, and as the basis, is also, to a certain degree, unlike that which it makes possible.

Briefly, if it is violence that makes clear the heterogeneity of law relative to the claim of justice, what is it that makes clear the heterogeneity of gift relative to economy? The answer, it seems to me, is something like excess or abundance. This thought of excess or of superabundance is first anchored in the story of Abraham and Sarah, for it is their God (the one associated with gift) who "gives life to the dead and calls into existence the things that do not exist" (4:17).

It is this "logic" of excess that then comes into play precisely where what is at stake is the clarification of the gift character of grace. The key phrase here is "much more" (*pollô mallon*). Thus the death of Christ (as that which separates us from the law) is compared with that which is to come (salvation, let us say). The difference is "how much more" (5:9). Similarly, if our resentment toward God is overcome, again by the violence that separates God (justice) from the law, then "much more surely will we be saved by his life" (5:10). This logic, if it is that, is then applied to the thought of gift as exceeding the need indicated by sin: "how much more the grace of God and the free gift . . . abounded to the many" (5:15). And if the "wages of sin is death," then we are also told of the "much more the abundance of the grace and the gift" (5:17) that will redound to our benefit, beyond debt. Without going into a detailed reading of these passages (we have encountered them before), it is enough simply to indicate that the reference to excess and abundance is what seems to separate the thought of gift from that of economy.[16]

It may be the case that Bataille may give us more help here than Derrida, for exuberance, excess, and abundance is not a prominent theme when Derrida thinks of justice and politics and ethics and so on. This is not to say it is alien to his thought or to his work. How could that be so for the author of *Glas* or *Ulysses Gramaphone*? But there is, it seems, a certain reticence with respect to this vocabulary in connection with the thought of justice.[17] Even so, it is unquestionable that for Derrida, it is also the case that it is precisely abundance that separates the thought of gift from economy.

This is already clear in his discussion of Mauss in *Given Time*, when

he notes that it is precisely at the point of having to give an account of potlatch that the economistic conceptuality within which Mauss tries to think
the gift goes into a kind of paroxysm. "His language goes mad at the point
where, in the potlatch, the process of the gift *gets carried away with itself*"
(46). But before the "madness of economic reason" (the name of this chapter of *Given Time*) is thus exposed, Derrida will have already noted in his
reading of Mauss: "The problem of the gift has to do with its nature that
is excessive in advance, a priori exaggerated. A donating experience that
would not be delivered over, *a priori*, to some immoderation . . . would not
be a gift . . . the most modest gift must pass beyond measure" (38). Gift to
be gift must be characterized by the "how much more," the excessive. Otherwise it is merely exchange.

Later we encounter other texts of Derrida that are even more explicit
in relation to this excess. In *The Gift of Death* he speaks of "two
economies": "one of retribution, equal exchange, within a circular economy; the other of absolute surplus value, heterogeneous to outlay or in-
vestment" (105), and then, in speaking of what he calls authentic filiation,
he says that this "occurs on condition that there is a gift, a love *without reserve*" (106). This notion of excess or surplus is indeed made the basis of
any talk of responsibility in *Points . . .* : "responsibility is excessive or it is
not responsibility. A limited, measured, calculated, rationally distributed
responsibility is already the becoming-right of morality" (286). (The question of excess relative to responsibility will return when we come to deal
with the question of duty beyond debt in the next chapter.) In these and
other texts, Derrida points to the way in which the gift is heterogeneous to
the law of economy precisely as excess, as surplus, as a "without reserve."
In these ways his reflections on gift seem to be in concord with Paul's emphasis on the "how much more" of gift or grace that separates it from the
economy of debt and death.[18]

Beyond Knowledge

We have noticed that for Derrida the thinking of gift takes us beyond
knowledge, even if not beyond thought. It is important to notice that there
is something similar going on in Paul, although it might be rash to conclude that it is precisely the same thing. Paul's ways of speaking of what we
have termed the messiah-event entails, he insists, a certain rupture with the
domain of knowledge. He makes much of the distinction between wisdom

and folly in order to subvert these categories in speaking about his own message concerning the messiah-event. Thus he speaks of his message (one that he has sought to make intelligible) as "folly" in contrast to Greek wisdom (1 Corinthians 1:18) while maintaining that "divine foolishness is wiser than human wisdom" (1 Corinthians 1:25).

This comes to expression in Romans precisely as he has been reflecting again on the effect of the messiah-event. Here again he will be thinking of divine wisdom that exceeds the order of knowledge, even if it is what he has been attempting to make intelligible. And in speaking of this wisdom that exceeds knowledge, he will also speak of gift beyond exchange or debt, of the gift of the divine grace that is not contained within the economy of debt and exchange. "O the depths of the riches and wisdom and knowledge of God! . . . who has given a gift to him, to receive a gift in return?" (Romans 11:33, 35). In the last reference to gift, Paul is citing while turning almost on its head a passage from Job 35:7 where Elihu, Job's friend, is, in effect, accusing him and counseling him to refrain from interrogating God for Job's misfortune. In the case of Paul, however, the aneconomic relation points not to a situation of deprivation (Job's misfortunes) but to one of astonishing abundance whereby the divine promise reaches out to include even those who seem to have rejected it. Thus it is a gift that is not motivated by any prior condition but that overrides all such preexisting conditions. It is this of which, according to Paul, we may and must speak, even if our thinking must exceed what can be ordinarily circumscribed within the order of knowing or of human (as opposed to divine) wisdom.

Event

It is not the case that Paul can simply say, as does Derrida, that the gift is impossible or even, as Bultmann would say, an impossible possibility. The difference between Paul and Derrida at this point is precisely that Paul is not restricted by a quasi-phenomenological bracket, with a reflection on the possibility, but rather is obligated to speak of an event, the actuality rather than the possibility of this event.

The messianic event for Paul has, in some sense, already come, even if the mode of this already remains still in the register of that which in a certain way is yet to come. But it is the former modality, that it has already arrived, that sets apart the mode of Paul's reflections from those of Derrida.

I do not say this in order to seek to adjudicate which is right. Both are constrained by the genre of discourse within which they operate. It is not that Paul is overly confident of an event that has occurred, or that Derrida falls short of a recognition of some sort of evangelical truth. Both are struggling within and against a certain "language game," but different language games too. Thus it is the homology that we notice, not the identity of content.

In his contribution to *God, the Gift and Postmodernism*, Derrida explicitly links the thinking of gift and the thinking of event: "An event as such, as well as the gift, cannot be known as an event" (60). The unknowability of event opens up onto the question of revelation, the appearing of gift, and so the question of the revelation of event or as event. Derrida places this into relation to Heidegger in order to open the question of revelation and revealability:

Translated into Heidegger's discourse, which is addressing the same difficulty, this is the distinction between *Offenbarung* and *Offenbarkeit*, revelation and revealability. Heidegger said, this is his position, that there would be no revelation or *Offenbarung* without a prior structure of *Offenbarkeit* without the possibility of revelation and the possibility of manifestation. That is Heidegger's position. I am not so sure. Perhaps it is through *Offenbarung* that *Offenbarkeit* becomes thinkable, historically. That is why I am constantly hesitating. That is part of—what can I call this here?—let us say, my cross. (73)

Although Derrida will go on to question this alternative in terms of what a reflection on *khora* may offer, he has already given us much to think at this point. For first we may recognize here in the possible inversion of Heidegger's priorities the position that has been emphasized by Karl Barth, namely that for theology at least, the possibility of revelation must be thought from the event of revelation—that is, from revelation as something that has happened. It would seem that there is not as much of a disjuncture here between Paul and Derrida as we had thought. But of course here Derrida is going beyond phenomenology, as he has said he must, if he is to think gift (66).[19]

Even more startling here is the linking of this indecision relative to the actuality or possibility of revelation to what, hesitantly, he calls his cross, a cross that is not unrelated to the cross that is also, if Paul is to be believed, the event in which we are given what he calls grace. Derrida also goes on to say that this is what he is trying to get at with *khora* and that this is aiming at a new basis for politics. But he also says, "Perhaps, and this is my hypothesis, if not a hope, what I am saying here could be translated after the fact into Jewish discourse or Christian discourse or Muslim discourse, if they can integrate the terrible things I am suggesting now" (77). The terrible things have to do with *khora*. And I must, for now, leave that aside. But what Derrida hypothesizes here—or even hopes—is that what he is saying can be translated "after the fact" into, for example, Christian discourse. This is precisely what we are trying to do here with respect to at least that part of Christian discourse that derives from Paul. But, and this is what must be emphasized, this translation can by no means be an exclusive one such that it would disqualify a Jewish or Muslim translation (and other translations besides).

Thus far, we have seen that the justice that exceeds, goes beyond, or is outside the law is a justice that is given its decisive impetus through a gift that is outside economy and that has the character of a certain excess or gratuity. But precisely how does this result in or give justice? It is to that question that I must next turn.

5

Duty Beyond Debt and / or the
Obedience of Faith

We have seen that grace or gift offers itself as the basis of the possibility of justice. But we have not yet seen how this claim of justice is made effective or put into effect "apart from the law" by means of something like gift. With respect to Paul, we have seen that somehow the result must be that the "just requirements of the law" are put into effect by gift or grace apart from the law itself. But this seems to be merely perplexing at first. What sense can such expressions as the obedience of faith (Romans 1:5; 16:26), or the law of Christ (Galatians 6:2), have as we move, if we do, beyond law to a gifted justice? In order to gain some leverage on this perplexity, we may be assisted by Derrida's reflections on a duty beyond debt, an attempt to think something like obligation beyond the economy of debt and exchange. This will then give us some help, I contend, in understanding what Paul is up to. It should be noted that this is crucial if we are to make good on our claim that Paul really is concerned with justice, that his critique of the law does not simply abrogate the claim of justice, that grace is not a substitute for justice (nor is that which corresponds to grace, namely faith), but is precisely that which leads to justice for real.

Duty Beyond Debt

I turn first then to Derrida and to his discussions of duty beyond debt. Although there are many texts in which this idea is treated, it is first announced in *The Other Heading* in connection with a discussion of Europe. Some of the ideas are then elaborated in a discussion with Kierkegaard in *Gift of Death* and subsequently in "Passions: An Oblique Offering" and then in *Aporias*. These texts build on one another in interesting ways.

The Impossible (Again)

The reflections on duty beyond debt may first be linked with what we have seen thus far of justice and gift, that these are, as we have repeatedly noticed, connected with the impossible, with what has often been termed the aporia. In thinking about the opening to the other and of responsibility to and for the other, something that has been linked before, following Levinas, with justice, Derrida writes, "I will even venture to say that ethics, politics, and responsibility, *if there are any*, will only ever have begun with the experience and experiment of the aporia." The aporetic is, as usual, linked with the impossible: "The condition of possibility of this thing called responsibility is a certain *experience and experiment of the possibility of the impossible*" (*Other Heading*, 41).[1]

The discussion moves closer to a direct approximation to the problem of duty in "Passions: An Oblique Offering" (in *On the Name*), written as a response to a number of essays in *Derrida: A Critical Reader*. Derrida says of what he writes here that it is written "as a token of boundless gratitude . . . to all those who have generously brought their tribute to this work" (7). But it is precisely this situation of gratitude and of the response that follows from gratitude that leads to the question here of a double or even contradictory duty: "Friendship as well as politeness would enjoin a double *duty*: would it not precisely be to avoid at all cost both the *language of ritual* and the *language of duty*?" (7). That there is a duty imposed by gratitude not to respond out of duty is what opens the question of a kind of obligation that is beyond obligation, that does not stand in the relationship of a discharge of debt. That the "one must" cannot be simply understood as duty in the ordinary sense is what places these reflections, as Derrida notes, in a certain tension with the ethical philosophy of Kant. "One must not be friendly or polite out of duty. We venture such a proposition, without a doubt, against Kant" (7).

The clarification of this tension takes place in a long and very instructive footnote (note 3). First Derrida gestures toward a tension between duty and the economic order. "Pure morality must exceed all calculation, conscious or unconscious, of restitution or reappropriation. This feeling *tells* us, perhaps without *dictating* anything, that we must go beyond duty, or at least beyond *duty as debt*: duty owes nothing, it must owe nothing, it ought at any rate to owe nothing. But is there a duty without debt?" (133). This seems to parallel what we have already heard of gift, that it is in some way aneconomic. But in connection with gift, we also heard that it nevertheless engages this economic order and we find something similar here with respect to the duty beyond debt: "But if debt, *the economy of debt*, continues to haunt all duty, then could we still say that duty insists on being carried beyond duty?" And answers: "Now, who will ever show that this haunting memory of debt can or should ever cease to disturb the feeling of duty? Should not this disquiet predispose us indefinitely against the good conscience?" (133). Here the inevitable contamination of duty with debt serves as yet another reminder of the impossibility of instantiating what he had earlier called "pure morality." It is precisely the impossibility of a clean distinction between duty and debt that rules out any good conscience, which, as we have seen, would be the very mark of a certain immorality and irresponsibility.

Derrida carries these reflections further in a discussion in *Aporias*: "The most general and therefore most indeterminate form of this double and single duty is that a responsible decision must obey an "it is necessary" that owes nothing, it must obey a *duty that owes nothing, that must owe nothing in order to be a duty*, a duty that has no debt to pay back, a duty without debt and therefore without duty" (16).[2] This may also be expressed as an "overduty," which recalls once again the situation of a certain justice outside or beyond the law: "Duty must be such an over-duty, which demands acting without duty, without rule or norm (therefore without law)" (16).

But once again, we are reminded that this "outside the law" must still have a certain relation, a presentable relation he will say, to the lawful order that it necessarily interrupts: "Who will dare call duty a duty that owes nothing, or, better (or, worse) that *must owe nothing*? It is necessary, therefore that the decision and responsibility for it be taken, interrupting the relation to any *presentable* determination but still maintaining a presentable relation to what it interrupts" (17). In speaking of this "presentable relation to what it interrupts," Derrida recalls us to the relation without relation to the law. That is, the duty that goes beyond debt both interrupts the law, but also maintains something like a "presentable relation" to it.[3] But here what is at stake is something like the law of morality itself in a Kantian sense: the requirement to give an account, a publicly intelligible account, of what it is that one does or has done or will do in the name of that morality. This would be possible and obligatory if the act or decision were within the order of debt (this is what I must do or am obliged to do) but an over-duty, or duty beyond debt, cannot present such an account of itself (and thus interrupts presentable determination) yet cannot absolve itself of this requirement (and thus maintains a presentable relation to the attempt and obligation to present an intelligible account).[4]

The question of a generally intelligible account here associated with debt necessarily raises the question of philosophy itself—or more precisely of the right to philosophy (or philosophizing) that both interrogates what is or may be meant by a "generally intelligible account" while still attempting to give such an account of itself.[5] Thus Derrida will also place philosophy itself within this same question of the debt and of that which exceeds debt: "Perhaps the right to philosophy passes henceforth through a distinction between several regimes of the debt, between a finite debt and an infinite debt, an internal debt and an 'external' debt, between debt and duty; a certain erasure and a certain reaffirmation of the debt—and sometimes a certain erasure in the name of an affirmation" ("The Right to Philosophy," in *Negotiations*, 342).

The Question of Love

The Gift of Death (1992) adds one other dimension to this question of a duty beyond debt that will be essential to our reading of Paul. It is here that we hear of love as the content of this duty beyond debt.[6] Here Derrida is commenting on Patochka: "On what condition does goodness exist beyond all calculation? On the condition that goodness forget itself, that the movement be a movement of the gift that renounces itself, hence a movement of infinite love. Only infinite love can renounce itself and, in order to *become* finite, become incarnated in order to love the other, to love the other as a finite other" (50/51). If we leave aside for now the extraordinarily suggestive (for a theologian at least) formulations concerning infinite love, incarnation, and so on, we realize that in any case, with the question of goodness beyond calculation, we are in the sphere of that "pure morality" that concerns a duty beyond debt and that the name suggested for this duty, if it is one, is love, even infinite love.

Concerning love, Derrida also writes in *On the Name*: "But why not recognize there love itself, that is this infinite renunciation which somehow *surrenders to the impossible*? To surrender to the other, and this is the impossible, would amount to giving oneself over in going toward the other,

to coming toward the other but without crossing the threshold, and to respecting, to loving even the invisibility that keeps the other inaccessible"
(74). Here we notice in particular the question of a love that renounces itself, renounces its claims or rights, in order to turn toward or go toward the
other, and, on the other hand, a certain reserve that respects the distance
from the other that preserves the otherness of the other. We will return to
these questions.

We have therefore an association of duty beyond debt that is tied to
the question of justice beyond law and of gift beyond economy or exchange, and that points us toward the question of love as the name of this
duty. As we shall see, this is something with which Paul is also concerned.

The Obedience of Faith

The phrase I begin with belongs in a series of paradoxical formulations in Paul concerning the new form of life that he believes to follow
from, or correspond to, the justice which is outside the law, the justice that
comes as a gift. Among those paradoxical formulations are also "The law of
Christ" and "obedience of faith." By attending to a particularly interesting
passage, we may see how what Paul is up to seems to correspond to something of what Derrida has been reflecting on. The passage in question is
from Romans 13:8. Paul has just been exhorting his readers to attend to
their obligations in the world, to be, in a certain way dutiful, including dutiful subjects of the law. The first few verses of this chapter have often
enough been taken to be the summary of Paul's "political ethics," an ethics
of subservience to rule, to the rule of Rome. We have already seen the
questionableness of such an interpretation. The material that follows, to
which I will be paying particular attention, has in contrast been supposed
to be something more like a personal ethic, for here Paul will speak of love,
and what can that be if it is not personal?

I have already indicated how I believe that the passage in Romans
13:1–5 should be read. But it is also important to contest the plausibility of
distinguishing between the subject matter there broached and the subject
matter of the following verses as a difference between public and private,
or even political and communitarian. Such a distinction, however hallowed
by tradition, and especially as it has come to seem self-evident in the modern period, cannot simply be taken for granted.[7]

Paul has just been speaking of what is due: "pay to all what is due them—taxes to whom taxes are due, revenue to whom revenue is due, re-spect to whom respect is due, honor to whom honor is due" (13:7). If we try to get at this a bit more literally, we get, "(Re)pay [*apodote*] to all the debts [*opheilas*]; to the taxes, taxes, to the customs, customs, to the fear, fear, to the honor, honor."[8] We are here speaking of what is owed, of debt and the discharge of debt. This debt goes beyond the realm of money and goods (taxes, customs) to include the symbolic order (fear, honor). What is in view is the need to discharge debt, to pay what is owed, whether in hard currency or in social and symbolic exchange. It is this discharge of debt, however incurred, that sets the stage for what is to follow.

It should be noted here that if this were where Paul ended, if this were the goal of his discourse, then he would in fact be the apostle of the good conscience, one who simply urges compliance with the law, with the economy of the law. But we have already seen that Paul at every point in-terrupts this economy of the good conscience. We may recall what Derrida has said in *Aporias* regarding this good conscience:

good conscience as subjective certainty is incompatible with the absolute risk that every promise, every engagement, and every responsible decision—if there are such—must run. To protect the decision or the responsibility by knowledge, by some theoretical assurance, or by the certainty of being right, of being on the side of science, of consciousness or of reason, is to transform this decision into the de-ployment of a program, into a technical application of a rule or a norm, or into the subsumption of a determined "case." All of these are conditions that must never be abandoned, of course, but that, as such, are only the guardrail of a responsibil-ity to whose calling they remain radically heterogeneous. (19)

In urging his readers to discharge their obligations, Paul has set up what Derrida calls a "guardrail" of responsibility; we may say the guardrail of accountability. But that this is only a guardrail is made clear by what fol-lows. Paul then goes on: "owe (be indebted) nothing to no one. But to love one another." Here Paul seems to go beyond debt to indicate a duty be-yond debt. Much hinges on this "but" [*ei mai*], on how it functions. It seems to me to function to indicate a different order than that which went before. Otherwise it could have been included in the list of things "owed," like taxes and fear. Instead, it stands in a different register, a register het-erogeneous to, or beyond, debt. At the same time it is enjoined upon the reader, much as the acquitting of debt was also enjoined upon the reader. It stands under the claim of an imperative, even if of a different sort of im-perative or claim: the claim of a duty beyond debt, we might say.

Love might be understood as the paying of a debt if it were to be directed toward one to whom one owes love—for example, if the love of the other responded to the other's love for me. We might read this as if the love were to be directed to the one who loves us, for example, in Paul's discourse until now, God or the messiah. Both have been said to be subjects or agents of a love directed to the reader or to all Romans (5:5, 8, 8:39). But Paul is not saying that one should love God (or Messiah); in fact, Paul never says this. Although Paul can say the "love of God has been poured out into our hearts" (Romans 5:5), he can never suppose that the idea is to "return" this love, to pay it back. To be rather too hasty here, we could say that this love is to be, can only be, disseminated.[9] It can only be, as it were paid forward.

In any case, here we have to do with the other person, the other human. It is this one who is to be loved in terms of a duty beyond debt. Here we recall what we have already read in Derrida: "Pure morality must exceed all calculation . . . of restitution or reappropriation . . . we must go beyond duty, or at least beyond *duty as debt*: duty owes nothing, it must owe nothing, it ought at any rate to owe nothing" (*On the Name*, 133). Derrida's formulation here seems to correspond quite closely with what Paul is speaking of: a duty "that owes nothing," that "ought to owe nothing"; or as Paul says, "owe no one anything." But the word used here for this duty beyond debt is love. I will not at this point undertake anything like an analysis of what Paul means by love and how this must be understood differently in relation to an entire tradition concerning love in western Christian discourse.[10] Here I only want to indicate some of its more formal or abstract features in order to show how it may be related to the question of a duty beyond debt.

We recall that the terminology of love is not alien to Derrida's discussion of duty, of the duty beyond debt. In *The Gift of Death*, reflecting on Patochka, he writes of "a movement of the gift that renounces itself, hence a movement of infinite love" (50–51). To be sure, Derrida is here explaining the thought of another, or perhaps we should say countersigning, the work of Patochka. In any case, love is the name of that which is beyond calculation, of that which is compatible with gift. Second, we should also note that the "one another" to whom Paul addresses himself here as an indication of the desideratum of this interhuman relationality is also consonant with at least some of the formulations put forward by Derrida. We recall that he had asked: "How to distinguish between two disadjusments, between the disjuncture of the unjust and the one that opens up the infinite symmetry of the relation to the others, that is to say, the place for justice?" (*Specters of Marx*, 22). That it is justice that opens the space for a relation to others, a relation that is not economic or exhausted or exhaustible by the economic, we have already seen. Thus the symmetry indicated here is not one of, for example, "I love the one who loves me." That would be a finite, a self-enclosed symmetry. Instead, we seem to have a different kind of symmetry, one that Derrida here calls "infinite," that is, in which there is a going beyond of the economic, a continual going beyond. In another text, Derrida can speak of a certain reciprocity, but one that is not the same as symmetry or at least a finite or self-enclosed symmetry.[11] Something like that seems suggested by Paul's indication of love spiraling out of (economic) control in that it is a love for "one another." We would have to see whether this love remains within a restricted economy of the "community" to which Paul addresses himself, or whether such a restriction, if there is one to be discerned in Paul's discourse, is in principle broken down by what it is that Paul otherwise wants to say. This will become clearer in a moment. In the meantime, we keep to the theme of justice, for we are concerned with a duty beyond debt that places us in a distinctive relationship with others: "'The relation to others—that is to say, justice,' writes Levinas" (23).

In the designation of a duty that owes nothing, that must owe nothing, Derrida goes on to say of the responsibility (and decision) that actualizes such a duty, "It is necessary, therefore that the decision and responsibility for it be taken, interrupting the relation to any *presentable* determination but still maintaining a presentable relation to what it interrupts" (*Aporias*, 17). In Paul's language, the duty that owes no one anything and so breaks with the competence of law (*nomy*) or economy, nevertheless maintains something like a "presentable relation" to what it interrupts. It is presented here precisely in terms of what Paul calls a fulfilling of the law. Thus he explains, "The one who loves another has fulfilled the law" (13:8); and he will conclude, "love is a fulfilling of the law" (13:10). Our earlier reflections on the law prepare us to understand this assertion as an assertion about fulfilling what Paul called in chapter 2 "the just requirements of the Law"—that is, the intent, aim, or goal of the law, that is, justice. It is this "love one another" that does this, that instantiates what it means to do justice, the divine justice.

The explication given of this by Paul is quite interesting. He cites the law, the superior law in his way of thinking, the law that may also be termed the Mosaic law: It is this law that is fulfilled, he maintains, by love: "The commandments, 'You shall not commit adultery; you shall not murder; you shall not steal; you shall not covet'; and any other commandment, are summed up in this word, 'Love your neighbor as yourself'" (13:9). It is noteworthy that in his summary of "the commandment(s)," here as everywhere, Paul makes reference only to those commandments that bear on what may be termed interhuman justice. That is, he does not here or elsewhere make direct reference to those commandments that bear on the relation to God (you shall have no other gods before me, you shall make no graven images, you shall keep the Sabbath, and so on). Indeed, at no point are these "commandments" reinscribed in New Testament discourse when the law, precisely the law as the "ten commandments" is rehearsed (for example, Mark 9:19 and parallels). In this, all other writers of the New Testament follow Paul. Whatever remains of these "other" commandments is summarized or comprehended in a single formulation: "love your neighbor as yourself," a formulation from Leviticus 19:18.[12] In any case, it is clear that for Paul, the law cannot be satisfied by a relation to the divine but only by a relation to the other, the neighbor, the other person.[13] And it is here that one encounters the duty that is beyond debt.

For Paul, the citation, if it is that, of Leviticus is not sufficient to establish the intelligibility of his claim that loving the neighbor adequately summarizes the commandments. Accordingly, he adds: "Love does no wrong [harm, violation] to the neighbor, therefore, love is the fulfilling of the law" (13:10). It is because love precludes harm to the other person, not because of something said by Moses or even Jesus, that it should be clear that love fulfills—that is, accomplishes—what the law aims at. This, of course, will not be true with respect to compliance with laws or given systems of legality. There are any number of laws that seem to run afoul of a concern for the neighbor. We will have occasion to look at the role played in this respect by laws that restrict while also allowing for a certain hospitality to the stranger or alien in the next chapter. And Paul will go to considerable trouble with respect to another set of laws that seem to restrict hospitality (with respect to food) in Romans 14, as he had also done in 1 Corinthians and in Galatians. That is, particular laws may, and regularly do, place one in the position where a positive regard for the neighbor or at least certain neighbors is "against the law." (I grew up in the Jim Crow South where this was an everyday occurrence.) Paul's argument here is not about each and every law but about the aim or "just requirement" of the law, that is, the law that aims at justice.

Even so, the formulation is remarkable because it remains entirely negative, "love does no harm." It does not seem that this is for Paul an adequate definition of love. The point is that it is a definition of love insofar as love is commensurate with a fulfilling of the law, that is, with doing what is required or ought to be required by law. But love goes beyond law to do that at which the law can only point, to which it can at best only testify.[14]

As is well known, Kant doubts that love can be the content of a duty. It cannot as such be required. Yet at the same time we know that the religions of the law (Judaism, Christianity, Islam) do in fact command love; in fact, if Paul is to be believed, they scarcely command anything else. That love cannot be a duty may be so, if duty is encompassed within debt. But this is not so if what is commanded, not by law but by justice, is precisely the love of the neighbor, and perhaps of the stranger, and even of the enemy as well.

Of these possible derestrictions of love, I will only at this point note that Paul has already had something to say about the enemy. Just after saying that his hearers/readers should "extend hospitality to strangers" (12:13), Paul says, "Bless those who persecute you; bless and do not curse them" (13:14); and later, "do not repay anyone evil for evil" (12:17); and goes on to say, "if your enemies are hungry, feed them; if they are thirsty, give them something to drink" (12:21). Here again we may note that the question is one of going beyond repayment, beyond economy. Indeed, the law of economy is precisely interrupted here at the point of not repaying "evil for evil" (although we are to "repay honor for honor" and even "fear for fear"). In the subsequent exhortation concerning feeding enemies, Paul is citing Proverbs 25:21–22, which also contains the obscure assertion that thereby one heaps coals of fire upon their heads. Whatever this refers to,[15] what is interesting is what Paul cuts off from this citation of the proverb. He eliminates the phrase that brings this back into a (deferred) economy: "The Lord will reward you" (Proverbs 21:22b). That is, even at the point of citation, Paul exercises great care not to fall back into the economy of reward or payment.

Which brings us back to the question of gift or grace and how this duty beyond debt may be understood as provoked by gift. On one level this is perfectly clear. For the gift or grace with which Paul is concerned, the one that provokes this duty beyond debt is the love "of God," a love that is unrestricted or unconditional. "I am persuaded," he has said, that "nothing can separate us from the love of God" (Romans 8:38–39). Hence it is not surprising that the consequence of love as gift is love as duty beyond debt. This is prevented, as we have seen, from being confused with a circular economic relation in that the responding love, the love that corresponds to the gift of love, is not a love that is returned to the one who loves—God, for example—but is directed to the other human. Thus the love that has been given is not returned (still less kept) but given, handed on.

The question of duty beyond debt returns us to the question of Paul's odd phrase "the obedience of faith," which, as it happens, brackets the whole of the letter to the Romans (1:5, 16:26). This is often (mis)interpreted as if faith itself, and especially faith as a set of beliefs or even of commitments to the church were what Paul was emphasizing here. Our reflections thus far would undermine this identification. It is important to notice that Paul avoids the language of debt, as we have seen, avoiding the return of the economic relation of works. But he does not similarly avoid the language of obedience to designate the life that responds to the gift. This must be understood in terms of the continuing validity of the intent of the law, that is, of the claim of justice. It is not that grace or gift abolishes or diminishes or reduces that claim, but that, on the contrary, gift makes that claim effective and efficacious. It is this that is signaled by obedience. This obedience is not simply a hearing, as he says also in Romans 2:13, but is also a hearkening, a doing of that which is required justly by the law, by the law's innermost intention or justification. What is at stake here, then, is a response to the gift that corresponds to it; that is, a faith as faithfulness that is set into motion through the gift that makes possible, and so gives, justice.[16]

In this connection, it will be important to note that for Paul, it is possible to speak both of the faith *of* the messiah (as opposed to faith *in* or belief *about* the messiah) and of the obedience *of* the messiah. These are extraordinary formulations in that they make considerable trouble for conventional "christologies." Exploring their significance would take us far from our more narrow focus on the question of justice and its becoming effective beyond the law, which is our theme in these reflections. But we can at least situate these notions within the set of issues that we are discussing here. The faith of the messiah, it seems to me, must be understood in terms of faithfulness, that is, an adherence to the divine aim and claim of justice and to the actualization of that justice through, or by means of, gift. It is this adherence, this faithfulness, that Paul can also say is the becoming obedient of the messiah in Philippians 2:8, who "became obedient to the point of death."

Moreover, when Paul speaks of this messianic faithfulness or obedience, it is in order to say that this is precisely what also comes to expression or should come to expression in the believer or adherent. Thus it is the believer who is to have the same mind-set as the messiah who has renounced what was properly his own (in that case "equality with the divine") in order to become obedient (Philippians 2:5, 8).

Something similar seems to happen in relation to Paul's understanding of the faith(fullness) of the messiah that is to be shared by the one who adheres to the messiah and so becomes just. Paul has been speaking of the justice of God that has been disclosed through the faithfulness of Jesus messiah for all who are faithful (3:22). It is thus the justice of God, or as we have been saying, divine justice, that is attested or demonstrated in the justice of those who have the faithfulness that was also that of the messiah. What he says is, "[God] did this to show his justice . . . it was to prove . . . that he himself is just and that he makes just the one who has the faithfulness of Jesus" (3:27). Thus the link between divine justice and our justice is precisely faith, or rather faithfulness, that is first of all attributed to Jesus messiah and then emulated in the one who adheres to the messiah. Thus the obedience of faith is precisely this messianic faithfulness, or faithfulness to the messianic, which has its origin and goal in divine justice.

That Paul is always thinking of justice and its actualization among those who adhere to the messianic, who engage in this messianic faithfulness, makes clear how he can be concerned with the accomplishment of a duty that fulfils what the law intends. But that this duty is one based on gift and so one that exceeds the economy of debt is what is marked out by the idea of faithfulness that is somehow incited or provoked through gift.

Before leaving the question of a duty beyond debt as a way of indicating the actualization of justice beyond law, we should note that for Paul the importance or urgency of the claim of this justice is related to a sense of eschatological imminence. Derrida has written that "Justice—or justice as it promises to be, beyond what it actually is—always has an eschatological dimension" (*A Taste for the Secret*, 20). In any case justice, the justice that is beyond the law cannot wait (*Force of Law*, 255). It is always invested with urgency.

For Paul, there is a somewhat different way of bringing this urgency to expression. In the words that immediately follow the discussion of the love that goes beyond debt but that is in its own way a fulfilling of what the law requires, Paul writes, "you know what time it is, how now is the moment for you to wake from sleep. For salvation is nearer to us now than when we became faithful; the night is far gone, the day is near. Let us therefore lay aside the works of darkness and put on the armor of light" (13:11–12). It is precisely the talk of a duty that exceeds debt but that fulfils the just requirements of the law that must be placed within the horizon of a certain imminence, an impending and radical transformation. On the one hand, that transformation has not yet occurred; it is still, in a certain way, night. Yet like the rooster crow that heralds the daybreak, Paul sounds the alarm. It is as if it is on account of a certain somnolence that humanity has been only going through the motions of justice, as justice based on, or in compliance with, legality. But now it is time to wake up, to be alert, to anticipate the day of lucidity and clarity. It is a kind of awakening to the coming of the other (the day of salvation, God, the messiah) that awakens us to the love of the neighbor and thus to justice. Thus Levinas could speak of a certain insomnia that is characteristic of the ethical relation,[17] a casting off and putting off of sleep, an awakening from a constitutional (one might even say ontological) drowsiness, and a becoming alert to what comes and so to the arrival of the neighbor, the other.

The ethical-political relation to the neighbor, to the other, is dealt with by Derrida (following and transforming Levinas) as hospitality, as the welcome extended to the other, the stranger. And it is to that discussion that I next turn.

6

Hospitality, Ethics, and Politics

Although there are many ways in which the question of a duty beyond debt, a gift beyond economy, and a justice beyond law, might be
made more concrete—through reflections on gratitude or forgiveness, for
example—the one that Derrida has seemed to find most fruitful for
broaching the question of politics has been that of hospitality. In this chapter I will turn to that question. In order to do this, it will first be appropriate to attempt to discern why this question, and how it is related to the political question. This in turn, I will contend, helps us to think the
significance given by Paul to issues that are in some way those of hospitality, particularly his treatment of this theme in Romans 14 and 15 as well as
in other letters under the heading of "welcome." This will open up the
question of what Paul has to offer to the question of cosmopolitanism, a
theme recently broached by Derrida and in which he has explicitly mentioned a certain Paul: the Paul of Ephesians.

Derrida on Hospitality

The question of hospitality as the question of ethics and politics has
come to have an increasingly explicit place in Derrida's thought. Already in
The Other Heading he had noted that the question of Europe opens up to
the question of something like hospitality: "The same duty also dictates
welcoming foreigners in order not only to integrate them but to recognize
and accept their alterity" (77). That the question of welcome and that of

politics are integrally connected is already announced here. And this question will continue to dominate the question of ethics and politics for Derrida both as one that requires a certain theoretical reflection (*Of Hospitality, On Cosmopolitanism,* "Hostipatality" in *Acts of Religion,* and so on), but also provoke some of his most overt interventions into the sphere of political debate in and beyond France.

That the question of welcome or of hospitality is not merely one example among others of the political "relevance" of deconstruction is made clear at a number of points. In *On Cosmopolitanism,* for example, he writes, "*ethics is hospitality*; ethics is so thoroughly coextensive with the experience of hospitality" (17). Moreover, he can also maintain that this is true not only of ethics but of what we might call ethos or rather, here, culture: "one cannot speak of cultivating an ethic of hospitality. Hospitality is culture itself and not simply one ethic amongst others" (16). This is not simply an ad hoc formulation but one that is repeated with a certain insistence. In *Of Hospitality,* for example, he writes, referring to his ongoing seminar: "We had also recalled the fact, at one point, that the problem of hospitality was coextensive with the ethical problem" (149). And in "Hostipatality," which are the notes for Derrida's seminar of 1997, he writes, "Hospitality—this is culture itself" (361). These representative assertions place the question of welcome and hospitality at the forefront of Derrida's reflections.

But we should also notice that the reference to welcome and hospitality are therefore also connected to, and virtually substitutable for, the questions to which we have already addressed ourselves. We recall that Derrida had maintained that "deconstruction is justice" in *The Force of Law* (243).[1] Here he maintains something similar regarding hospitality: "Hospitality—this is a name or an example of deconstruction" ("Hostipatality," 364). In the discussion of justice relative to law, we had already had occasion to refer to Derrida's reflections in *Of Hospitality,* where the formulation is most often that of the relation of law to the laws. But the connection to the theme of justice, of justice outside the law, is also explicit in that discussion: "The law of absolute hospitality commands a break with hospitality by right, with law or justice as rights" (*Of Hospitality,* 25). Something similar to this formulation is also found in "A Word of Welcome" in *Adieu to Emmanuel Levinas*: "discourse, justice, ethical uprightness have to do first of all with *welcoming*" (35).

Accordingly, we will not be surprised to read that true hospitality is heterogeneous to hospitality by rights, but it can "set and maintain it in a perpetual progressive movement; but it is strangely heterogeneous to it as justice is heterogeneous to the law to which it is yet so close, from which in truth it is indissociable" (*Of Hospitality*, 27). Hospitality here stands to "right" as the claim of justice stands to law. As we would expect, this relation is one of both heterogeneity and of indissociability. And hospitality instantiates this in an especially clear way by bringing us back to the by now familiar problematic: "It is a question of knowing how to transform and improve the law, and knowing if this improvement is possible within an historical space which takes place *between* the Law of an unconditional hospitality, offered *a priori* to every other, to all newcomers, *whoever they may be*, and the constitutional laws of a right to hospitality, without which The unconditional Law of hospitality would be in danger of remaining a pious and irresponsible desire" (*On Cosmopolitanism*, 22–23). The parallel, or even in a certain way the "substitutability," of hospitality and justice would also lead us to expect a clear relation between the question of hospitality and that of gift in relation to economy, and that is precisely what we find:

For to be what it "must" be hospitality must not pay a debt, or be governed by a duty; it is gracious, and "must" not open itself to the guest [invited or visitor] either "conforming to duty" or even, to use the Kantian distinction again, "out of duty." This unconditional law of hospitality, if such a thing is thinkable, would then be a law without imperative, without order and without duty. A law without law, in short. For if I practice hospitality "*out of* duty" [and not only "*in conforming with* duty"], this hospitality of paying up is no longer an absolute hospitality, it is no longer graciously offered beyond debt and economy. (*Of Hospitality*, 83)

All the themes or questions to which we have directed our attention in these reflections on Derrida and Paul come together in this formulation: that of law beyond law, of duty ("must") beyond debt, of gift (or grace) beyond economy.

But what are we speaking of when we speak of an absolute hospitality that is so like justice beyond the law, or gift outside economy, or duty without debt? What is at stake here is the welcoming of the other as other. These reflections are generally a kind of appropriation and transformation of what has been developed in the reflections of Levinas concerning the welcome to the other; although Derrida characteristically transforms the question of welcome into that of hospitality.[2] In any case, what is at stake is the openness to the other, to that which is not the same and is not to become the same as "myself." It is precisely, we might say, the otherness of the other that is welcomed, that is received with hospitality, with a certain gladness in contrast to the allergic reaction to the other that wishes to reduce the other to an extension or echo of oneself. Already in *The Other Heading* Derrida had formulated this as the question of a duty to welcome the other, the stranger, the foreigner, not in order to integrate or assimilate them (in that case to Europeanize them), but respecting, indeed in a certain way celebrating, their otherness or alterity.

In developing the complications of the notion of hospitality, Derrida is dependent on some of the formulations of Levinas. For example, we would normally suppose that the host would be one who is without need, one who simply remains the same in self-plenitude while graciously making space for the other as a temporary extension of the household to encompass the other. Derrida, however, is able to make use of the resources of the French language in order to play on the way *hôte* may refer to either the guest or the host and so to trouble the distinction that otherwise would seem self-evident. With the aid of Levinas (and the latter's change in terminology from *Totality and Infinity* to *Otherwise than Being*), Derrida will speak of the host/guest as hostage[3]—that is, as surrendering self-identity to and for the sake of the other. That the guest is in a certain way at the mercy of the host may seem more or less thinkable but that the host should be at the mercy of the guest requires a bit more thought. The idea actually has a double character. On the one hand, the host is fundamentally a guest in that his or her at-home-ness in the world is always in some way derivative and dependent. But it is also the case that the identity of host as host is dependent on there being a guest. In order to be a host, I need a guest, and without that guest, I may neither be a host nor "at home." Thus my "identity" as host is dependent on or hostage to the guest. Thus Derrida can ask, "Is not hospitality an interruption of the self?" (*Adieu*, 51).

There are ways in which this becomes even more radical, implicating the whole idea of what it means to be a subject or a self as a subject; the way in which one is constituted in advance by the relation to the other; and so on. The exploration of these paths is extraordinarily helpful, I think, for theology, but at this point, we must confine ourselves to noticing how some of these ideas help us to see what Paul is up to, above all in Romans.

Welcome in Paul

Paul's explicit development of the theme of ethics as welcome comes in Romans 14 to 15:7, and we will turn to this shortly. But first, we should notice the way in which this theme is already presupposed in his earlier discussion of Abraham, for this will help us to see the connection of parenesis to the more familiar themes of grace, faith, and justice.

Abraham

Derrida, in his discussion of hospitality, has had occasion to refer to the way in which this theme is rooted in the narrative of Abraham and so in the "origin" of the "Abrahamic faiths." "The three monotheistic religions, as Abrahamic religions, are issued from a patriarch that came to this earth as a 'stranger, a hôte, *ger*,' and a kind of saint of hospitality" ("Hostipatality," 369). The reference to Abraham comes in Derrida's reflections on the writing and career of Louis Massignon, who had established a house of hospitality and prayer to welcome Muslims, not in order to have the latter change their religion (Massignon was a Christian), but simply in order to represent the hospitality that is at the heart of faith. This is a doubly rich example, not only because of the attempt both to enact this and to reflect on it, but also because Massignon was a "guest" among those to whom he offered hospitality. This strange interchangeability of host and guest recalls and opens up a reflection on Abraham, who was a stranger in the land, having left his own family and country in response to a call (Genesis 12:1–3). The story of Genesis is first a story of the sojourner who is at the mercy of the hospitality of strangers.

Derrida turns then to the events of Abraham's receiving a visitation from the Lord, first in the form of a vision in which the promise that had initially spurred Abraham to leave his home and father's house is iterated (Genesis 15). Here is where the narrative says that "Abraham believed the LORD and the LORD counted it as justice" (15:6). After the apparent fulfillment of the promise in the birth of Ishmael, Abraham again receives a visitation of the LORD in which the promise is once again uttered and displaced. But here is an event that Derrida takes to be exemplary of the situation of the host and guest, for here the name and so the identity of the host is transformed (from Abram to Abraham), as is that of his wife (from Sarai to Sarah). The coming of the guest, the reception of the guest, does not leave the "host" unchanged. A new identity is represented by the new name. "This is indeed hospitality *par excellence* in which the visitor radically overwhelms the self of the 'visited' and the *chez-soi* of the hôte" ("Hostipatality," 372).

Very briefly, then, we see in this narrative several of the features of the puzzling situation of hospitality. The host is also a guest (Abraham is a guest in the land but is host to the visitation of the other); the guest is also a host (who is the "owner" of this land?); the host is dependent for his very identity on the visitation of the guest; and so on. This very situation is brought to the reader's attention by Paul in Romans 4 when he attempts to think a justice outside or beyond the law. What Abraham does that is called both faith and justice by Paul is to welcome the coming of the visitant and to rely for his identity on the word or promise of the visitant. The origin of faith is the scene of hospitality in which the other is welcomed, trusted, and relied on.[4]

Welcome

With this in mind, we may now turn to the more explicit treatment of this theme in Romans. This comes in the so-called paranetic section of Paul's text, in which he attempts to indicate some of the consequences that follow for his readers from the development of the themes of a justice beyond the law, a justice that is gift. Already in 12:13 Paul had articulated the principle in the form of an imperative—"extend hospitality to strangers"— but in the next section, he takes this up again, not in the first place in the sense of strangers who are of a different nationality, but in the sense of those who are of a different opinion or, as we shall suggest, a differing religion.

The section begins with the injunction: "Welcome those who are weak in faith, but not for the purpose of quarreling over opinions" (14:1), and concludes with the injunction: "Welcome one another, therefore, just as Christ has welcomed you" (15:7). The occasion for the injunction to welcome has to do with some rather deep-seated differences of opinion. What differences? There appear to be those who think one should abstain from meat, while others think it is OK to eat meat.[5] Some also (the same ones?), it would appear, are opposed to the drinking of wine, whereas others suppose that wine is good. There is also a potential dispute about whether one day is better or more appropriate than another, or whether all days are equally good. It is not altogether clear how these differences are to be lined up: is it one group who opposes eating meat or drinking wine, and who favors observing the specialness of a particular day? Or is more than one group designated here? And is Paul talking about groups that are influenced by Jewish law or by pagan perspectives? These are intractable questions.[6] Fortunately, their solution is not necessary to get an idea of what Paul is struggling with here. What is important is that these differences of opinion certainly threaten the life of the community, or rather, that what they threaten is the very possibility for the community to embody the new justice, the justice beyond the law, the justice that is based on gift. Certainly nothing so threatens the possibility of giving and receiving hospitality as differences in principle over what one may or may not, should or should not, eat. In another connection, Derrida also makes this point:

The infinitely metonymical question on the subject of "one must eat well" must be nourishing not only for me, for a "self," which would thus eat badly; it must be *shared*. . . . One never eats entirely on one's own: this constitutes the rule underlying the statement "One must eat well." It is a rule offering infinite hospitality. And in all differences, ruptures, and wars (one might even say wars of religion), "eating well" is at stake. ("Eating Well," in *Points . . .* , 282)

Here two issues are joined: that the question of hospitality is the question of the sharing of food, and that what is at stake in ruptures, even wars of religion, is precisely the question of eating and sharing food. The question, then, of a welcome to the other is immediately threatened by differences over what it means to eat well, over what it is appropriate to eat and to share.

We may say that what is at stake here is precisely a difference in "religion." Indeed, differences of religion are far more about differences in eating than about anything else. This is especially true when religionists come into contact with one another, are in a position to welcome (or not) one another. Hindus and Muslims are divided in India by the question of eating meat. And this is by no means a trivial matter for those who must find a way to live together. Christians and Jews are distinguished from Muslims by, among other things, whether one may drink wine, and this is scarcely a trivial matter, for example in Saudi Arabia. Jews and Muslims are distinguished from Christians by whether one may eat (among other things) pork and so on. Although theologians may focus on things like ideas of divinity and interpretation of texts, and priests may worry about worship styles, the "faithful" are most often confronted by differences of religion as differences in what it is to eat, or eat well. It is here that difference as difference of religion comes to sharpest focus in the everyday, with the possible exception of the question of holy days: Friday, Saturday, Sunday, or some other, or none.

What Paul recognizes is that these are not trivial matters but matters, as he will say, of conscience. That is, they are matters that involve the self-understanding of the person in relation to the divine. To be sure, Paul places himself here (at least rhetorically) on the side of those who suppose that there is no need to worry about food, drink, or days: "I know and am persuaded that nothing is unclean in itself," he says (Romans 14:14), a position that we might be tempted to associate with a secular humanist today; that is, with one who adopts not only a nonreligious attitude toward food and drink and days, but one who is rather suspicious of all these religious ideas that make such a fuss about food and drink and days. Of course, even in a world without God, these same kinds of differences seem to surface interminably, even if today they most often march under the banner of health, diet, and so on—another way of trying to be safe, of trying to save the other; that is, other (or the same?) quests for salvation.

In any case, Paul is here dealing with the question of differences that are in effect differences of "religion." And they are differences that threaten the very possibility of hospitality to, or welcome of, the other as other. For what such differences provoke is the attempt to insist on the rightness of one's own view and thus to invite the other in order to "convert" the other to the rightness of one's position or religion.

This is by no means the first time that Paul has found it necessary to deal with this kind of issue. In Galatians it seems to have had to do at first with the question of the observance of something like kosher. He and other Jews like Peter had eaten together with pagans, putting aside their own religious customs for the sake of being in the position of giving and, especially, receiving hospitality. But when more observant Jews (who were of course also Christians) came to town, Peter withdrew from the common table with pagans. This at least is how Paul recounts the story (Galatians 2:11 ff.); and he accuses Peter of duplicity in this regard. For what is essential here, he believes, is putting aside religious scruples for the sake of welcoming one another, breaking bread with one another. A quite different set of circumstances seems to have arisen in Corinth with respect to the question of eating meat sacrificed to idols—that is, to an at least virtual participation in pagan sacrifices and so religion (1 Corinthians 8–10).[7] There is no need to go into the details of these discussions in Paul's texts at this point, although they provide endless food for thought. What is crucial for our purposes is to see that for Paul, in very concrete ways, what is at stake in his attempt to nurture groups that will somehow instantiate a new and more radical form of justice quite typically comes down to addressing the question of the conditions of possibility of giving and receiving hospitality or of "welcoming one another."

In this rather fraught situation of threatened hospitality, Paul's response is one that brings into question the subjectivity of those with whom he identifies (called here "the strong"). For what Paul in effect argues is that they should put aside their own religious convictions in favor of the position of the other. That is, to be able to welcome or to be welcomed in this context of a kind of mutual welcoming, that which is distinctive of the subjecthood of those whom he addresses must be sacrificed. Otherwise hospitality and so justice beyond the law will not happen. It would be all too easy to begin such an argument by simply saying those who have scruples should put them aside. That is what he seems to have argued in relation to Peter in Galatians. But Paul is aware that even this, rather liberal, opinion is a kind of scruple, indeed is a religious difference, and because it seems to be his own view as well, he begins by saying that it is the "enlightened one" who must yield to the religious one. Precisely because the reign of God (or even the democracy to come) does not consist in imposing religious views on others, therefore it follows that the position of a certain enlightenment should also not be imposed.[8] We have seen that the situation of hospitality places the guest and the host (and not only the guest) in the position of surrender of a self-assured and self-contained identity. And this is what we find here as well in Paul's admonition directed to the strong (and perhaps later to the weak as well)—namely, that for the sake of what is really important, for the sake of the coming of that justice that is based on gift or grace, one must put aside one's "identity" in order to receive one another. Thus he says, "Do not for the sake of food, destroy the work of God" (14:20). But this "work of God," as we have seen, is precisely the bringing of justice, a justice that is outside the law, based on gift, and issuing in a duty beyond debt.[9]

We may also note that for Paul the question of whether or not to eat, especially in 1 Corinthians but also here in Romans, is, in a certain way, "undecidable." That is, in either case, what is at stake is an unconditional reference to the messiah, to God, to justice. Yet either the eating or the not eating, the drinking or the not drinking, may and must instantiate this loyalty to the messianic. That each "be fully convinced" in their own minds acknowledges at the very least that neither decision is "programmable" or simply automatically deducible from the unconditional "principle." A full development of these discussions in Paul would also lead us into the fruitful reflections of Derrida into questions of responsibility, decision, and negotiation. At this point, these connections may simply be noted and a discussion of them reserved for another occasion.

Messianic Welcome

At the end of his discussion of this problem, Paul has said, "welcome one another as Christ has welcomed you." This is a rather curious phrase. Why does he say as Messiah has welcomed you? How have Paul's readers been welcomed by the Messiah? How does this substantiate the call to welcome one another?

The substantiation of the call to welcome the other finds a somewhat different basis in Hebrews 13:2: "for thus some have received angels unawares," a probable reference to the hospitality of Abraham in welcoming the divine messengers (Genesis 18), a hospitality immediately followed by the antihospitality of the people of Sodom toward these same messengers (Genesis 19). But it is also a theme announced in Ovid concerning the welcome given by Philemon and Baucis to strangers who turn out to be gods (*Metamorphosis*, book 8).

But Paul does not substantiate the injunction to welcome one another by recourse to these illustrious narratives. Instead he says, "as the messiah has welcomed you." The form of this justification is rather like that which we find in Leviticus, where the Israelites are told to be hospitable to strangers for they were strangers in Egypt: "You shall love the alien as yourself, for you were aliens in Egypt" (Leviticus 19:34), a connection often enough repeated in the Law (Exodus 22:21; Deuteronomy 10:19). Because we were strangers, dependent on the kindness of those who received us, let us also receive the vulnerable wanderer with kindness. But Paul cannot use this content even if he will use this form. For he is addressing gentiles or pagans rather than Jews. Those to whom he speaks cannot think of themselves as having been sojourners in Egypt. Thus instead of the welcome extended to Israel and his sons in Egypt, Paul refers to the welcome extended to the gentiles by the messiah. It is this antecedent welcome that serves as the basis for the injunction to welcome one another. But how have those Paul addresses been welcomed by the messiah? In what way have they been welcomed or received by Israel's messiah?[10]

This brings the reader back to Paul's difficult argument in Romans 9–11 concerning the way in which the gentiles have been made welcome in a promise originally directed only to the Jews. That this is the argument that he intends to substantiate his admonition concerning welcome is clear from what immediately follows that admonition: "For I tell you that Messiah has become a servant of the circumcised on behalf of the truth of God in order that he might confirm the promises given to the patriarchs, and in order that the gentiles might glorify God for his mercy" (15:7–9a). This terminology immediately points us to Paul's discussion of how it is that the promise to the patriarchs is confirmed and to how the gentiles have received mercy. To a significant degree, that argument had been anticipated and provoked by what Paul had already said about Abraham (the patriarch par excellence) in Romans 4. But this had left the question of the fate of contemporary Israel hanging, and Paul cannot find that situation satisfactory: "For I could wish that I myself were accursed and cut off from Messiah for the sake of my own people" (9:3). This is not the place to unravel all that Paul attempts to do in this rather extended argument. However, the upshot of Paul's argument is that the rejection of Messiah by (many) of his own people has the unexpected result that the gentiles receive mercy—that is, that the good news comes to be proclaimed directly to them, apart from the law. It is, however, Paul's argument that the opening to the gentiles and their being grafted onto the rootstock of patriarchal promise does not mean that Israel has been rejected. On the contrary, "the gifts and the calling of God are irrevocable" (11:29). In consequence, Paul is led to conclude that his own beloved mission to the gentiles is but a detour by which in the end "*all* Israel will be saved" (11:26). And it is this detour that also means that the promise to the patriarchs that Israel would be a blessing to the gentiles, would be the way in which justice will come to the gentiles, is to be accomplished in an unforeseen way. It is quite possible that Paul did not know where his argument would lead him, that he is astonished by it at least as much as the reader. That at least is how he seems to conclude with an outbreak verging on glossolalia: "O the depth of the riches and wisdom and knowledge of God! How unsearchable are his judgments and how inscrutable his ways!" (11:33). He then goes on to speak precisely in terms of gift, "who has given him a gift to receive a gift in return?" (11:35), thereby bringing us again to the question of gift beyond economy and of the unknowability of the gift.

Now the point of this extraordinary argument, what may even be called a bravura performance on the part of Paul, is that he is able then to bring it forward as the basis for the exhortation to hospitality: welcome one another as messiah has welcomed you. For in the end, the messiah has welcomed all, both Jews and gentiles, and so all beyond all religious scruples, practices, and principles. It is therefore this all-embracing welcome that is to be brought to concrete expression in the life of those who are found within the new sociality brought into being by this welcome, this gift of hospitality.

Cosmopolitanism

For Derrida, the question of hospitality or welcome is not only *the* ethical question, it is also in a certain way, *the* political question, *the* question of politics today. And it is in connection with this thesis that he has occasion to refer to Paul as the basis of a cosmopolitanism that is at stake in contemporary political life. In order to see how the question of politics is at stake here and how it is that Paul plays a crucial role in the articulation of the possibility of such a politics, and thus how Paul is finally to be understood as a political thinker, as a political philosopher even, we will therefore explore this dimension of Derrida's thinking and see to what extent we may verify the reference to Paul in this regard.

Speaking of the importance of *mondialisation* as opposed to globalization, Derrida, in a speech to UNESCO in November 1999 entitled "Globalization, Peace and Cosmopolitanism," says the following:

> it is because the concept of world gestures toward a history, it has a memory that distinguishes it from that of the globe, of the universe, of earth, of the *cosmos* even (at least the cosmos in its pre-Christian meaning, which Saint Paul then christianized precisely to make it say *world* as *fraternal* community of human beings, of fellow creatures, brothers, sons of God and neighbors to one another). For the world begins by designating, and tends to remain, in an Abrahamic tradition (Judeo-Christian-Islamic but predominantly Christian) a particular space-time, a certain oriented history of human brotherhood, of what in a Pauline language—the language that continues to structure and condition the modern concepts of the rights of man or the crime against humanity (horizons of international law in its actual form to which I would like to return, a form that conditions, in principle and by right, the beginning of globalization [*mondialisation*])—of what in this Pauline language one calls *citizens of the world* (*sympolitai*, fellow citizens [*concitoyens*] of the saints of the household of God), brothers, fellow men, neighbors, insofar as they are creatures and sons of God. (*Negotiations*, 374–75)

In this extraordinary passage, Derrida makes clear that the thinking of world as an historical process and reality, what is inadequately today spoken of as "globalization," depends in important respects upon the ideas that are brought into focus by Paul even as they are the common property of the Abrahamic traditions. It is common to the Abrahamic traditions precisely as the law of hospitality that can accept no ethnic and religious boundaries and that therefore comes to expression in a kind of citizenship of a new world (what Derrida likes to call a democracy to come) composed of "fellow men, neighbors . . . creatures and sons of God." The ideas that Derrida puts forward here had been developed in an essay first published in 1997 but translated into English in 2001, "On Cosmopolitanism." Here Derrida links Paul's contribution to that of the Stoics: "Finally at this juncture, we could identify the cosmopolitan (*cosmopolilitique*) tradition common to a certain Greek stoicism and a Pauline Christianity, of which the inheritors were the figures of the enlightenment, and to which Kant will doubtless have given the most rigorous philosophical formulation" (18–19).[11] Note that in *Adieu to Emmanuel Levinas*, Derrida also refers to "the great tradition of a cosmopolitanism passed down from stoicism or Pauline Christianity to the Enlightenment and to Kant" (88).[12] The reference to Kant is precisely what links this discussion both to "cosmopolitanism" and to the question of hospitality because it is Kant's discussion of the "Third Definitive Article for a Perpetual Peace: Cosmopolitan Right Shall Be Limited to Conditions of Universal Hospitality," in the essay *To Perpetual Peace, a Philosophical Sketch* of 1795, that often provokes Derrida's reflections on hospitality.[13]

The reference to stoicism is made more precise in relation to Cicero: "It was Cicero who was to bequeath a certain cosmopolitanism. Pauline Christianity revived, radicalized and literally 'politicized' the primary injunctions of all the Abrahamic religions. . . . Saint Paul gives to these appeals or to these dictates their modern names" (*On Cosmopolitanism*, 19). There is a certain sense in which the stoic notions of a kind of universal humanity were somewhat depoliticized given the imperial conditions within which they were articulated. That is, the disappearance of the polis as the basic political unit, replaced by empire, made the notion of citizenship in empire nonsensical. But Paul does seem to want, as Derrida says, to "politicize" this sense of universal humanity. It is the case that Derrida will want to put in question "the secularized version of such Pauline cosmopolitanism" (20), but what is put in question by Derrida are the limits to hospitality of not residence but visiting; and that it be dependent on state sovereignty. These are the limits placed on the notion of universal hospitality by Kant in articulating the "secularized version" of Pauline cosmopolitanism. That is, it is not yet the Pauline formulations but their secularized versions that Derrida is particularly inclined to put in question.

The Paul to whom Derrida refers in these texts is not explicitly the Paul of Romans but the Paul of Ephesians and in particular Ephesians 2:19–20. We will not attempt to adjudicate the century-old dispute concerning the Pauline authorship of Ephesians. But we will see what it is that has drawn Derrida's attention to this text and seek to determine whether the views expressed there are consonant with what we have read in Romans.

The text to which Derrida refers when he gives Paul credit for developing the terms in which cosmopolitanism gives itself to be thought in the tradition of the West is Ephesians 2:19: "So then you are no longer strangers [*zenoi*] and sojourners, but you are fellow citizens [*sumpolitai*] of the saints and members of the household [*oikeioi*] of God." This assertion of common citizenship comes as the conclusion to the argument of Ephesians' concerning the bringing together of Jews and gentiles. The argument is addressed to the gentiles and recalls that they were once alienated from the commonwealth (*politeios*) of Israel and thus *zenoi* or strangers. They were, that is, the "ones far off." But the work of God in and through the messiah is to break down the dividing wall of hostility, a wall that is here identified with the "law of commandments and dogmas [*dogmasin*]" (2:15a). It is this dividing structure of "religion" that has been abolished to the end of the constitution of a new humanity (*anthropos*) that replaces the divided and mutually antagonistic humanities (2:15b). It is this new human being that is pluralized in order to be termed fellow citizens and members of the same household or family.

Although the terminology in which the idea of overcoming division based on law is quite different in this text from that which we find in Romans, there is nevertheless a strong relationship. For as we have seen in Romans, the intention of Paul was to articulate the overcoming of the rupture between Jews and gentiles. This occurs in a number of ways, but it is especially focused in the way in which the narrative of Abraham is deployed (making grace rather than law the basis of justice for both the "circumcised" and the "uncircumcised") and by the "history of salvation" narrative that Paul elaborates in Romans 9–11, which has the consequence that "all will be saved." This overcoming of religious and "ethnic" difference is then applied to the internal politics of the community under the heading of "welcome one another," as we have seen. That the point of view in Ephesians is determined by the same general conception of law and gift and so on is also evident: "For by grace you have been saved through faith; and this is not your own[14] but of the divine gift; not of works lest anyone boast" (2:8).

There is another way in which this notion of a single humanity is worked out in Romans. It is through the idea of the unity of humanity either as "Adamic humanity" or as "messianic humanity" in Romans 5. This contrast is one that Paul had developed in 1 Corinthians 15, where he deployed it in quite a different way because his theme there was resurrection. However, what Paul does by the development of this contrast is gesture toward the unity of humanity in two contrasting but interdependent ways. Adamic humanity is indeed the whole of humanity understood both as creation and as under the dominion of sin and death. It is the human being as earthling, as a being unto death, as somehow embedded in guiltiness. Paul invokes the name of the supposed ancestor of the human race not in order to talk about a once upon a time mythical figure, but in order to indicate a universal condition: "and so death spread to all humans because all sinned" (5:12). Although all humanity may be understood from the perspective of this earthling as characterized by guilt and death,[15] this is also supposed to be a preindication of another unity of all humanity now named "messiah." Adam (earthling) "was a type of the coming one" (5:14), the arrivant we might say, the messianic. Once again with respect to the coming of the messiah, we have not an isolated figure of saga but an inclusive designation of humanity as such: "Then as through one offense condemnation comes to all humans, so also through one event of justice [*dikaiomatos*] comes to all humans being-made-just to life" (5:18). This difficult passage presents us with a definite parallel:

One offense > all humans > condemnation [> death]
One justice-event > all humans > made just > life

The claim, then, is that the single humanity designated as messianic is that humanity in which the free gift of justice will reign, thereby producing not death but life.[16] How all of this is supposed to occur through what I have called the event of justice or the justice-event is a matter for another discussion, one that would explore the messianic in Paul and so the coimplication of what is called christology and what is called eschatology. This is a crucially important issue for working out the way in which reading Derrida can help us to think Paul. That, however, takes us away from the focus on the question of justice at this point and thus of hospitality. What the reference to Adam and Messiah does do for us at this point, however, is to emphasize that for Paul, each of these terms gestures toward humanity regarded as a single "thing." Each term points to what might be termed the species unity of the human being.[17] It is this unity of the human being, whether as Adamic or, more importantly, as messianic, that makes intelligible Paul's supposition that all humans are summoned to justice and all receive, or are intended to receive, or actually will receive, the gift of justice and so of life. It is this unity of humanity that then makes it possible to suppose that divisions of religion or culture or even gender are secondary to the common "citizenship" of all human beings in one creation/cosmos.[18] And it is therefore this that lies behind the specific admonition concerning a mutual welcome. Indeed Paul gestures toward this when he supposes that "all things are clean" (14:14), even if our scruples or our habits of separating things into categories of clean and unclean are more than mere conventions but have a certain performative force: "it is unclean for anyone who thinks it is unclean" (14:14).

The Political

My discussion thus far has shown that the theme of hospitality or welcome is important in comparable ways for Paul and Derrida. I have moreover shown that Derrida's emphasis on the question of cosmopolitanism is rooted in Pauline conceptuality, as he has himself indicated. What remains is to show how for Derrida this is to be understood as a decidedly political matter—as, perhaps, definitive of the political as such— and how this comports with what we have been discovering about Paul.

For Derrida, the question of hospitality or welcome to the stranger or foreigner is not only what might be termed a theoretical issue. It is also one that has been the occasion of some of his most direct engagements in the political disputes of France and Europe. As a consequence, it is here that the question of the relation between an unconditional like hospitality and the concrete political, juridical order comes most clearly into focus in his work. He writes: "The law of absolute hospitality commands a break with hospitality by right, with law or justice as rights" (*Of Hospitality*, 25). Here it is clear that there is a fundamental distinction between the claim of hospitality that sets it "above" or outside the law. But even though true hospitality is heterogeneous to hospitality by rights, it can "set and maintain it in a perpetual progressive movement; but it is strangely heterogeneous to it as justice is heterogeneous to the law to which it is yet so close, from which in truth it is indissociable" (27). That unconditional hospitality is both heterogeneous to and indissociable from hospitality as this is encoded in the law (for example, governing refugee status) should by now seem familiar. But this relation means that an engagement with the political becomes unavoidable: "I nonetheless claim that a politics that does not maintain a reference to this principle of unconditional hospitality is a politics that loses its reference to justice. It may retain its rights (which I again distinguish here from justice), the right to its rights, but it loses justice" (*Negotiations*, 101).

That politics must maintain a reference to justice, that this provokes the political-legislative-judicial sphere into continual questioning from the side of justice and thus of hospitality, means that one is made to confront the question of the transformation of existing law: "It is a question of knowing how to transform and improve the law, and knowing if this improvement is possible within an historical space which takes place *between* the Law of an unconditional hospitality, offered a priori to every other, to all newcomers, *whoever they may be*, and the constitutional laws of a right to hospitality, without which *The* unconditional Law of hospitality would be in danger of remaining a pious and irresponsible desire" (*On Cosmopolitanism*, 22–23). It is then this reference to the concrete situation of the law that brings Derrida into the arena of political controversy with respect to the formulation of laws and policies concerning immigration and the question of the so-called undocumented immigrants in France. In "The Deconstruction of Actuality" (1993), Derrida characterized the standard political discourse as follows: "The common axiom, the consensus, as they say, is always: stop illegal immigration, no excessive, unproductive, disruptive hospitality" (*Negotiations*, 100). Already here he brings into question the received wisdom about the distinction between political and economic exile (101 ff.). But Derrida becomes far more pointed in his critique of actual legislation in a 1996 intervention, "Derelictions of the Right to Justice." Here it was a question of the revision of the law to make things more difficult for illegal immigrants or the undocumented (*sans-papiers*). As part of this enforcement, the government actually used the phrase "the crime of hospitality" to refer to those who knowingly offered refuge to the undocumented (taking a page from the antiimmigrant legislation in the United States in the early 1990s). It is the invention of this "crime *of* (rather than against) hospitality" that provokes some of Derrida's most incandescent prose. He asks, "What becomes of a country, one must wonder, what becomes of a culture, what becomes of a language when it admits of 'a crime of hospitality,' when hospitality can become, in the eyes of the law and its representatives, a criminal offense?" ("Derelictions of the Right to Justice," in *Negotiations*, 133).[19]

This is an extraordinary text that situates the question of the tightening of "border controls" as exemplary for what is happening with globalization (140). Although the economic boom of the 1990s in the United States put much antiimmigrant legislation on the back burner, the terrorist attacks of September 11, 2001, brought back the legal question of limits to hospitality with a vengeance.[20]

As Derrida has maintained, the question of absolute hospitality calls into question the very structure of the political as it exists today, for it calls into question the character of the nation-state as an entity that has the right and duty to defend its borders, define its citizens, identify those who have political, economic, and indeed human rights, and so on. These questions have become increasingly urgent in our time on account of what in English we call globalization, as the basic social and economic forces at play escape any meaningful relation to national borders and the control of nation-state politics. Thus the question of cosmopolitanism that Derrida traces back to Paul and that we have seen to be rooted in the conception of Abrahamic, Adamic, and Messianic humanity and expressed in the new society for which Paul assumed responsibility in the exhortation to mutual hospitality becomes all the more "relevant" to all that can be called "politics" in the brave new world unto which we are embarked.

It is, however, not simply that there are contemporary political consequences to, and effects of, what Paul was struggling to bring to expression so many centuries ago. It is rather that what Paul was attempting in his own time was the creation of something like a new politics that stood in contrast to the dominant political orders (*politeia*) within which he worked as both a Pharisee and as a citizen of Rome.[21] Paul was not content, as were many of his stoic contemporaries, to simply give up on the social reality that confronted him and to make justice the attribute and aim of individual existence alone. Rather, Paul was concerned to foster the emergence of a new kind of society or sociality that would instantiate justice outside the law and so bring to expression the duty beyond debt that he called love. It is because of this that he spends so much time focusing on the question of the conditions of possibility of welcome or mutual hospitality,[22] and hence for him the importance of overcoming those divisions (religious, as we have seen) that make the giving and the receiving of hospitality so difficult. Paul did not so much seek to reform the political order as to replace it. (In this sense, Nietzsche was right about the extent of what he saw as Paul's ambition.) But he sought to replace the existing order not with a new law, but with that justice which is outside the law.

The irony is that although Paul could articulate the unconditional principle of such a new society—"there is neither Jew nor gentile, Greek nor barbarian, slave nor free, male nor female"—his greatest difficulties come in the process of "negotiating" this unconditional of the messianic society under concrete social, cultural, and, indeed, political, circumstance. Whatever may be the very real challenges that must be put to the outcome of such negotiations, especially as they may be thought to apply to our own time, it is crucial to see that it was this that Paul was attempting to do: to articulate concrete arrangements within which the unconditional character of human solidarity could come to expression in society.[23] What has too often prevented Paul's readers from understanding this has been the inability to see that he is wrestling with real political problems on the basis of grappling with some of the most fundamental issues of what might be termed political philosophy. It is this that reading Derrida may help us to think afresh.

7

Pardon

In this chapter, I turn to what is in a certain sense the most difficult question in attempting to think Paul with the aid of Derrida. The question of forgiveness in Paul's thinking is difficult first because Paul does not use the term. It simply has no place in his vocabulary.[1] But what makes the discussion of the question all the more difficult is that long centuries of the reading of Paul's letter to the Romans have nevertheless contrived to find the theme of forgiveness everywhere, as if it were all that Paul had to say. Indeed, it is this by now well-established orthodoxy in the reading of Paul that makes divine absolution for all sins of the past the sole meaning of justification and thus eliminates from Paul any interest in the question of the call and claim of justice. This call and claim is eliminated in favor of an announced absolution whose only condition is the agreed price of faith understood as belief and/or adherence to the institution that is authorized to administer this absolution on behalf of the divine. The difficulty, then, that we incur in turning to this question is that of again installing forgiveness as a substitute for, rather than the instigation of, justice.[2]

Derrida on Forgiveness

It is precisely with respect to this conundrum that I believe Derrida's own reflections on forgiveness may offer us some help. However, the discussion of forgiveness in Derrida is itself not without daunting challenges for the reader. This is true above all now because the issues associated with this term have been the theme of Derrida's ongoing seminar for the last several years, and he had even suggested that this might continue to be true so long as he continued to teach.[3] As a consequence, whatever one says based on already published texts of Derrida is certain to be superseded by subsequent publication of work already well underway.

Fortunately, it is not our task here to present an essay on "forgiveness according to Derrida," but rather to see how Derrida's thinking about forgiveness can give us some perspective on the way in which something like forgiveness may play a certain role in the thought of Paul in spite of the fact that it is not thematized as such. The challenge will be to see whether we may be helped to see in what way divine pardon serves rather than opposes divine justice and the claim of that justice on those who are addressed by the "good news" concerning messiah Jesus.

I will follow my normal procedure of first seeking to clarify the place of the thinking of forgiveness in Derrida's work, especially in relation to the other issues with which I have been dealing. I will then look at some of the specific features of forgiveness that also distinguish it from those prior themes, that is, in what way it leads us beyond what we have heretofore learned from our reading of Derrida. Thus armed, I will attempt to think the terminological absence as well as the prodigious effects of this question in the thought of Paul, especially in Romans. This will enable me to indicate how the traditional reading of Paul may need to be revised if the question of justice is not to be abrogated by talk of forgiveness and its cognates.

Forgiveness and the Aporia

We begin by noticing that Derrida's reflections on forgiveness tie it directly to the aporetic structure that we have come to see with respect to such issues as gift and hospitality. As recently as *Without Alibi*, the question of forgiveness and those of gift and hospitality have been linked—for example, in terms of a certain passivity that "marks the experience of all unconditional and pure events as such (gift, forgiveness, hospitality, death)" ("Provocation," xxxiii). As such an unconditional or pure event, forgiveness "(granted or asked for), the address of forgiveness, must forever remain . . . heterogeneous to any determination in the order of knowledge" ("To Forgive," in *Questioning God,* 36). As that which is heterogeneous to knowledge, it is in a certain sense "mad." But Derrida explains, "if I say, as I think, that forgiveness is mad, and that it must remain a madness of the impossible, this is certainly not to exclude or disqualify it. It is even, perhaps, the only thing that arrives, that surprises, like a revolution, the ordinary course of history, politics, and law. Because that means that it remains heterogeneous to the order of politics or of the juridical as they are ordinarily understood" (*On Cosmopolitanism*, 39). As is regularly the case, Derrida can say of forgiveness, as he says of other aporetic structures (the gift, for example), "if there is such a thing." But because this phrase is regularly misunderstood to mean that Derrida denies the reality of that which is so qualified, he has had to explain, "When I say, 'if there is such a thing,' I do not mean that I doubt the possible occurrence of such a thing. I mean that, if forgiveness happens, then this experience should not become the object of a sentence of the kind 'S is p'" (*Questioning God*, 53). Forgiveness, then, like hospitality and duty without or beyond debt, and the gift share a similar character. In order to see how they are related to one another beyond such a similarity of aporetic structure, I turn to the way forgiveness has been implicated in his discussion of these questions.

We have seen that the theme of welcome or of hospitality is one that has been decisive for Derrida in developing his views on a sort of politics, or cosmopolitics. It may be helpful to see how forgiveness is related to this theme of hospitality. The main text where this has been discussed is in the seminar notes published as "Hostipitality" in *Acts of Religion*. In the session of February 12, 1997, the theme is forgiveness. The question of forgiveness is first broached as the request of the visitor whose arrival is an interruption of, or intrusion on, the "host." "Whoever asks for hospitality, asks, in a way, for forgiveness and whoever offers hospitality grants forgiveness" ("Hostipitality," 380). Perhaps this is the most obvious sense in which forgiveness is implicated in the scene of hospitality. The other approaches and says, "pardon me." And the host insofar as host—that is, as welcoming or receiving the visitant—grants forgiveness by precisely dismissing the request: it is nothing, don't worry about it, you are welcome. But perhaps things are not at all so simple as this first impression might lead us to expect. Derrida suggests, "one should not only say that forgiveness granted to the other is the supreme gift and therefore hospitality par excellence. It is also because, inversely and first of all, the welcoming one must ask for forgiveness from the welcomed one even prior to the former's having to forgive. For one is always failing, lacking hospitality" ("Hostipitality," 380). And he explains: "forgiveness for my lack of preparation, for an irreducible and constitutive unpreparedness" (380).

Is this an exaggeration? It depends on whether there is a real hospitality to be thought—that is, one that defines itself by its very welcome and thus by its readiness to welcome, to make way for, place for, home for, the other. But one can never be ready for this; one can never succeed in being, in the full and necessary sense, a host. One's welcome is always too little, too late. "Please come in," we might say; "the house is such a mess," we might say; "I have only soda in the fridge and two-day-old cookies; please pardon my lack of hospitality." Is this mere "formality"? Or is what is at stake here the very heart of what it means to be welcoming of another, any other? Is it not the case that whenever it is a question of giving and the giving of hospitality, I must ask for "forgiveness for not having known how to give" (381). Derrida continues: "Thus, I have to ask the hôte for forgiveness because, unable to ever receive and give him enough, I always abandon him too much, but inversely, in asking for forgiveness and in receiving from him the forgiveness of him, I abandon myself to him" ("Hostipitality," 389). It is precisely here that we again encounter the motif of the host as hostage to the other, as one who must abandon "himself" to the forgiveness of the other.

In this discussion of forgiveness and hospitality, we are returned to the question of duty and the duty beyond debt. If the host must forgive the guest for the intrusion, and if the guest must forgive the host for not knowing how or not being prepared to welcome—all this in order for the event of hospitality, if there is such a thing, to take place—then what is the character of this duty, the duty to forgive? Derrida returns us here to the by now familiar logic, if that is what it is, of duty beyond debt:

Must one do the impossible for forgiveness to arrive as such? Perhaps, but this could never be established as a law, a norm, a rule, or a duty. There should not be any *il faut* for forgiveness. Forgiveness "must" always remain unmotivated and unpredictable. One never gives or forgives "in accordance with duty" (*pflichmässig*), or even "from duty" (*eigentlich aus Pflicht*), to use the Kantian distinction. One forgives, if one forgives, beyond any categorical imperative, beyond debt and obligation. And yet one *should* [*il faudrait*] forgive. (*Negotiations*, 351)

Forgiveness and Gift

Although the bulk of Derrida's reflections on forgiveness come later, it was already the case in *Given Time* that forgiveness had been linked to the question of hospitality and so to that of gift, for there he speaks of the unrest "of the gift as well as forgiveness . . . but beyond duty and debt" (69). And this linkage is all the more evident in the seminar notes for

"Hostipitality": "Here perhaps is a condition [the possibility of the impossible, the impossible of the possible] that forgiveness shares with the gift—and therefore with hospitality, which gives without return or else is nothing. Beyond the formal analogy, this perhaps also means that one affixes its condition of impossibility to the other: the gift to forgiveness or forgiveness to the gift, hospitality to forgiveness and forgiveness to hospitality" (386). Here it is no longer, as he suggests, simply a matter of a formal analogy, a similarity or even identity of structure, but a rigorous concatenation or mutual coimplication of these ideas or (quasi) concepts.[4] It is, however, in a subsequent essay, "To Forgive: The Unforgivable and the Imprescriptible," in *Questioning God,* that Derrida makes some of his boldest statements about the relation of gift and forgiveness. Here he begins with the play between *don* (gift) and par-don and will suggest again a basic structural similarity: "Thus forgiveness, if it is possible, if there is such a thing, is not possible, it exists only by exempting itself from the law of the possible . . . and this is what it would have in common with the gift" (48).[5] But he suggests the importance of not confusing these notions, of not confusing, that is, gift and forgiveness. "One must neither yield to these analogies between the gift and forgiveness nor, of course, neglect their necessity" (22). Above all, this means making clear that they are not simply the same thing: "Thus no gift without forgiveness, and no forgiveness without gift, but the two are, above all, not the same thing" (22). Now already here we may begin to see the potential relevance of Derrida's reflections for the problem that we noted at the outset, namely that the gift or grace that is the center of Paul's attention in much of Romans has in turn been understood entirely in terms of forgiveness. Thus if it is possible to institute here a rigorous distinction as well as indissociability, then we may be on our way to a better understanding of Paul than has been afforded by the tradition that has swallowed up gift in forgiveness, a forgiveness that then becomes the whole meaning of justification, thereby abolishing the claim of justice. But in what would such a rigorous distinction consist? How, given the indissociability of gift and forgiveness, of *don* and par-don, and given their structural homology, will it be possible to clearly distinguish the one from the other?

Derrida suggests that the, or one of the, basic differences between forgiveness and gift is that forgiveness concerns itself above all with the past: "The past is the past, the event took place, the wrong took place, and this past, the memory of this past, remains irreducible, uncompromising.

This is one way forgiveness is different from the gift, which in principle does not concern the past" (31). If the gift does not primarily concern itself with the past, we should also recall that it cannot, as we saw in the earlier discussion of the gift, be located simply in the present either without abolishing itself as "present"—that is, as gift. Thus the gift aims itself toward the future. But forgiveness necessarily deals with the past, with what has already come to pass, or with what has already failed to be done. Yet precisely here, in this distinction of times, this temporalization, we may also see the necessary relation between forgiveness and gift. Indeed, in order to open itself toward a future, the grip of the past, its fatality, must be interrupted. Accordingly, forgiveness may be the necessary antecedent of gift. This is how Derrida says it: "as if forgiveness, far from being a modification or a secondary complication or a complication that arises out of the gift, were in truth its first and final truth. Forgiveness as the impossible truth of the impossible gift. Before the gift, forgiveness" (48). It is as if in order to launch the giving of the gift, in order to break open the law of the past, its iron determination, there had to be a suspension or interruption of the past, a suspension named here "forgiveness."[6]

This will mean, as we shall see, that gift or grace is by no means exhausted by a reference to the past (as forgiveness), but rather it has the structure of a promise. This, of course, was true for Paul as well, because the model of grace or gift had been the promise given to Abraham concerning the future, a future of land and progeny, and this promise has been expanded, according to Paul, to include the resurrection of the dead and liberation of creation. Thus, however much forgiveness may be necessary to gift (and so to promise), it cannot be taken to be the whole of the gift, but rather its necessary, if insufficient, condition.

Forgiveness and Law

If, despite their difference, forgiveness does have something of the character of gift, then we would expect it to stand in some basic tension with law.[7] And this is precisely what we do find in "On Forgiveness" in *On Cosmopolitanism and Forgiveness* (2001), where Derrida writes, in a now familiar gesture: "Forgiveness is often confounded, sometimes in a calculated fashion, with related themes: excuse, regret, amnesty, prescription, etc.; so many significations of which certain come under law, a penal law from which forgiveness must in principle remain heterogeneous and irreducible" (27). This may also be expressed in relation to the way in which forgiveness has in view a return to normalcy as is sometimes or even normally the case in political instances of amnesty or a "truth and reconciliation commission." He writes, "each time it aims to re-establish normality . . . then the work of forgiveness is not pure. . . . Forgiveness is not, it *should not be*, normal, normative, normalizing. It *should* remain exceptional and extraordinary, in the face of the impossible: as if it interrupted the ordinary course of historical temporality" (32). In this way, forgiveness, like the gift, may be understood as the interruption or exceeding of a certain economy. And it is this precisely as also interrupting "the ordinary course of historical temporality"—that is, as breaking the hold of the past, its over and doneness, in such a way as to make place for the coming of the new.

The regular way that this impossibility of forgiveness comes to expression in Derrida's thought is in the relation between a conditional and an unconditional forgiveness. He writes, "I remain 'torn' (between a 'hyperbolic' ethical vision of forgiveness, pure forgiveness, and the reality of a society at work in pragmatic processes of reconciliation). But without power, desire, or need to decide. The two poles are irreducible to one another certainly, but they remain indissociable" (51). This situation of irreducibility and indissociability will remind us of the relation between gift and economy or that between justice and law. And Derrida makes this explicit:

if our idea of forgiveness falls into ruins as soon as it is deprived of its absolute reference, namely its unconditional purity, it remains nonetheless inseparable from what is heterogeneous to it, namely the order of conditions, repentance, transformation, as many things as allow it to inscribe itself in history, law, politics, existence itself. These two poles, *the unconditional and the conditional,* are absolutely heterogeneous, and must remain irreducible to one another. They are nonetheless indissociable. (44)

Just as the gift must enter into the structure of exchange from which it also remains heterogeneous, and the claim of justice be inscribed in the structure of law from which it always remains fundamentally alien, so also with true forgiveness and the conditionality of forgiveness with which it is often confused.[8]

The heterogeneity of conditional and unconditional forgiveness comes to expression in a certain tension within the western tradition concerning forgiveness. Speaking of the equivocation of tradition (but here it is the Christian tradition, it seems), Derrida writes, "Sometimes, forgiveness (given by God, or inspired by divine prescription) must be a gracious gift, without exchange and without condition; sometimes it requires, as its minimal condition, the repentance and transformation of the sinner" (44) This answers well to what we find in certain New Testament texts, perhaps most especially in Matthew, where there is an attempt to think the relation between divine forgiveness and the forgiveness that is extended to the neighbor, the brother or sister. This New Testament text is one to which Derrida has given considerable attention, most notably in *The Gift of Death*. In Matthew we find the insistence that the divine forgiveness is in a certain way dependent upon the forgiveness of the neighbor: just as you forgive, so also will you be forgiven (Matthew 6:14–15). In one way, both are unconditional in that they do not seem to depend on a prior worthiness, a prior repentance, or even a prior confession. Nevertheless, the forgiveness granted by the divine is said to echo the forgiveness that we grant to one another.[9] What will have to become clear, however, is in what way what we can discover in Paul answers either to the conditionality or the unconditionality of forgiveness as Derrida has distinguished them.

However, the heterogeneity between unconditional and conditional forgiveness cannot be permitted to become simply one of opposition. It must also be clear that they are indissociable. Thus Derrida writes, "Yet the distinction between unconditionality and conditionality is shifty enough not to let itself be determined as a simple opposition. The unconditional and the conditional are, certainly, absolutely heterogeneous, and this forever, on either side of a limit, but they are also indissociable. There is in the movement, in the motion of unconditional forgiveness, an inner exigency of becoming effective, manifest, determined, and, in determining itself, bending to conditionality" ("To Forgive," 45). We shall see how this plays itself out on the public or political stage in a moment.

One of the most important ways in which Derrida has sought to clarify the aporetic structure of forgiveness or "pure forgiveness" or "unconditional forgiveness" is by means of associating this forgiveness with the question of the unforgivable. It is precisely here that the "impossibility" of forgiveness and thus its distinction from an economy of conditionality comes properly into view. Thus, in *Negotiations*, "As if it were possible," referring to his ongoing seminar, Derrida writes, "one only forgives the unforgivable. By only forgiving what is already forgivable, one forgives nothing. Consequently forgiveness is only possible, as such, where faced with the unforgivable, it seems thus impossible" (349). A similar point is made in his seminar on hospitality that preceded the seminar theme of forgiveness (and perjury): "The impossibility of forgiveness offers itself to thought, in truth, as its sole possibility. Why is forgiveness impossible?. . . . Simply because what there is to forgive must be, and must remain, unforgivable. If forgiveness is possible, if there is forgiveness, it must forgive the unforgivable—such is the logical aporia. [. . .] If one had to forgive only what is forgivable, even excusable, venial, as one says, or insignificant, then one would not forgive. One would excuse, forgive, erase, one would not be granting forgiveness" (Hostipitality, 385).

As we can readily see, the conditionality of forgiveness is precisely related to the forgivable, to that which can, under certain circumstances, be excused, be erased from memory. Here no radical break with the past is involved; the past fault is simply erased as having had no ineluctable consequences for the present or the future; it can become past, really past: "forget about it," we say. Or the past fault is integrated into the economy by means of a kind of countereconomy of supplemental effects (confession, repentance, amendment) that remain within the horizon of a retributive economy. You confess, I forgive, tit for tat. In either case, the past fault is completely forgivable, either because it was trivial (or venial) or because a supplemental causal nexus is established alongside the one set in train by the fault, one that depends on the work of confession, contrition, and so on. In each case, the law remains in force: the law of temporality, the law of legality, the law of retributive economy. Nothing astonishing has happened; nothing new has arrived.

But forgiveness, if there is such a thing, has, as we have repeatedly seen, a far different structure. It has to do with the impossible. And this means that forgiveness, if it happens, is the forgiveness of what cannot be excused, cannot be forgotten, cannot be erased—in short, with what cannot be forgiven, with what is unforgivable. But what is it that is unforgivable? What is it that is so monstrous a crime, a violation, that it cannot fall within the scope of legality, or of an economy of mitigation or excuse or worthiness?

Here Derrida's reflections are determined by his observations concerning a certain geopolitical phenomenon that is closely associated with what we saw in the last chapter concerning cosmopolitanism and the emergence of something like international law. Accordingly, in order to clarify the character of the unforgivable, we must return to the scene of the *mondialisation* of politics. In *Negotiations*, Derrida remarks, "Today there is a globalization, a global dramatization of the scene of repentance and of asking forgiveness. It is conditioned both by the ground swell of our Abrahamic heritage and the new position of international law" (381). He refers here, first, to the way in which governments acknowledge complicity in past crimes and ask for forgiveness. Thus, for example, he refers to the Japanese prime minister asking for forgiveness for certain crimes committed by Japanese forces in the period of World War II. More recently, Derrida has discussed the acknowledgment of responsibility for the actions of the Vichy government in France during the same period, an acknowledgment that had been rejected by Mitterrand but that has now been admitted by Chirac on behalf of the French state.[10] Similarly, the United States has even gone so far as to admit to responsibility for the mistreatment of its Japanese American citizens during World War II (but not for the staggering civilian casualties of Hiroshima and Nagasaki), and even with respect to the institution of slavery (although not admitting to the appropriateness of claims for reparations).

In general, these are actions undertaken by officials far removed from actual responsibility. A recent exception is the resignation of the Dutch government on account of responsibility for not halting genocidal practices in areas of the former Yugoslavia under its (at least nominal) protection. However unevenly, and with quite divergent degrees of candor, there is nevertheless a noticeable phenomenon of governments and quasi-governmental agencies (the Vatican, for example, or even the Southern Baptist convention with respect to slavery, if not racism) acknowledging culpability with respect to actions taken or not taken in the past that resulted in widespread violation of the dignity and life of multitudes of human beings. It is of this phenomenon that Derrida is speaking when he says, "the globalization of forgiveness resembles an immense scene of confession in progress, thus a virtually Christian convulsion-conversion-confession, a process of Christianisation which has no more need for the Christian church" (*On Cosmopolitanism*, 31).[11] What is notable, as Derrida suggests, is that peoples and states that have no connection with Christianity (the government of Japan, for example) seem nevertheless to be engaged in a quasi-Christian exercise of public acts of confession, contrition, and repentance and to be seeking some sort of absolution thereby. It is in this situation that Derrida sees the coming to pass of a kind of Christianity without the church, without explicit reliance upon the "Christian tradition," but that still has an unmistakable connection to that tradition.

If the matter were left here, we would still be in the order of an economy of excuse or confession that seeks to restore normalcy (smoothing relations between Japan and Korea, for example, or between the Vatican and Israel).[12] But this phenomenon is intimately connected with another. For the crimes that are thus confessed are or seem to be "crimes against humanity." "Nothing less than the human race would suddenly come and accuse itself publicly, dramatically, of all the crimes that have indeed been committed by it against itself, 'against humanity'" (*Negotiations*, 383). That which links the public dramas of confession and repentance to the unforgivable is precisely that the terms in which this scene is articulated is that of crimes against humanity. It is the monstrosity of such crimes, that they violate humanity "as such," that seems to make the dramaturgy of confession and asked-for forgiveness so compelling.

The very idea of crimes against humanity derives from the Nuremberg trials but has gained ground quite rapidly in the last decade or so. It has become the subject of the tribunals dealing with what occurred in the former Yugoslavia and is at work in a quite different way in Rwanda. It was the subject of an unparalleled attempt to arraign Pinochet for crimes committed against his own people when he was head of state and now with attempts on the part of Chile's government to depose Henry Kissinger. There is obviously something going on here that has achieved an astonishing momentum, in spite of the fact that the United States seeks to exempt itself from any possible application of the international law it so often piously invokes. But in this case, what is so astonishing is not the arrogance of the hegemon (when has that not been true in history?) but the fact that this self-claimed exemption is so clearly seen to be inexcusable by the overwhelming majority of governments and peoples.[13]

For what has happened is that quite suddenly, and no doubt as a consequence of the Holocaust and its unspeakable enormity, the very notion of crimes against humanity has become common currency in international political discussion and institutionalization. As this has become more and more a feature of thought in relation to the *mondialisation* of something like international law, it becomes increasingly clear that it is impossible to contain the notion of crimes against humanity to certain exceptional regimes or periods. For as Derrida has noted, "All humans are the heirs, at least, of people or of events that were marked, in an indelible way, by 'crimes against humanity'" (*Negotiations*, 383). Although this is certainly coming to be visible in relation to the history of the West, at least as concerns the inextricable association of that history with colonial conquest, slave trade, and world war, it is also not limited to the West, as the example of Japan suggests.

However, what still remains to be clarified is how it is that certain crimes, even if these are not isolated instances but are somehow common to all nations and thus all peoples, come to be seen as especially monstrous and as being therefore not crimes against certain humans, for example, but crimes against humanity as such.[14] It is precisely here that Derrida sees the relevance of a certain Abrahamic tradition and above all of a certain residual or implicit Christianity. Here is what he writes in *Negotiations* (and the end of this citation will be familiar to one who has read, as we did earlier, what he has said in "On Forgiveness"): "if consequently, any crime against humanity touches what is most sacred in the living, and thus already touches the divine in man, some God-become-man or some man-become God-by-God (the death of man and the death of God would betray the same crime here) then the globalization [*mondialisation*] of forgiveness resembles a huge process in progress, an endless procession of repentants, thus a virtually Christian convulsion-conversion-confession, a work of Christianization that no longer needs the church or missionaries" (384).

What Derrida says here is rather allusive. But what is clearly at stake is that the character of a crime against humanity is that it is felt to be in some way an assault upon what is divine, even if it is "the divine in man" or what is sacred or divine in the human as such. Now we know that for Derrida "every other is wholly other" and that this suggests that the violation of any other is the violation of that which is "wholly other" and is in that sense at least the violation of the divine, the divine in or as human.[15]

But what Derrida does indicate here seems to go rather beyond his more characteristic formulation of *tout autre est tout autre*, or "every other is wholly other." For instead he provocatively invokes an entire theological tradition concerning something like incarnation or inhumanation. "Some God-become-man" or even "some man-become-God-by-God." Now here it seems to me that Derrida is deliberately flirting with something like a "christological" tradition. And his formulation, which begins with something like a traditional (Johanine) christology of God-become-man, is corrected (almost) to reflect what seems in fact to be a Pauline formulation, one that leads off Paul's discussion in Romans when he speaks of the messiah Jesus as having been designated "son of God in power according to the spirit of holiness by the resurrection from the dead" (1:4)—that is, the messiah designated or made divine by the divine (spirit) precisely in or through the resurrection from the dead, that is, in the overturning of the verdict of public authorities whose verdict is therefore not only unjust but also impious.

It is not clear how much we should read into this rather remarkable formulation of Derrida's. But at the very least it may be read as an invitation to explore further the question of the way in which violation is a violation of the divine because it is a violation of the human (and vice versa) and that therefore pardon, if there is such a thing in Paul, is directed precisely to what is, in this sense, unforgivable. Is it the case, for example, that what is unforgivable, or inexcusable, or infinitely grave, is the damage inflicted on the neighbor that is at the same time a violation of the sanctity of life, of the dignity of that which is "the image of God"?

Paul on "Amnesty"

We have already indicated the twofold problem in speaking of forgiveness in Paul. The first is that Paul himself does not speak of forgiveness. The second is that (many of) his readers have scarcely found anything else and so have lost sight of the claim of justice. Thus, if, in spite of the absence of forgiveness as a theme, we find it to be of significance, we run the risk of abolishing the claim of justice in favor of a forgiveness that abolishes justice. Let us deal with the first issue first, and the rest of the discussion will attempt to deal with the second.

Forgiveness and/or Blessedness

We begin with the letters that are now by a kind of scholarly consensus attributed to Paul. In these letters, the only use of the term for forgiveness (*aphiein*) is found in Romans, but it is in the middle of a quotation from the Psalms (attributed here to David).[16] In addition, the term appears in two letters whose Pauline authorship is in dispute, namely Ephesians and Colossians. The term does not appear in any of the other letters that are now attributed to Paul: 1 and 2 Corinthians, Galatians, Philippians, Philemon, 1 Thessalonians.

This is remarkable in itself, because one would be led to suppose from the history of western theology, and especially Protestant theology, that Paul is the author of the doctrine of the forgiveness of sins as the basic, indeed exclusive, meaning of the term *justification*.

The occurrence of the term for forgiveness comes in Romans 4:7. Paul has just introduced the figure of Abraham and has begun to make clear the distinction between faith as trust and faithfulness on the one hand, and work, wages, debt on the other. Thus it is the reliance on the one who makes just the ungodly that itself produces justice (4:5). He then writes, "So also David speaks of the blessedness of those to whom God reckons justice apart from works: 'Blessed are those whose iniquities are forgiven, and whose sins are covered; blessed is the one against whom the LORD will not reckon sin.'" Paul then continues, "Is this blessedness, then, pronounced only on the circumcised, or also the uncircumcised?" What introduces the citation and follows from it is precisely "blessedness," and it is this that seems to connect what Paul is saying to the citation from Psalm 32:1–2, in which the term also occurs twice. At no point is it Paul's argument, for example, that Abraham was a "sinner," that he was guilty of an infraction of the law or of a disregard for justice. Indeed, it seems that all that could at this point be alleged against Abraham was that he was ignorant of God, that he had not yet been called or encountered by the divine. In any case, it is no part of Paul's argument to emphasize either that Abraham was a sinner or that he was "forgiven"; indeed, Paul is at pains to separate Abraham from the imputation of sin, because as he himself says, "where there is no law there is no violation"(4:15).

Instead, what Paul emphasizes is Abraham's "blessedness," which comes from his being called by God and his responding to that call with trust and obedience. Thus the emphasis of Paul's argument is not on the past of Abraham (who he was before hearing and heeding the call of the divine), but on Abraham's future. For it is this to which he is pointed by the call of the divine which is therefore "promise": "the promise that he would inherit the world."

But if Paul had no intention of dealing with the question of forgiveness announced in the Psalm, why does he then invoke the Psalm? The most obvious answer is that he has the Psalms on his mind because he has quoted a number of them in a lengthy catena of Psalms regarding universal or general injustice (3:10–18). Thus this last citation marks a new beginning that turns away from the past indicated by the indictments of 3:10–18. The model for this beginning is not, however, the "blessedness" of something like forgiveness, but rather the blessedness of inclusion in the promise made to Abraham, an inclusion made real through sharing in the same sort of reliance on the word of promise itself. Thus forgiveness has here the place simply of making it possible to assert that the new can begin, the new that is indicated by the promise. Forgiveness has the role of putting humanity again in the position of Abraham, a position anterior to the law (which as Galatians has said came 430 years later but which in Romans 4 appears to be the situation anterior to the command regarding circumcision). It is then the necessary condition of gift or grace but is not yet that gift or grace itself, not yet the promise to which faith and so the gift of justice corresponds. Because Paul is most concerned with precisely that gift or grace, he is not preoccupied with forgiveness. Here, as elsewhere, he is not looking backward to the past but pressing ahead (Philippians 3:13), in response to the promise that makes justice possible beyond the law.

Accordingly, whatever is to be said about forgiveness in Paul must respect the rather preliminary and presuppositional character of this idea in his thought. If we respect the tacitness and preliminary character of the idea of forgiveness, we can nonetheless verify certain features of this question that are illuminated by what we have read of Derrida.

Graciousness and/or Forgiveness

There is one point at which we may find rather surprising confirmation of some of the things that Derrida has maintained about forgiveness in what may also be an illuminating mistranslation of Paul. The English reader of the Bible will recall that there is another point at which Paul seems to speak of forgiveness in his letters. It occurs in 2 Corinthians, where what is in view is a person who had been excluded from the community on account of some outrageous act. It is possible (I think probable) that the case in point is that referred to in 1 Corinthians 5:1–5 of the man who is having carnal relations with his (step) mother. In 2 Corinthians, Paul writes, "this punishment by the majority is enough for such a person; so now instead you should forgive and console him, so that he may not be overwhelmed by excessive sorrow. So I urge you to reaffirm your love for him. . . . Anyone whom you forgive, I also forgive. What I have forgiven, if I have forgiven anything, has been for your sake in the presence of messiah" (2:6–8, 10). The unwary may suppose that Paul is using a term that would normally be translated as "forgive" (*aphiein*) here.[17] But in fact, Paul is using a term that, although it appears elsewhere in his writings, is never otherwise translated as "forgive." The term is the verb form of *charis* (*chariszomai*), that is, gift or grace, and has the sense of be gracious to or favorable to. We may get some sense of how this works if we attempt a retranslation of the passage trying to bring out the sense of grace or favor. If we take the punishment suggested in 1 Corinthians 5 as our starting point, a kind of excommunication or expulsion from the community, this will be even more evident. The passage in 2 Corinthians would then read: "This punishment by the majority is enough for such a person; so now instead you should welcome [or be gracious to] and console him, so that he may not be overwhelmed by excessive sorrow. So I urge you to reaffirm your love for him" (2:6–8). Actually we can see that the idea of welcoming and of being favorably disposed or gracious to someone comports better with the sense of "console" and "love" than what is often known and practiced as "forgiveness." This may even come to expression in the odd phrase to which we may return that concludes the admonition: "Anyone you favor, I also favor. What I have welcomed (or been gracious to) if I have favored any, has been for your sake" (2:10). To be sure there is a change of heart that is at stake here, but it is a change of heart on the part of the community (and subsequently on the part of Paul). Although such a change of heart may be expressed as forgiveness, it is all the more the case that it comes to expression as a gracious welcome and inclusion of the one who had been excluded. And this is precisely conformable to the situation that Paul has expressed by means of the nominative form of grace (*charis*) as the action of the divine that includes the excluded. It is then this gift, rather than the forgiveness that may accompany or even anticipate it, that is the focus of Paul's concern.

Thus, what Paul is saying has nothing to do with a penitential situation. Rather, what Paul is doing is suggesting that one who had been excluded now be welcomed and this by means of a term that has generally been associated with gift. What comes to expression here then is the intimate association between gift and welcome and something like forgiveness that Derrida has claimed to be true in his discussion of forgiveness, even though he has not to my knowledge availed himself of the semantic resources in Pauline Greek to drive home this point. It may therefore be useful to attend further to this semantic field.

The point may be even clearer if we include the use of this term in so-called Deutero-Pauline texts. Thus in Colossians we have, "Bear with one another and, if anyone has a complaint against another, forgive each other; just as the Lord [or Messiah] has forgiven you, so you also must forgive" (3:13); and in Ephesians, we have, "and be kind to one another, tenderhearted, forgiving one another, as God in messiah has forgiven you" (4:32). In neither case is the word for *forgiveness* used in the Greek; in both cases it is the word normally translated as being favorable or gracious to another. In both cases, we have what appears to be a rather exact parallel to Paul's exhortation in Romans to "welcome one another" (Romans 15:7). That is, what is in view is the coimplication of gift and welcome that goes beyond debt and that seems to presuppose something like forgiveness even if, contrary to the translated appearances, that is not what seems to be foregrounded by the language itself. In the text from Ephesians, indeed it is clear that we should actually prefer a translation that avoids the sense of forgiveness. Thus the passage would read: "Be kind to one another, tenderhearted, being gracious to one another just as God in Messiah has been gracious to you." Being kind, tenderhearted, gracious, favorable, or even hospitable to one another are notions that seem to comport better with one another than the insertion of the idea of "forgiveness" here. Of course, we might say with Derrida that gift and welcome presuppose forgiveness in general and so also here, but the emphasis for Paul seems to lie elsewhere, as we have seen to be characteristic of Paul, even where the term for forgiveness does (fleetingly) appear.

The related text from Colossians does seem to at least suggest somewhat more prominently the situation of a presupposed forgiveness because it takes into account the possibility that the members of the community may have a "complaint" against one another. That is, the welcome or graciousness must overcome what may be a preexisting situation of irritation or even animosity. (There is no suggestion, however, of something like sin here in the ordinary sense.) The overcoming of such a past animosity or barrier to gift or hospitality is precisely what may suggest the sense of forgiveness even if that is by no means all that is at stake here.

I have been emphasizing the predominance of the notion of graciousness or even hospitality or welcome in the passages where *charizomai* is translated as "forgive." The grounds for emphasizing this is perhaps more evident if we recall that in the majority of the occurrences of this term, the translation is unarguably one of gift or grant. Thus, for example, in Romans 8:32, 1 Corinthians 2:12, and Galatians 3:18, the English translation correctly emphasizes gracious gift, freely given. It does seem, then, that the favor of gift (grace) and the welcome of the other, in spite of all differences, seem to suggest, at least to translators, something like forgiveness as the presupposition, although sometimes this sense seems to be accorded an undue prominence, even to the point of an exclusive meaning.[18]

This is not, however, entirely an innocent decision in translation, for it conforms only too well to what we will have to contest: the absorption of gift or grace by forgiveness and the severance of both from justice, even the justice that is based on, and instigated by, gift or grace. Accordingly, we must at every step remind ourselves that Paul's thinking about something like forgiveness is never at the center but is always, at most, an implication or presupposition of his thinking about gift or grace.

Unforgivable and Unconditional

Even if the idea of forgiveness is at best implicit in Paul's argument, rather than an explicit theme or question, it still may be the case that Derrida's reflections on forgiveness may illuminate for us some of what is going on in Paul's thinking of the gift. This we would expect to be true if, as Derrida has suggested, the idea of gift or grace entails something like the idea of forgiveness. Derrida has suggested that forgiveness, if it happens, is addressed to what is fundamentally unforgivable and hence must occur, if it does, in such a way as to be unconditional. In what way does something like this come to expression in Paul's argument?

We may note first that there is in Paul's argument a sense in which injustice is "unforgivable." This is evident in the way in which Paul links together the ideas of impiety and injustice in his blanket indictment of Greco-Roman society: "For the wrath of God [divine wrath] is revealed from heaven against all impiety [*asebeian*] and injustice [*adikia*] of humanity—imprisoning the truth in injustice" (1:18). Although the controlling term here is "injustice" (which, of course, the reader of an English translation would not know because it is rendered as "wickedness"), this is nonetheless linked with impiety as if injustice were in and of itself also and at the same time, impiety. That is, the violation of the other human is at the same time a violation of the divine. And this not as a matter of the infringement of a specific legality but as the violation of justice itself, which, as Paul is at pains to remark, and not only in Romans, is divine.[19] It is because this is so that Paul may conclude his indictment of the rampant injustice in Greco-Roman society as a whole with the assertion that "They know God's decree, that those who practice such things deserve to die— yet they not only do them but even applaud others who practice them" (1:32). So pervasive has injustice/impiety become that there is no longer any sense of guilt or shame, but rather what is unjust is treated as if it were just, what is impious as if it were piety itself. At several points Paul underlines the inexcusability of this situation: "they are without excuse" (1:20) he says at the beginning of the indictment, and he concludes, "Therefore you have no excuse" (2:1). It is the inexcusability of this conjunction of impiety/injustice that means that anything other than the administration of the sentence of death (and thus something like forgiveness) must be unconditional if it is to occur at all.

If we take this as our point of departure, we can ask to what extent we may speak of the unconditionality of something like pardon in the thought of Paul. This may be seen in a part of the argument that Paul makes in Romans 5. Here his theme is the orientation of messianic life by hope, a hope that is homologous to the hope that had provoked Abraham to respond with trust and faithfulness and so to be just. The issue, then, is the turn from a past mired in injustice toward a receiving of the gift of justice. It is in this connection that Paul speaks of a certain kind of nonconditionality: "For while we were yet weak, at the right time Messiah died for the impious. Indeed rarely will anyone die for a just person—though for a good person someone might actually dare to die. But God proves his love for us in that while we were yet sinners Messiah died for us" (5:6–8). At least two points here call for comment. The first is the association that we have already noticed between impiety and injustice. Here four terms are closely coordinated that together specify the lack of merit (and so of conditionality) for the divine response: weakness, injustice, impiety, sin. These four terms are related ways of designating something like the unfittingness of the divine favor and hence its nonconditionality. It is not that these anticonditions are in any way mitigated, excused, or compensated for. Rather, they are allowed to stand as the antipresupposition of the act of kindness, love, generosity of the divine in and through the messiah.

The messianic event is here summarized in terms of the death of the messiah. As we have already seen, it is the death of the messiah that ruptures the hold of law on history; it is what makes evident that justice comes not from the law as such but from divine gift or grace, and so from hearing and heeding the divine promise, as in the case of Abraham. It is then this death that ruptures the hold of law and so makes way for a new provocation to, and "capacity for," justice. It is in this sense that this death produces the justification or being made just of those who are now included in the messianic event: "Much more surely then, now that we are made just through his blood will we be saved through him from the divine wrath" (5:9). The divine wrath, as we know, is what is directed against injustice and impiety. The messianic event is what will have produced, on the contrary, justice and fidelity and thus "saves" from wrath.[20] But it does this without antecedent condition, that is by demonstrating that precisely in spite of the condition of injustice and impiety, nevertheless humanity is given a new beginning by means of an event that breaks the hold of law, even the divine law of retribution for injustice and impiety.

The effect of this event then is not that injustice is excused, or mitigated. Nor is there any possibility of the presence of antecedent conditions such as confession or repentance. The effect of the messianic event is that persons become just (not, as we have seen, by compliance with legality, but by means of gift that incites duty beyond debt and so on) and so are saved from the (divine) wrath.

Throughout, Paul's emphasis lies not in the question of the past but in the new freedom for justice that is opened up. Thus his emphasis is on how greatly the new exceeds the past. In our discussion of gift, we noted the "how much more" that corresponds to talk of gift in Paul and that dominates the passage that follows the one we have been discussing (for example, 5:15, 17, 20).

In his subsequent argument, Paul will develop several analogies to make clear how the new situation differs from the old that was under the law—indeed, the law of sin and death. But it differs precisely in this: that now there is freedom for justice. Thus in 6:3–14 Paul uses the analogy of death (we have died with messiah) in order to point to the liberation from sin and injustice in order that we become "instruments of justice." Similarly, in 6:16–23 he uses the analogy of slavery, of being the property of another, in order to show how before we were slaves to sin/injustice but now are to become slaves of justice (6:20). A subsequent analogy of marriage suggests that as the wife is subject to the husband until he dies, upon being widowed, she is free. This freedom, Paul makes clear, is freedom with respect to the law (7:6), but not with respect to justice.

The series of analogies, then, places the emphasis on the new reality that exceeds the old. It exceeds it precisely in the sense that it provides an opening for the arriving of justice. That Paul does not speak of forgiveness here means that his attention is not on the past but on the new that has come and has separated us from the past. If in order to speak of that separation from the past we speak of forgiveness, it must be clear that this has to do only with what may be termed the presupposition for what it is that Paul really wants to say and to stress.

Double Bind

Perhaps it is in these terms, then, that we can seek to understand what it is that Paul is driving at in the last part of the seventh chapter, the place where Paul has been read as laying bare the inner conflict of the will that subsequently becomes so important to Augustine (and, often, to Derrida's explicit reading of this passage).

What is remarkable here is that Paul does not seem to be continuing with his temporalizing structure (before and after). If we were to seek to place this new discussion within the "before and after" schema, then we would ask whether Paul is speaking of those who are unjust, whose behavior is thus like that which he has indicted earlier, or whether we are here dealing with the situation of those who are being made just, who are responding to the call and claim of justice. It seems clear that the latter is what Paul has in mind because the one who speaks here "wants to do good," "delights in the law of God," and is consciously "slave to the law of God." These are characteristics of the "after" that Paul has so assiduously emphasized in the previous three analogies. But if this is true, how is it that the "before" of flesh (and thus the law of sin) seems still to have a certain power? Has nothing been changed, save in the realm of a divine attitude toward sin, becoming now indulgent where before it was severe? This is what one might suppose to be true if one consulted what has often passed itself off as the tradition of interpretation.

In order to think this differently, it may be that we can be helped by some of Derrida's reflections on justice and on the situation of the one who seeks to be just, that is, who responds to the call of justice. As I have intimated before, and indeed already in the first chapter, this may come not from what Derrida explicitly says about Romans 7 (where I have contended he remains under the spell of Augustine), but rather in his reflections on the difficulty of one who seeks to be just.

Already in *The Gift of Death* Derrida had exposed this structure. Here he speaks of duty and responsibility and sacrifice as he seeks to make clear something like the exemplarity of Abraham (another Abraham here, the one who is about to sacrifice his son, but is this really a different Abraham?). He writes: "Duty or responsibility binds me to the other, to the other as other, and ties me in my absolute singularity to the other as other . . . [. . .] There are also others, an infinite number of them, the innumerable generality of others to whom I should be bound by the same responsibility. . . . I cannot respond to the call, the request, the obligation, or even the love of another without sacrificing the other other, the other others" (68). If justice means that one responds to the other, then as soon as one seeks to be just with respect to this or that one, one is, it seems, necessarily unjust. Of course Derrida is not yet using here the language of justice. This will come later. But let us stay with the language of this text a bit longer: "As soon as I enter into a relation with the other, with the gaze, look, request, love command, or call of the other, I know that I can respond only by sacrificing ethics, that is, by sacrificing whatever obliges me to also respond, in the same way, in the same instant, to all the others" (68). Now what is critical for our purposes here is that the situation being described is not that of the so-called divided will. It has nothing to do with the way in which, for example, my desire overpowers my good intention, or the way I am controlled by the libidinal impulses of my unconscious. Rather, it is that precisely in responding to the claim of any other, I turn my back on the equally legitimate and urgent claim of all the others. We are then not speaking of the condition of one who has become callous to the call of the other, or who has only in view his or her own advantage, or who is driven by anxiety and fear to be so self-regarding as to close off the other's call and claim. What is at stake here is neither the captivity of the will nor its impotence but rather the situation of one who really seeks the good of the other, and therefore sacrifices the good of other others.

In a later text, Derrida will return to this situation. But now the terminology that will be deployed is not that of ethics and sacrifice but that of justice and perjury (betrayal) and of forgiveness. This is how Derrida rewrites the dilemma that we have seen sketched out already in other terms:

I must ask forgiveness—*pour etre juste.* Listen carefully to the equivocation of this "*pour.*" I must ask forgiveness in order to be just, *to be* just, with a view to being just; but I must also ask forgiveness for being just, for the fact of being just, because I am just, because in order to be just, I am unjust and I betray. I must ask forgiveness for (the fact of) being just. Because it is unjust to be just. I always betray someone to be just; I always betray one for the other. ("To Forgive," 49)[21]

Here we have related two problems with being just. On the one hand, in order to intend to be just, I must ask for forgiveness. This is what we have seen, for example, in the relation between forgiveness and hospitality. I am never really prepared to welcome enough and so begin by asking for forgiveness in order to begin. But what if somehow I have begun?

What if I am, however incompletely, launched on this enterprise of welcoming another, responding to the claim of the other, being in this way, however imperfectly, just? Then I am already being unjust. For there is always another, another other, with a claim on me. And in order to be just to the one, I am already betraying the other. Of course it is not here that I actively seek to be unjust to the "third." On the contrary, I seek to be just. But it is precisely in thus seeking to be just that I discover at work another law, the inexorability of injustice, inscribed in the act of seeking to be just, of desiring to be just with all my heart.

The way Derrida speaks of this betrayal of the other other, of the third, is by speaking of perjury. In responding to one I neglect others, the third; in respecting the claim of one, I already commit to more than I will do; in the moment of responding to the claim of justice I deny it, in vowing to one I necessarily, ineluctably perjure, that is, betray my commitment to justice. "This is what I have called the congenital perjury of justice, justice as perjury. But this also means where I have to ask forgiveness for being just, to ask forgiveness of the other, of every other; where for justice, I have to take account of the other of the other, of another other, of a third." This can even appear to be something like the structure of faith, of fidelity, an infidelity inscribed at the heart of fidelity: "forgiveness for infidelity at the heart of fidelity, for perjury at the heart of sworn faith" ("Hostipitality," 388). That is, it is precisely the situation of fidelity, of faithfulness, of faith in short, that places one in the situation of ineluctable infidelity. Only if I am committed to justice (faithfulness) do I discover this infidelity, here named perjury. "Perjury is inscribed in advance, as its destiny, its fatality, its inexpiable destination, in the structure of the promise and the oath, in the word of honor, in justice, in the desire for justice." And this is so because since there are always at least three "it is justice itself that makes me perjure myself and throws me into the scene of forgiveness" ("To Forgive," 49).

Now this, it seems, is very like the problem with which Paul is wrestling in Romans 7. At the least, several of Paul's formulations seem to be in accord with what we have been reading in Derrida: "I do not understand my own actions. For I do not do what I want, but I do the very thing I hate" (15). "I can will what is right but I cannot do it. For I do not do the good I want, but the evil I do not want is what I do" (18b–19). Or again: "So I find it to be a law that when I want to do what is good, evil lies close at hand" (21). Here it is quite clear that the situation being described is that of one who desires, wills, intends the good; who seeks justice, who is, or wills to be, faithful. And it is precisely this one who discovers the dilemma of being utterly in need of something like forgiveness.

Moreover, there are a number of indications that for Paul this has precisely to do with the embeddedness of our action, not in a divided will, but in our interaction with the other. Here Paul speaks therefore of another law, not in the will but in the action. Evil lies close at hand, not in the recesses of the heart or the divided will; "I see in my members another law at war with the law of my mind, making me captive to the law of sin that dwells in my members" (23). Since Augustine, the interpretation of this conflict as an interior conflict of the will has also settled upon the interpretation of members here as sex, most especially "visible" as the absence of male control over a recalcitrant penis (that either erects or remains flaccid at inopportune moments, thereby betraying the inefficacy of the [divided] will).[22] But this seems quite far from Paul's intention here, for he has earlier spoken of "presenting our members as tools or instruments of justice." It seems clear that he means by this our ways of engaging with the world, the community and the other. The difficulty is that in precisely willing and doing justice we discover that we are already embedded in a world of injustice in which to respond to the claim of the one I betray the claim of the other.

This is the bind in which not the unjust but the just find themselves, not the one without faith, but the one who is responding to the claim of faithfulness to the call of justice. But how then seek to be just? What is the point of trying to be just, if always already I am bound to be unjust even in seeking to be just? "Wretched man that I am, who will rescue me from this body of death?" (24). The body here as otherwise in Paul (for example, Romans 12:1) refers to that by virtue of which I am in the world—visible, interactive, and so on. It is this that will be said to be offered to justice, to God, to the other (12:1). But here I have discovered a problem; it is precisely here, at the site of my engagement with the other, that I find injustice to be inscribed; and so also death is inscribed: death of the other, and my own deserving to die on account of injustice. How can one (precisely the just one) be delivered from this conundrum? Of course it is impossible (wretched man that I am). "So then with my mind I am a slave to the law of God, but with my flesh am a slave to the law of sin" (25b). Paul's way of speaking of this bind is to say that it is flesh, that is my very limited and vulnerable being in the world that seems to make it inexorable that I betray my sworn faith, and thus to turn faith into faithlessness.

Derrida has said that it is precisely in being just that I am unjust, and that in order to be just, I need something like forgiveness, something impossible that breaks the hold of the ineluctable perjury or betrayal at the heart of seeking to be just. In a related connection, Derrida has spoken of the need to be able to hope for forgiveness in order to sur-vive. What he writes is, "This being-there, this existence, would be both responsible and guilty in a way that is constitutive ('sin of existing') and could only constitute itself, persevere in its being, sur-vive by asking for forgiveness (knowing or not knowing of whom or why) and by assuming forgiveness to be, if not granted, at least promised, hoped for, enough to be able to continue to persevere in one's being" ("To Forgive," 43). Here, then, in order to be, and all the more in order to be just, one must hope for what is impossible, for what breaks with knowledge and normality, for forgiveness.

Paul writes, "There is therefore now no condemnation for those who are in Messiah Jesus" (8:1). That is, it is the messianic event that summons us into justice and that at the same time assures us that there is no condemnation, no accusation for those who turn toward this messianic event, who seek to be faithful to the justice that comes. Thus Paul supposes that it is indeed the case that those who seek to be just are delivered from the bind that he has been describing and they are delivered precisely by the assurance that for them there will be no condemnation.

Again, here Paul does not explicitly speak of forgiveness. The closest he comes is in the assurance that there is no condemnation. And we may say that this seems to imply forgiveness, or at least what Derrida was speaking of when he spoke of the need for forgiveness for being just and in order to be just—"to keep on keeping on" as folk say who are engaged in the struggle for justice—to "sur-vive," as Derrida says.

Double Pardon

If, in spite of the absence of the term for forgiveness in Paul we were to apply what we have read in Derrida to an attempt to understand Paul, we might have to make an initial distinction between two very different situations or contexts and so "meanings" of forgiveness. On the one hand, there is that which ruptures the fatedness to injustice in which humanity is embedded through the universality of the regime of injustice. Here we have in view the great disruption by which the hold of the law is broken and humanity is offered a new beginning in which the hold of the past is broken through. Here in general Paul speaks of the cross. The aim of something like forgiveness (or amnesty) here is that the call or claim of justice now be heard and responded to. But it is precisely in this new situation that another sense of forgiveness seems to come into play. Here it is a question not so much of a new beginning but of the injustice that accompanies, precisely, justice, the intending, willing, even the doing, of justice. Here it is not a question of the unconditional amnesty that opens up a new future but of the abrogation of condemnation for those who are caught up in the new, in the messianic, in the justice project.

The first (we are calling it amnesty) is unconditional, universal. It is the gift of justice or justice as a gift. But it impels faithfulness. Where it does not provoke faithfulness, it has not (yet) become an event (for us). There is no anterior condition, but there is a kind of telos: in order that there be justice. And this lays upon the one who is caught up in it the claim of a duty beyond debt, the claim of unrestricted hospitality and so on.

But here there is the problem, the dilemma (the aporia) of the injustice of being just, of the struggle for precisely that justice that is outside the law yet complies with what it is that the law really or truly intends. And that conundrum or aporia is that even here, perhaps especially here, for the one caught up in the messianic quest for justice, we discover that "evil lies close at hand." So now there is a need for something like forgiveness again, not in the first sense, for here it is only a question of those who are faithful, who seek justice, who are bound by the messianic. And here it is therefore a question not of a general amnesty, but of the suspension of condemnation.

In a way, this double situation of forgiveness will remind us of what Derrida, following Benjamin, detected as the double violence of the law: the violence that inaugurates law, that founds it, and the violence that sustains or maintains the legal order. Here we have the gift of forgiveness that inaugurates the new (that in a way abrogates the law in the name of justice), and on the other hand the forgiveness/gift that sustains the possibility of seeking to be just.

Here also no absolute distinction can be maintained. For they both have the character of the "impossible" and the structure of breaking the hold of a certain fatedness, or embeddedness in the situation of injustice. Yet they are not simply the same either. For the one is directed at all, at humanity as such. The other is directed at those of that humanity who are caught up in the messianic project launched by the first amnesty. The first aims at or entails the second; the second continues the first and has the same origin and structure (what I have been calling the messianic).[23]

Above all, what predominates in Paul's argument is not forgiveness but gift as the basis of justice. The gift is opened up by something like forgiveness in the sense of amnesty that ruptures the hold of law and so makes way for a justice that is in a certain sense outside the law. But this gift would be no gift at all if it simply placed us within an impossible situation: that of being unjust because we are attempting to be just. For the gift of justice to be truly gift, then, something else is necessary: precisely the abrogation of condemnation for those who are caught up by the messianic. Otherwise the call of justice would be simply cruel, a poisoned gift. But because justice is gifted, it entails not simply a universal amnesty (or unconditional pardon for all) but it also entails the abolition of condemnation for all who are thus impelled by faithfulness to the gift to seek justice.[24] The claim of justice is inexorable, unavoidable, but it is not merciless. It is mercy, that is, it is gift, through and through.

It is not our task to unpack all that Paul is up to here, and so we will not at this point follow him as he tries to make the difference in relation clear in connection with the messianic event (the one called messiah Jesus), nor to seek to test the hypothesis that when Paul has in mind the first amnesty, he is more inclined to speak of something like the execution of the messiah, and when he speaks of the second he is more inclined to speak of the spirit: "For the law of the spirit of life in messiah Jesus has set you free from the law of sin and death" (8:2). For our concern here and throughout has been to see how what Paul is concerned with is justice. And of course this is precisely what the end of condemnation here also means for him, "so that the just requirements of the law might be fulfilled in us" (8:4).

The lodestar of Paul's argument is precisely justice, divine justice that is outside the law but that is nevertheless precisely justice. The difficulty with respect to talk of forgiveness is that this functions so often to break the hold not only of law but also of the claim of justice. If, with the help of Derrida, we are to speak of something like forgiveness in Paul, we may do so only in such a way as not to dismiss or to render ineffectual the call and claim of justice. And this also means not in such a way as to excuse or mitigate injustice. It has seemed to me that this is precisely what Derrida helps us to think through his thinking of forgiveness, a forgiveness that is always "impossible" but that also is necessary if there is to be justice.

We however should not leave this discussion of forgiveness without noting that in a certain sense talk of forgiveness "as such" is not appropriate in the case of Paul. In the first case, that of the general or universal amnesty that comes to pass in the messianic event, it is certainly not the case that it is without a telos or goal, for this is what precisely Paul wants to insist on, namely that the goal of this event is that we become just and so be saved "from the wrath" that comes to those who are unjust. Thus, although it is unconditional, it is not without a goal outside itself, and this is what Paul is most concerned with.[25] In the second case, that of the abrogation of condemnation for those who are caught up in and by the messianic event, this abrogation is not simply universal and in that way without conditions, for it presupposes precisely the desire and will to be just, to do justice. Thus in neither case is forgiveness simply and purely as such Paul's concern. Hence it is not something that Paul himself speaks of, however much something like the concept of forgiveness may help us to think some aspects of what he is arguing in the letter to the Romans.

Political Effects

We have seen that much of Derrida's concern for the question of forgiveness has been articulated through a concern for the question of the politics of *mondialisation* and the emergence of international law concerning crimes against humanity and the question of amnesty, confession, and so on. In this global scene, Derrida has also detected the work of a kind of Christianization without the church, a sometimes unconscious appropriation of certain themes from the Christian tradition.

But it is also important to notice the global political effects of a certain Christian tradition that has understood grace as swallowed up in forgiveness and a forgiveness that has moreover been severed from the call and claim of justice. Throughout this study, I have maintained that Paul is concerned with justice, a justice beyond or outside the law to be sure, one that comes as or on the basis of gift, but one that is nonetheless to be understood as justice, even divine justice. If, within this context, we are to speak of forgiveness, then that forgiveness must be understood as related to the call and claim of justice. Forgiveness must not be allowed to obviate or substitute for that claim. To be sure, it is an interruption of the legal order, as is justice itself. But it is not a suspension of the call and claim of justice.

However, much of the tradition of reading Paul has been oblivious exactly at this point. Justification has meant simply forgiveness, and its connection to justice has been lost. Instead of being an incitement to or provocation of justice, justification as a certain kind of forgiveness has come to substitute for justice. Faith has accordingly been separated from faithfulness and so from the obedience of faith—from the form of life that corresponds to the gift of justice. Instead, faith has often come to mean "belief" in the sense of public assent to certain dogmas or in the sense of associating oneself with an institution that claims for itself the capacity to dispense plenary pardon in return for a certain institutional doctrinal conformity. Thus not justice as a consequence, but belief as a prior condition, has been made the concomitant of talk of forgiveness.

The history of this interpretation of Paul has been a history written in blood. For crimes against humanity have been "excused" or "expunged" and sometimes even incited on the basis of the supposition that indulgence is available for the price of belief without reference to the call and claim of justice. Only in this way can we begin to understand, I believe, how the history of the West is also a history of atrocity. The atrocities of crusade, inquisition, and *conquista* can be perpetrated with a "good conscience" on the basis of the supposition that justification does not entail justice—certainly not the kind of justice that can only be expressed as the welcome granted to the other, to any other.

The Reformation, with its emphasis on justification, does nothing to reverse this history. On the contrary. It is Luther whose anti-Semitism provides the template for *Mein Kampf* and whose instructions to the princes concerning the rebellion of the serfs was simply to exterminate them by any means necessary. Nor does Calvin's attitude toward "heretics" provide a more encouraging example. Nor does modernity, whether religious or secular, provide a more encouraging illustration, whether we think of the slave trade or the secular and Protestant robber barons, or the singular good conscience of modern states in the prosecution of world wars, cold war, or even the war on terrorism.

As Derrida has often noted, we are not simply the passive recipients of tradition. Tradition requires to be read, to be appropriated, to be thought. If we are to make headway against this history of blood, a history of unjust suffering inscribed with the torturers' instruments upon the bodies of suffering humanity, then this will require, among other things, a rethinking of our tradition. There is a part to be played in this work, I believe, by a rethinking of Paul and by a rereading that is attentive to his complex and difficult, but ultimately rewarding, attempt to think through divine justice as messianic gift. And it is this work for which, I have contended, a reading of Derrida may offer us important help.

Conclusion

The Faith of Deconstruction

The argument of the preceding chapters has had the intention of re-situating the reading of Paul's Letter to the Romans in such a way that the overriding concern for the question of justice comes to the fore. In this way Paul may be extracted from the clutches of his ecclesial and dogmatic jailers who have all too often done what Paul accused the empire of doing: "imprisoning the truth in injustice." For the result of what has become the traditional appropriation of Paul has been that the question of justice has been effectively silenced, substituting in its place a doctrine of justification that absolves the believer from the claim and call of justice.

In order to show that Paul may be understood (I believe, *should* be understood) in relation to the issues that arise when one considers the question of justice, I have suggested that invaluable help may be found from reading Derrida's reflections on justice and related questions. I have attempted not so much to argue as to exhibit the illuminating effects of the juxtaposition of deconstruction with the thought of Paul. In so doing, I find myself, somewhat to my surprise, doing what I find Derrida had already suggested might be done. In an extraordinarily interesting interview on "Deconstruction in America,"[1] Derrida is asked by James Creech to talk about how religion in America may have affected the reception of deconstruction. In reply, Derrida mentions the necessity of analyzing "a whole history of exegesis, of modern hermeneutics in German and European protestant thought, centering around Heidegger, Karl Barth etc." The mention of these names (I don't know of any other mention of Karl Barth in Derrida's work) immediately points us to the question of the interpretation of Paul, and this not only because Barth was above all an interpreter of Paul, beginning with his shattering commentary on Romans, but also because Heidegger to a certain extent, and certainly his close associate at Marburg, Rudolf Bultmann, were also interpreters of Paul.[2] But Derrida goes on to specify that "the point would seem to be to liberate theology from what has been grafted on to it, to free it from its metaphysico-philosophical super-ego, so as to uncover an authenticity of the 'gospel,' of the evangelical message. And thus, from the perspective of faith, deconstruction can at least be a very useful technique when Aristotelianism or Thomism are to be criticized." To this I would add, as Derrida might not, that it may even be a useful tool for criticizing a certain Augustinianism, although this could not be excluded from what is involved when he continues, "or even from an institutional perspective, when what needs to be criticized is a whole theological institution" (surely a certain Augustine, not to mention a certain, at least "canonical," Luther and Calvin are implicated in what might be termed "a whole theological institution") "which supposedly has covered over, dissimulated an authentic Christian message." Derrida goes on to mention certain theologians "who applaud deconstruction, who need deconstruction, not against their faith but in service to their faith, against a certain theology, even against a certain academic theological institution" (12).[3]

Given what I have been seeking to demonstrate in the preceding pages, I could certainly associate myself with those who are said to "need deconstruction" and even those who find it of significant service "to their faith," especially if I could clarify that this would mean in service to a certain faithfulness to the claim of justice inscribed, as I believe, in the argument of Paul in Romans. That deconstruction enables a rethinking of the question of justice in a way that stands over-against a certain theological (but also ecclesiastical) institution and institution of "reading" Paul in particular is what I hope to have shown. It may even be that the reading of Derrida I have attempted will not only help to resituate the reading of Paul but also serve to dispel certain misconceptions about the character of Derrida's own project. If this essay could serve also to encourage others to read Derrida in spite of certain rumors rampant in academic circles about the character of deconstruction, this would be but a token of my gratitude to deconstruction for its service to the clarification of faithfulness, at least as this may come to expression in certain formulations of Paul.[4]

In order to thus resituate the thinking of what Paul is up to in Romans, I have first attempted to show that the critique of law is made in the service of the call and claim of justice—indeed, of what Paul thinks of as divine justice. Thus it is precisely in the name of justice and not in abrogation of the claim of justice that law may and must be deconstructed. This by no means entails a one-sided opposition to the law but rather accounts for the rather ambiguous situation of the law as that outside of which justice must occur, if it is to occur, and as that law which is not thereby abolished but in a certain way fulfilled as regards its intention to instantiate the claim of justice under the conditions of what might be termed history and sociality.

Whereas for Derrida, in keeping with his reading of Benjamin, the deconstructibility of law (as opposed to the indeconstructibility of justice) is determined by its inevitable association with violence both of institution and of preservation, for Paul, I have suggested, the deconstructibility of law is focused in the violent event of the execution of the messiah in the name of the law (both of Israel and of Rome). It is this event, I have argued, that manifests for Paul the fundamental (and not just episodic) incompetence of law to establish or produce justice. Accordingly, if justice is to be produced, it must happen outside and, in a certain way, against the law.

In order to clarify how it is that justice may be produced outside, or otherwise than through, the law Paul has recourse to the notions of gift and grace and I have argued that Derrida's reflections on gift as a kind of impossible possibility serve to illumine Paul's thinking of grace and in particular its association with justice. In order to clarify how this is related to "works," I have had recourse to Derrida's reflections on the relation of gift to economy and debt and have maintained that although gift may and must enter into the sphere of economy from which it is nonetheless utterly heterogeneous, it "transcends" economy though the very excess (or as Paul says the "how much more") that is constituitive of gift as gift.

Many readings of Romans seem to suppose that Paul's argument reaches its climax in chapter 5 or 8, or, in some more recent expositions, in chapter 11. But I believe that the subsequent "paranetic" chapters are indispensable to Paul's argument because there it finally becomes clear in what sense justice really comes into play among those who are caught up in the messianic event that somehow produces "justice as a gift." Accordingly, I have found Derrida's reflections on duty beyond debt to be of great value in showing how Paul's own suggestion that we should "owe nothing . . . but love" serves to clarify what it means to say that justice that is outside the law nevertheless complies with what the law intends and even exceeds what may be thought of as a duty owed to, or on the basis of, the law.

Some of Derrida's most significant reflections on the question of justice outside the law—and on the question of gift and duty as well—come to a head in his reflections on hospitality. I have accordingly attempted to show that Paul's concern that we welcome one another in and despite our differences, most especially including what may be understood as "religious" differences, may be understood as an especially telling example of what it means to exhibit a certain justice—a justice, indeed, that may serve as a template for what, paraphrasing Kant, may be called cosmopolitan justice, the sort of justice that is urgently needed today and without which we seem doomed to biocide (whether or not we speak of this, in Pauline fashion, as divine wrath).

In connection with the question of hospitality, Derrida has also more recently considered the question of forgiveness as it also becomes a feature of international law and practice. In spite of the fact that Paul does not make use of the term for forgiveness in his own argument, several of Derrida's perspectives on forgiveness in relation to gift and hospitality and even duty beyond debt helpfully illuminate what may be termed the forgiveness edge of gift, that is, the way in which gift, in order to be gift, must interrupt the determination of the past in order to launch itself toward a future that exceeds rather than prolongs the past (and the present). In thus taking up the question of forgiveness, I have tried to maintain that it is not itself the meaning of justification, for this would sever the connection between justice and justification. Rather, it is that which makes the impossible gift of justice possible and so inaugurates the provocation to/of justice. In this way, I hope to have interdicted the tendency of talk of forgiveness to swallow up the question of gift and so the question of that justice outside the law that comes as a gift. It is my hope that this will make possible a reconsideration of Paul that will overcome the history of atrocity that has accompanied the traditional reading of Romans.

For Further Reflection

In these reflections, I have by no means exhausted the number of Pauline issues that may be helpfully illuminated through a reading of Derrida. In general, there are two or three groups of issues that seem to me at this point to call for further reflection. One set of issues has to do with the way in which Paul attempts to work out concrete questions of corporate life in the new societies that he is fostering and guiding. The other set of issues to which our reflections have often led are those that have to do with Paul's messianism. I will briefly indicate something of the scope of these issues in a somewhat programmatic fashion.

Negotiating Paul

We have seen that Paul's concern for a justice beyond the law and a duty beyond debt bring him to consider the unity or solidarity of humanity within, and in spite of, concrete differences among persons. And we have seen that the political entails a negotiation of the unconditional (justice, hospitality, and so on) in the concrete context of a particular sociality.

Derrida's reflections on the negotiation of the unnegotiable,[5] as well as his reflections on responsibility and decision provide a helpful framework for understanding what Paul is up to when he wrestles (not always perhaps successfully) with how to bring this to expression in his communities. The question of food and days, and so of "religious" differences, is one that we have seen to be crucial to his development of a politics without or beyond law. What he attempts here may have a certain relevance in our world that continues to be riven by differences of religion that not only do not welcome the other but that turn positively murderous in relation to the other.[6] But Paul's remarks about circumcision have also undermined his otherwise clear intention to overcome differences of religion.[7] How is this to be thought?

There are other issues where we may be less certain how Paul's negotiations remain helpful. For example, it is clear that Paul seeks to find some way to develop a corporate life in which the differences between slave and free, the basic class divisions of Greco-Roman society, would not destroy the basic principle of unity in messianic humanity (Philemon, 1 Corinthians 7:20–24). Unfortunately, Paul's attempts to negotiate the actual circumstances of the emergence of a new sociality within the context of a massive social fact of Roman slaveocracy became a way for subsequent slaveocracies to use his concessions to "reality" as a cover for the perpetuation of these systems.[8]

With perhaps even greater reason, the abolition of the absoluteness of gender differences may seem to have been betrayed by Paul's puzzling concessions with respect to veils (something to which Derrida refers)[9] and the rather strange exhortation to women to be silent in the assembly (if that can indeed be attributed to Paul). Even more perplexing are Paul's concessions to the patriarchal household despite his manifest misgivings about what may be termed the institution of marriage and family (1 Corinthians 7:1–16).

Perhaps related to this are Paul's manifest concerns with alternative forms of sexuality. Although this is by no means as big a deal in Paul's letters as subsequent interpreters make it out to be (in part by supposing that questions of passion are always only questions about sex narrowly construed), this is also an area in which Paul seeks to bring into relation the unconditional and the concrete decisions with which he and his readers are faced.

My contention in any case would be that what Paul is doing in these particular discussions, which take up considerable space in his letters, is wrestling with the question of how to foster the kind of alternate society that would constitute evidence for the claim and promise of a justice beyond the law. Here it is not so much a question of second-guessing Paul's "decisions" but of seeing what is at stake in them. It is simply not pertinent, I think, to suppose that because we are in a position to make different decisions (the abolition of slavery, the context of formal democracy, the emancipation—still woefully incomplete—of women, and so on), our decisions will somehow succeed in being immaculate in our own circumstances where Paul's gave too much away in his own circumstances.

One of the issues that we have alluded to in our question about the "political" tendency of Paul's thought is the role that his own societies or assemblies played in attempting to work out issues of justice beyond the law. Paul's so-called ecclesiology gestures toward the formation of a new form of sociality beyond law and so beyond institution. Yet this sociality takes on institutional or at least quasi-institutional form in Paul's letters, and all the more so in later texts that bear, rightly or wrongly, the name of Paul. What is crucial here is that Paul supposes that justice must have a corporate or social character. It is this, as we have seen, that actually brings Paul's thought into the sphere of the political where many of his stoic contemporaries resigned themselves to an individual instantiation of justice. Although Derrida has been criticized for not having a sociology, a sense of the ineradicably social character of justice (as opposed to a "relational" view), there are ways in which Derrida's reflections point to the necessity of a kind of cosmopolitan informal institution of intellectuals, activists, and so on committed to justice.[10] This, together with his pointers to a "democracy to come," suggests a way of attempting to understand what Paul is engaged in, through his attempts to foster new communities where a nonlegal justice can take shape. Unfortunately, Paul is generally read from within the institutional structure(s) known as the Church, as if his thinking about sociality were simply a precursor to the institutionalization of "Christianity" in the form of church. Even where the institutional framework of interpretation is abandoned, what results is a radical individualizing of his "ethical" reflections that render Paul as an oddly pious stoic or as an existentialist. The latter reading fails to come to grips with what seems to have been Paul's obsession with forming and nurturing assemblies of the faithful. The former (institutional) reading ignores the ad hoc character of Paul's positions and deprives them of any significance outside the ghetto of ecclesial self-confinement. In both directions, the relevance of Paul's thought for what may be termed political philosophy, for an attempt to think human sociality beyond the law, has been obscured. Reading Derrida is one way to begin to rethink what Paul is up to in these reflections.

Messianicity and the Messiah

Throughout Derrida's attempts to think justice beyond law, gift beyond economy, and even hospitality or welcome, he points to the necessity of something like a messianicity without messianism. At several points in our reflections, we have come up against Derrida's insistence on the necessity of an eschatological bearing for the attempt to think justice as gift beyond the law.

The basic problem in terms of trying to rethink what Paul is up to in Romans and elsewhere in his texts is that everything is predicated on something like the Messiah having already come. To be sure, it is also the case that everything in Paul's reflections is set within an eschatological expectation that is both imminent and all-encompassing and that therefore hope for what is unseen (Romans 8:24–25) remains the basic character of faithful or messianic existence.

It still remains the case that the coming of the messiah is, for Paul, the coming of one who is in some sense already known. And it is precisely this that has permitted an institutionalized form of Christianity to dispense with any significant role of messianicity in order to claim something like absoluteness for itself. In consequence, Christianity has been enabled to become a new religion, replacing or competing with Judaism and, later, Islam, as well as other religious institutions and traditions. Instead of an open-ended and essentially borderless sociality of expectation, it has become an institution with carefully policed frontiers. Is this an inevitable outcome of thinking that the messiah has already shown up in history, in advance?[11] So that the messiah becomes the prisoner of ecclesiastical self-interest, self-pre-occupation, self-preservation? So that access to the messianic hope for all humanity is mediated by an institution that therefore claims for itself hege-monic prerogatives? So that salvation, instead of arriving as an uncondi-tional gift, becomes the property of an institution or group that may charge entrance fees of belief, membership, or what have you?

This is an issue or set of issues with which the most creative theolo-gians of the past century have wrestled: Bultmann with his attempt to think the distinction and relation between an already and a not yet; Barth with his early attempt to think faith outside and against religion; Altizer with his attempt to think gospel against Christianity. It may be that several of the ideas developed by Derrida may enable us to rethink these problems in a fresh way, one that grapples with messianicity and the messiah, and so one that brings us closer to Pauline discussion anterior to the presupposi-tions of a Chacedonian formulation of the grammar of christology.

We have already seen that the having appeared of the messiah pro-vides the indispensable catalyst for Paul's thinking of the disjuncture be-tween justice and law. It is the fact of the messiah's being condemned by the force of law that necessitates for him a thinking of justice beyond law and thus leads him to the idea that justice is founded on gift. At least at this point Paul's thought seems to require the past appearance and fate of the messiah. Is this merely fortuitous? That is, is it possible to think this disjuncture without that claim? Derrida has himself wondered whether, as Heidegger might suggest, revealability is anterior to revelation[12] (a position made much of by Karl Rahner) or whether revealability as an idea or cate-gory of thought is itself dependent on something like an anterior event of revelation (a position in theology associated with Karl Barth). Or is there some other way of thinking this relation that brings both into question, that deconstructs this opposition without subjecting it to dialectical reso-lution? Certainly the supposition that the messianic event is one that re-mains both powerless and folly and which therefore cannot be permitted to become a covert form of religious self-assurance would be indispensable here. But would it be enough?

One of the ways of getting at this is through an exploration of the question of exemplarity. How is an example "more than" an example without effacing the singularity and so the nonideal or nongeneric character of example or instance? Derrida's reflections on this issue have been occasioned to a significant degree by the question of Europe, a question not unconnected, as he has suggested, to a certain Christianity. But he has also more directly confronted the issue of exemplarity as it relates to something like christology in dealing with certain remarks of Kant concerning the nonexemplarity of the death of Jesus. What Derrida shows in these reflections is the irony that the negation of exemplarity at one point reproduces it at another.[13]

Although the discussion of Kant has to do with the question of the obligation to die for another, in Paul's thought there is a sense in which the death of the messiah is a death that offers or gives something to humanity. At least a part of what it offers is the abolition of the power of the law to condemn (Romans 8:1). But there is another sense in which the death of the messiah is exemplary in Paul's thought. It is that the self-sacrifice of the messiah becomes exemplary for the renunciation of privilege vis-à-vis others in the messianic society. It is remarkable that Paul's most famous "christological" assertions come in the midst of exhortations to "have this mind in you that was in messiah Jesus" and that therefore urge his readers to not attempt to gain advantage, or even attempt to maintain themselves, themselves as selves, over against one another (Philippians 2:5 ff.; 1 Corinthians 1:10 ff.). What becomes exemplary here is the relinquishment of a certain subjectivity or subjecthood that is at least homologous to the necessary interruption of the subject in openness to, or welcome of, the other, any other.

These reflections obviously entail some engagement with the notion of sacrifice and with the issues raised by the impossibility of dying for another. Certainly Paul does deploy the cultic notion of sacrifice in his argument in Romans and elsewhere. But he seems immediately to deritualize it in terms of the more "secular" notion of one who dies for another (on the battlefield, for example). I have argued in another place that at least in the Gospel of Mark, there is the sense that the messiah dies for his followers in the sense of demonstrating for them how to engage in a deliberate strategy of martyrdom at the hands of the powers so as to delegitimate those very powers and so make space for the incoming of that which deposes them (something like the "reign of God," for example).[14] That is not something that Paul has worked through, even if he can also suppose that the sufferings from legalized opposition to the messianic movement are a participation in the formally similar fate of the messiah (2 Corinthians 4:10–11; Philippians 1:29). But what Paul does do is attempt to articulate what might be termed the ethical significance of "dying with the messiah" in terms of a renunciation of the prerogatives of subjecthood vis-à-vis the other and thus the instantiation of justice beyond the law. The general significance of these reflections has been short-circuited by attempts to make participation in that death a cultic phenomenon as well as by attempts to wrest Paul's reflections on the exemplarity of the death of the messiah from their "ethical" context in order to launch a reflection on the identity of Jesus with the divine. Again we may find help from a reading of Derrida in thinking differently what Paul is trying to articulate within and against the dominant religious, philosophical, and political discourses of his own time.

To what extent is the having come of the messiah thinkable as an event, what some have called "the Christ event"? Can one speak of an event in the past tense without it thereby being deprived of its character precisely as event? That some occurrence be an event is somehow dependent on its not being simply the outworking of a plan, a progressive or dialectical movement, the "logical deduction" from preexisting premises. This at least is how Derrida attempts to think about event, and this offers the interpreter of Paul some assistance, I think, in trying to think about how Paul thinks of the fate of the messiah, whether as executed or as resurrected or as both together. There is a tension in Paul's thought between the supposition that the messiah event is one that accomplishes something that was "kept silent for long ages" (Romans 16:25, cf. Colossians 3:26) that was, as it were, programmed from the very beginning according to some sort of divine plan, and, on the other hand, the view that something radically new and unanticipatable has happened that may and must be made the subject of the announcement of astonishing—life- and world-shattering, life- and world-healing—news. Moreover, there is the tension between the supposition that this event may and must be spoken of in the past tense and the no less urgent sense of its impending arrival. To what extent is this the physiognomy of event "as such"?

One of the ways—perhaps the decisive way—that Paul speaks of event is in terms of promise. It is the promise of progeny and land that comes to Abraham and to which Abraham's response counts as or toward justice. We have already indicated that the promise to Abraham is formally like the promise of "peace upon this house" that is the promise of any event of hospitality. But for Abraham, it is specified in this, perhaps we should say, patriarchal (progeny, property) way. But whatever it is that is promised to Abraham is in any case impossible. Paul underscores this in remarking on the age (impotence) of Abraham and the age (infertility) of Sarah (Romans 4:19), not to mention their helplessness as wanderers whose only land is the piece of dirt that Abraham acquires in which to bury his wife.[15] The promise promises what is actually impossible. And this promise of (impossible) progeny is formally like creation out of nonbeing or resurrection from among the dead.

In Galatians, Paul had the tendency to suppose that the promise had been fulfilled in the messiah event and, most especially, in the response of the gentiles to the "good news." But in Romans, what becomes clear is that the fulfillment of the promise is but the widening of the "horizon" of promise. It is not that those who are "in Messiah" already have taken possession of what the promise promises. Rather, they have been made those who are promised, those who await the still future arrival of what is promised. But the scope of the promise has been widened almost beyond recognition. Instead of progeny, we hear of the resurrection of (all) the dead. And instead of land, we hear of a new creation. To some degree, these altered dimensions of what is promised derive from the very character of justice itself, for as Derrida has already suggested, the question of justice places us in relation to those who have died (which he develops as a kind of hauntology)[16] and the question of justice places us before the questionableness of a concern only for the human being as opposed to an entire violated creation.[17]

The question of faith for Paul is a question of the orientation to promise conceived as entailing this unlimitable horizon. It is the orientation to or by messianicity that functions as faith, that produces the obedience of faith; that is, a hearkening to and anticipation of the coming of a justice that entails the resurrection of the dead and the new creation. As the reference to Abraham proves, wherever there is that orientation to a justice to come, a justice of unlimitable horizon for the living and the dead, and "all things" then there is what Paul calls faith, the faith that in some sense already counts as or toward justice, the faith that "saves." The other name for faith, then, is precisely hope, a hope that cannot be confused with optimism but is hope against hope, a hope oriented toward that which is not seen and thus not known, not calculable or demonstrable—in short, the impossible.

There are points in his reflections where Derrida suggests that attempting to give any content whatever, any identity whatever, to that which comes amounts to erasing its character as that which comes.[18] If this were all there were to be said, we would be at a loss to know how Paul's apparent confidence in certain formulations, the *parousia* of the crucified messiah, the resurrection of the dead, and so on could be understood as not abolishing the very idea of the "to-come." And it seems to me that Derrida is quite right in supposing that a determination of the character of that which is to come tends to make the future only the unfolding of what already is and so to deprive it of any real futurity, just as the supposition in our own time of the end of history with the arrival of democratic capitalism seeks to eliminate any true future, to make the future but the mopping-up operation of an already in principle accomplished hegemony.[19] There is no doubt that this is often or even typically the way that Paul has been understood, even by those who seek some role for eschatology in his thought.

We seem, then, caught in a double bind: either a contentless awaiting that provides no orientation at all for what it means to await, or a characterization of the future that eliminates it as future. One of the ways that Derrida has attempted to negotiate this double bind is by way of speaking of a "democracy to come." As he realizes, this is a very risky move. The very ideas that make democracy thinkable—subjects who possess themselves, nations with meaningful borders, and so on—are the very things that need to be deconstructed.[20] At the same time, the notion of democracy as an inclusive sociality characterized by difference without division or domination and thus by justice seems indispensable. What would have to be thought in relation to Paul is whether his version of the messianic, a messianicity whose contours are sufficiently clear to make it function somewhat like a "regulative idea" but whose features are sufficiently unclear to make it truly future, bears any formal resemblance to what Derrida is trying to think with talk of a democracy to come.

The Question of God

In indicating these sets of issues for further reflection on the possible intersections of Pauline thought and deconstruction, I have not directly mentioned the question of God. This is not because I believe this to be an unimportant question, but because I think it is one that is too often thought about in abstraction from everything else that may be important.

This appears to me to be a kind of hangover from the late Enlightenment, in which theology imagined its principle business to be the defense of some or other way of speaking about God as the lowest common denominator of a kind of religious or theological consensus. Thus questions of grace and law, of christology and eschatology, were relegated to the backwater provinces of "confessional" theology, whereas the higher ground was marked by an ostensibly more philosophically respectable focus on the question of the existence and nature of God, or more recently on the possibility or impossibility of speaking of God. As a consequence, theological discourse has tended, I believe, to become rather sterile and often quite arcane, severed from any possible pertinence for concrete human struggles for justice, for liberation, for peace, for life.

This is certainly the impression that what I am inclined to call NATO theology (the theology generated in the sphere of Euro-American affluence) leaves those who struggle outside and against the centers of globalizing hegemony to think a faith meaningful for, or pertinent to, our time. Although interrogating how the western traditions have thought about the divine is a crucially important task, and one that also bears on the task of rethinking Paul, it is one that also needs to be repositioned relative to issues of justice and the hope for wholeness if it is to have any purchase on the life of the world, life that can destroy itself without end. In this connection as well, it seems to me that Derrida's ventures into the precincts of "negative theology" have the merit of keeping a close relation to the question of the other (person). The attempt to think with the phrase "every other is wholly other" (or [the] wholly other is every other) rightly interdicts hyperousiological daydreams that disconnect the thought of the transcendent, or that which is beyond being, or what have you, from the question of responsibility to and for the neighbor, the other, humanity, creation.

Thus, even beyond the issues that I have discussed still somewhat cursorily in the body of this book, there are a number of other issues in the attempt to understand Paul, where I believe that a reading of Derrida may be especially helpful in getting at what Paul is thinking toward. This certainly does not mean that I suppose that either body of text, whether that signed by a certain Paul or that signed by a certain Derrida, are reducible to one another, that they are simply saying the same thing, even after making allowances for differences in culture and so on. Rather, what I suppose is that both are wrestling with crucially important questions, questions that were important then and are important now, and not important only for a select circle, whether that circle be called philosophy or theology, but important for a humanity yearning to become human. There were and are other thinkers, other "intellectuals," who were and are struggling with these issues as well. Neither Paul nor Derrida nor both together comprise all that is important or true. Even in the New Testament Paul is not the only writer that Derrida illumines; his own readings—for example, of the apocalypse of John or of the Gospel of Matthew—point beyond any exclusive preoccupation with something like Pauline themes.

What I hope to make clear, however, is not only that Derrida may help us to understand Paul, but that the series of issues to which it has been possible to devote some attention in this thought experiment opens up to other kinds of questions within the framework of the overall task of illuminating Paul through a reading of Derrida. At a minimum, this may make clear that Paul may be helpfully understood outside the ghetto of a narrowly confessional or even historical investigation. Thus, what I do hope to have done is to have suggested the importance of reading and thinking Paul outside the ghetto of Christendom and even a specifically Christian theology.

Derrida as "Christian Philosopher"

The reading of Derrida that we have taken up here as a way of provoking thought about Paul, especially the Paul of Romans, has indicated a number of significant parallels in the thinking of Derrida and of Paul. What are we to make of these parallels, especially of the fact that precisely where we have found them is not where we find Derrida explicitly referring to Paul? Is Derrida after all a Christian, or at least a Paulinist?[21] Or is his thought haunted by Paul, the specter of Paul that we encountered so early in his texts, in the text "Before the Law"? What is the strange role that this philosophy plays in relation to Paul, or Paul in relation to deconstruction?

At a number of points in his reflections on other thinkers and on the modern western tradition, Derrida has had occasion to wonder about the way in which their thought stands in relation to a certain Christian tradition or archive. In the *Gift of Death*, Derrida, in reflecting on Patochka, remarks:

In different respects and with different results, the discourses of Levinas or Marion, perhaps of Ricoeur also, are in the same situation as that of Patochka. But in the final analysis this list has no clear limit and it can be said, once again taking into account the differences, that a certain Kant and a certain Hegel, Kierkegaard of course, and I might add for provocative effect, Heidegger also, belong to this tradition that consists of proposing a nondogmatic doublet of dogma, a philosophical and metaphysical doublet, in any case a *thinking* that "repeats" the possibility of religion without religion. (49)

Here Derrida begins with thinkers whose religious identification is more or less clear—Levinas (Judaism), Marion (Roman Catholic), and Ricoeur (Protestant)—but then opens the list to include others who are less often (save for Kierkegaard) thought of in this connection. Here Heidegger is included, as Derrida says, for provocative effect, but as we shall see, there is considerably more here than a simple desire to have a provocative effect. He can even go further in going beyond the generic religious to suppose that it is thinkable that Heidegger and Levinas are Christian or at least suppose that "it is far from being clear" that they are not.

"Let us follow the hypothesis that in what they say in general Heidegger and Levinas are not Christian, something that is far from being clear" (48). In thus placing in play the doubt ("it is far from clear") that Heidegger and Levinas are not Christian, Derrida may also open the door for such a question or doubt regarding himself.[22] The question of such a Christian identity or identification arises not in the confessional, still less institutional sense (this can hardly be what is in question with respect, for example, to Levinas), but in the sense that the reflection on fundamental, or basic, or urgent matters in the world of the post-Latin civilization one may expect a certain infection or even saturation by a certain "Christianity," even if it is, as Derrida remarks elsewhere, a "christianization which has no more need of the Christian church" (*On Cosmopolitanism and Forgiveness*, 31).

In the case of Heidegger, Derrida had already gone to considerable lengths to indicate how the latter is in some (odd) way a Christian thinker. Much of the last chapter of *Of Spirit: Heidegger and the Question* deals explicitly with this question, beginning with the suggestion that Heidegger's attempts to clarify the relation between spirit and psyche seem to bear an uncanny resemblance to a Pauline reflection, itself dependent on not Greek but Hebrew (101). The self-conscious attempt of Heidegger to de-Christianize the poetic insight of Georg Trakl (in *Unterwegs zur Sprache*) is "deconstructed" by Derrida, most notably in an imaginary discussion between Heidegger and "those I called theologians and all they might represent" (110) who maintain that what Heidegger is proposing to think as non-Christian is precisely something like the essence of Christianity. Derrida represents the theologians as saying, "When you say all that, we who would like to be authentic Christians think that you are going to the essence of what we want to think, revive, restore, in our faith, and even if we have to do it against those common representations with which you wish to confuse Christianity" (*Of Spirit*, 111). It is perhaps already clear that there is a parallel between what I have been doing in relation to the reading of Derrida and what Derrida imagines certain theologians to do or to have already done with respect to Heidegger. I am not, of course, accusing Derrida of having confused Christianity with certain common (mis)representations.[23] As Derrida notes, this question of whether there is not some basic agreement between Heidegger and the essence of Christianity is not restricted to Christianity as such: "it is not certain that you would not receive a comparable reply and similar echo from my friend and coreligionary, the Messianic Jew. I'm not certain that the Moslem and some others wouldn't join in the concert or the hymn" (111). Derrida does mention the possible reply of Heidegger—that he is only trying to think the basis on which such religious or nonreligious assertions can be thought, that he is going to a more fundamental reflection (111–12).

But Derrida does not give the philosopher the last word here. It is the theologians who seem to be those who seek to draw Heidegger out further, who draw him into the theological question "of the other," the other of philosophy, the other as such (113). Subsequently, Derrida will refer to what he had written in this text and will say, "I have tried to suggest, notably in *Of Spirit*, that in spite of many denegations, Heidegger was a Judeo-Christian thinker" ("Eating Well," in *Points . . .* , 284). And in "Faith and Knowledge: The Two Sources of 'Religion' at the Limits of Reason Alone," he will refer again to the question of Heidegger, "who seems unable to stop either settling accounts with Christianity or distancing himself from it— with all the more violence in so far as it is already too late, perhaps, for him to deny certain proto-Christian motifs in the ontological repetition and existential analytics" (*Religion*, 12).

Heidegger is not the only thinker upon whom Derrida performs a similar operation. In his "Dead Man Running: Salut, Salut," which is a reflection on Sartre and Derrida's own relation to Sartre and the journal the latter founded (*Les Temps Moderne*), we find a parallel gesture. Reflecting on the soteriological language of Sartre in the essay that launched the journal, Derrida wonders, "In what does this existentialism-humanism remain

Jewish and Christian, 'secularized' in spite of so many de-negations" (*Negotiations*, 279), and later speaks of "the unavowed, unavowable secularization of a religious thematic" (285). The thematic in question is that of a kind of salvation or even redemption—that is, "salut."

Even Nietzsche (in "Nietzsche and the Machine") is subjected to a similar treatment:

> There will always be someone to say, "Yes, your deconstruction of the Judaic and Christian aspects to St. Paul is made in the name of a message that is hidden in Judaism, in Christianity, in Islam, even in twentieth century thought. You are 'hyper,' you speak 'hyper' at the very moment you are speaking 'against.' You are in the process of developing a discourse that is hyper-Jewish, hyper-Christian against these very instances." And in a sense, this person is right. . . . And the point does not just apply, of course, to Nietzsche. (*Negotiations*, 227)

What is especially intriguing in this passage is not simply that Derrida makes this increasingly familiar gesture even in relation to a thinker most would have thought, not without reason, to be anti-Christian or even anti-Jewish but that it seems such a clear invitation to think of Derrida in the same way. This is true not only because of the reference to the relation between Nietzsche and Paul here (which relationship has played a role in our own interpretation) but also on account of the reference to Nietzsche as really engaging in a hyper-Christianity precisely when he appears to be engaged in an anti-Christian (and Jewish) reflection. But Derrida has quite clearly identified himself with a kind of hyperbolism that marks all his thought (*Monolingualism of the Other*, 49 ff.). It is almost as if he were signaling from some nearly transparent hiding place. "And the point does not just apply, of course, to Nietzsche." Not only to Nietzsche but perhaps also to one whose thought has been so often associated, especially by some of its detractors, with a certain Nietzsche.

In the listing of certain thinkers who are to be thought as religious thinkers, a list that then included Heidegger (for provocative effect) but now should be expanded to include Sartre and even Nietzsche, Derrida characterized the relationship as a "doubling": "this tradition that consists of proposing a nondogmatic doublet of dogma, a philosophical and metaphysical doublet, in any case a *thinking* that 'repeats' the possibility of religion without religion" (*Gift of Death*, 49). It is precisely this way of thinking of Derrida that has been so brilliantly, even dazzlingly, developed by John D. Caputo in his *Prayers and Tears of Jacques Derrida*, whose subtitle, moreover, repeats the concluding phrase of Derrida in the last quotation: *Religion Without Religion*.[24]

In any case, what is at stake in the reading that I have attempted, as well as in those that I have proposed, is something like noticing whether we have in Derrida something like a "nondogmatic doublet" of a set of issues with which Paul is dealing.[25] I am not at all sure that what Paul is doing should in any case be called "dogmatic" or even, without further ado, "religious." But it does seem to me to be clear that both are wrestling with some of the same issues.

Is there a sense, then, in which we may say that Derrida is a religious, even a "Christian," thinker? Of course, as commonly understood, it would be obviously not the case that Derrida is a Christian thinker. He has more than a birth relationship to Judaism (see "A Silkworm of One's Own" in *Acts of Religion*). He has concerned himself at various points with a direct engagement with contemporary Jewish thinkers with whom his own work has a striking affinity (Levinas, Cixous, Jabes). In this way, he has contested the view of a certain (Aryan) purity of the western canon going back to Plato and insisted on a certain hybridity of that canon and tradition.

We may on the other hand (but is it a different hand after all?) note the way in which Derrida has concerned himself with certain texts of the "Christian canon," in the first place with thinkers like Augustine but also the "negative theology" of Angelus Silesius or Meister Eckhard as well as, of course, Kierkegaard. Even more striking is his reading of New Testament texts such as those of Matthew and of the Apocalypse of John, and, of course, Paul.

One way of understanding this is quite simply in terms of the opening of the tradition to what is always already there: its having already been shaped by Judaisms[26] and Christianities (and, since the European Middle Ages, Islams). That is, the very task of thought within Europe cannot be undertaken without reference to the hybridity[27] of the philosophical tradition in terms of Judaism, Christianity, and Islam alongside and deeply permeating the reception also of Plato and Aristotle and other monuments of antiquity. In this sense, Derrida is simply making philosophy and the humanities come clean about their often suppressed "other" by which they are inexorably shaped and also challenged. Thus all thinking in the "western" tradition is haunted by its religious other: spooked, in the sense of fearful, haunted in the sense of bothered and worried and preoccupied, as one would be if there were a ghost in one's house.

But there may be more at stake here than a recovery of an archive or than the summoning of the repressed into consciousness. It is rather that there are certain things that can only be thought, or certain ways of thinking the thought and the unthought, that are the province of a certain Judeo-Christian-Islamic way of thinking the relation of the transcendent to the worldly. In this recognition, certainly Levinas has been the pioneer. But deconstruction as a thinking of the limit of language and of knowledge is necessarily engaged in relation to modes of thinking that are endemic to these traditions and for which these traditions provide essential resources, precisely for that mode of thinking that is called deconstruction. This is all the more true of a thinking that privileges the ethical (as Levinas has shown) or the political, as this reading of Derrida has sought to make evident.

But perhaps there is even more here. It is to a certain extent signaled in what Derrida has said about Heidegger or even Nietzsche. It is that what is at stake may even be a certain recovery of "the essence of Christianity," beyond and even against what has been known as Christianity. This was certainly at work in one of Derrida's favorite thinkers (he says so in *A Taste for the Secret*, 40), Søren Kierkegaard, whose attack on Christendom is an attack precisely in the name of that which Christendom claimed to represent.

In a remarkable body of work for nearly half a century, Thomas J. J. Altizer has maintained that something like what Christianity is really all about had been banished from Christianity itself and that in the modern period something like the "truth of the gospel" (let's call it the gospel of Christian atheism) had had to take up residence outside and over against Christianity or what passed itself off as Christianity. Thus he has suggested a number of modern-day prophets of such an "essence" of Christianity that includes Kierkegaard and William Blake, Dostoyevsky and Nietzsche, and another of Derrida's favorite writers, James Joyce. I am certainly not the first of Altizer's students and associates to have thought that Derrida might well be added to this list of those who seek to bring to expression the heart of a certain Christianity that has been too often excluded, not unintentionally, from what calls itself Christianity. I am reminded here of a formulation that Derrida uses in *The Gift of Death* to characterize what he supposes Patochka may be up to: "Something has not yet arrived, neither at Christianity nor by means of Christianity. What has not yet arrived at or happened to Christianity is Christianity. Christianity has not yet come to Christianity" (28). And in reference to the globalization of something like the Truth and Reconciliation Commission of South Africa, Derrida has spoken of a certain Christianization of the world that has no more need for Christianity.

One of the things that distinguishes Derrida from some of the nineteenth- and even twentieth-century prophets of a gospel without Christianity or what calls itself Christianity, is that he actually works within a context that is quite clearly "post-Christian." Unlike Kierkegaard struggling against the Lutheran orthodoxy of his time, or Nietzsche struggling within and against a certain evangelical Lutheranism, or Joyce writing in the heavily Catholic atmosphere of Ireland, or Dostoyevsky within an intellectual landscape determined by the Russian Orthodox Church, Derrida works within the framework of an Enlightenment culture that has even been able to become somewhat oblivious to Christendom in its various manifestations. Thus his work is not characterized by something like an attack on Christendom but instead by a rather calm consideration of what the Abrahamic traditions may have to offer to thought. Thus as we have seen, he can even say concerning his thinking of the gift that what interests him in thinking the gift is precisely the gift in the sense of a certain Christianity: "I am interested in Christianity and in the gift in the Christian sense" (*God, the Gift, and Postmodernism*, 57). Indeed, one could say that the "orthodoxy" against which Derrida is thinking is the orthodoxy of an Enlightenment thinking that supposes it has left the Abrahamic traditions behind. (One is reminded of Bonhoeffer saying that although one cannot really talk religion and God with one's coreligionists, it is possible to do this quite calmly and nondefensively with an atheist, or even one who rightly passes for an atheist.)

The point of these reflections, however, is not to ask or answer whether Derrida is in some odd sense a Christian or even a Paulinist, or whether Paul is a protodeconstructionist. The point, rather, is that both Paul and Derrida are wrestling with questions that are urgent for their respective civilizations, above all the question of justice. And it is because they are wrestling with precisely these questions that they may be seen to engage one another's projects in interesting and illuminating ways. The question of justice and the impossible possibility that justice comes not through the refinement of the law but by way of a gift that awakens us to a messianic promise and vocation is one that concerns us all, I think, whether or not we call ourselves Christians or deconstructionists or some other term. It concerns us quite simply as human beings who share the doom and the promise, if there is one, of this planet, and who have the obligation to think unflinchingly about our common lot, even if that which we are given to think surpasses knowledge and science, even if it leads us to embrace what may seem foolishness to those who are deemed knowledgeable and weakness to those who think they have and exercise power.

Notes

CHAPTER I

1. Levinas writes: "The world in which pardon becomes all-powerful, becomes inhuman." Emmanuel Levinas, *Difficult Freedom: Essays on Judaism,* trans. Sean Hand (Baltimore: Johns Hopkins University Press, 1990), 20. Later, he writes, "The efficacity of the work is replaced by the magic of faith; the austere God appealing to a humanity capable of Good is overlaid with an infinitely indulgent divinity that consequently locks man within his wickedness and lets loose this wicked but saved man on a disarmed humanity" (104). This is connected to the extermination of six million Jews which poses a certain crisis in that "the monstrosity of Hitlerism could be produced in an evangelized Europe." This shatters "the plausibility which Christian metaphysics could have for a Jew used to long acquaintance with Christianity. This plausibility involved *the primacy of supernatural salvation with regard to justice on earth.* Has not this primacy made at least possible a great deal of confusion on earth, and this extreme limit of human dereliction?" (161). These are the questions that any reading of Paul on justification and justice must be accountable to from now on.

2. Many of these will be more systematically indicated in the conclusion.

3. There is a growing interest in Paul among contemporary continental philosophers. Among the most important attempts to think what Paul may contribute to contemporary issues are Slavoj Žižek, *The Fragile Absolute, or Why Is the Christian Legacy Worth Fighting For?* (New York: Verso, 2000); also by Žižek, *The Puppet and the Dwarf: The Perverse Core of Christianity* (Cambridge: MIT Press, 2003); and the remarkable study by Alain Badiou, *Saint Paul: The Foundation of Universalism* (Stanford: Stanford University Press, 2003). Another notable Continental philosopher, Giorgio Agamben, has written an alternative interpretation to that offered by Badiou in Agamben's *Il tempo che resta: Un commento alla Lettera ai Romani* (Toreino: Bollat Boringhieri, 2000). Žižek's reading of Paul is partially influenced by the perspec-

tive of Jacques Lacan, who deals with Paul in his *Ethics of Psychoanalysis*, trans. Dennis Porter (New York: Norton, 1992). This reading of Paul is taken up as well by Julia Kristeva in *Strangers to Ourselves*, trans. Leon S. Roudiez (New York: Columbia University Press, 1991). In the course of subsequent chapters, there will be occasion to indicate some of the perspectives put forward by these thinkers insofar as they illuminate the juxtaposition that we will seek to bring into focus between Derrida and Paul.

4. Hendrikus W. Boers, *Theology out of the Ghetto: A New Testament Exegetical Study Concerning Religious Exclusiveness* (Leiden: E. J. Brill, 1971). The character of this project has also been explained in my "What Is Humanistic Interpretation," in *Text and Logos: The Humanistic Interpretation of the New Testament*, ed. Theodore W. Jennings Jr. (Atlanta: Scholars Press, 1990), ix–xvi.

5. Thus Alain Badiou, in *Saint Paul*, claims: "Basically I have never connected Paul with religions. It is not according to this register, or to bear witness to any sort of faith, or even antifaith, that I have, for a long time, been interested in him" (1). In this, he follows the example set many years ago by Jacques Lacan, who, in his *Ethics of Psychoanalysis*, recommends to his audience that they read the best of the religious authors (97) and defends his own reading of Paul (to which I will refer later) by claiming that "the knowledge in question is like any other, and for this reason it falls into the field of inquiry that we should conduct on all forms of knowledge" (171). Lest this be (mis)understood as simply a reductive reading, Lacan speaks of accepting as such the idea of other forms of knowledge than the kind that is founded scientifically and indeed, he points to the Pauline notion of grace as "irreplaceable," yet one for which there is nothing "equivalent in classic academic psychology" (171). As will become clear, the present discussion is concerned not with the psychological value of Pauline concepts, but rather their political significance.

6. The restriction to the interiority of the individual has been the basis not only for a specifically theological interpretation of Paul, for example in Augustine, but has also in the twentieth century been taken as the basis for reading Paul in connection with existentialist and even psychoanalytic interpretations of the divided self.

7. José Porfirio Miranda, *Marx and the Bible: A Critique of the Philosophy of Oppression* (Maryknoll, N.Y.: Orbis, 1974). Miranda refers to the antecedent work of Käsemann, Michel, Lyonet, and Jüngel that approximates to the concerns that he raises (173–77).

8. The extent of the difficulty that we are indicating here may be gauged by the example of the translation of Jean-Françoise Lyotard's "On a Hyphen." The translators note that "Lyotard translates *diakaiosune* throughout as *la justice*, justice; we have in several places followed Lyotard in this translation while also maintaining the translation of the New Revised Standard Version as 'righteousness.'" Thus the depoliticizing translation of Paul infects the translation of Lyotard. See

Jean-Françoise Lyotard and Eberhard Gruber, *The Hyphen: Between Judaism and Christianity*, trans. Pascale-Anne Brault and Michael Naas (Humanity Books, New York, 1998), 27, n. 6.

9. We may note that Miranda is not alone among Latin American liberation theologians in his reading of Levinas; there is also Enrique Dussel. But for our purposes here, the work of Miranda, riveted as it is on the question of justice, is of far more immediate concern. In this concern, Miranda is followed by Elsa Tamez, whose excellent study of the idea of justification by faith also details the work done by a number of more recent Latin American theologians. *The Amnesty of Grace: Justification by Faith from a Latin American Perspective*, trans. Sharon H. Ringe (Nashville: Abingdon, 1993; translation of *Contra toda condena: La justificacion por la fe desde los excluidos*, which originally appeared in 1991).

10. Dieter Georgi's *Theocracy in Paul's Praxis and Theology* was translated in 1991 (Minneapolis: Augsburg Fortress, 1991) but was first published in German as part of a collection edited by Jacob Taubes on *Theokratie* (Paderborn: Ferdinand Schöningh, 1987). Taubes's own political reading of Romans thus stands as the forerunner of Georgi's work. Taubes's work in this area was published after his death as Jacob Taubes, *Die Politische Theologie des Paulus*, ed. Aleida Assmann and Jan Assmann (Munich: Wilhelm Fink Verlag, 1993). This has now been translated by Dana Hollander as *The Political Theology of Paul* (Stanford: Stanford University Press, 2004). In the United States, the ongoing work of the Paul and Politics Group of the Society of Biblical Literature has been published as Richard A. Horsley, ed., *Paul and Empire: Religion and Power in Roman Imperial Society* (Harrisburg: Trinity Press, 1997); and Richard A. Horsley, ed., *Paul and Politics* (Harrisburg: Trinity International Press, 2000).

11. In the essay "Before the Law," which we will refer to below (in Derrida, *Acts of Literature*, ed. Derek Attridge [New York: Routledge, 1992], 217).

12. First published as "Deconstruction and the Possibility of Justice" and now available in its entirety as "The Force of Law" in *Acts of Religion*, ed. Gil Anidjar (New York: Routledge, 2002).

13. I do not subscribe to the view that Derrida has only recently become a thinker to be taken seriously on ethical issues. Already, in the conclusion to my *Beyond Theism* (Oxford: Oxford University Press, 1985), I insisted that deconstruction and dissemination (terms meant to evoke the thought of Derrida) were indispensable allies for an emancipatory theological project concerned with questions of justice.

14. Derrida's reflections on a wide range of contemporary ethical and political themes may now be found in Jacques Derrida and Elisabeth Roudinesco, *For What Tomorrow . . . : A Dialogue*, trans. Jeff Fort (Stanford: Stanford University Press, 2004).

15. Derrida makes a similar point, albeit less polemically, in "Faith and

Knowledge: The Two Sources of 'Religion' at the Limits of Reason Alone," in *Religion*, ed. Jacques Derrida and Gianni Vattimo (Stanford: Stanford University Press, 1998), 49.

16. Although in many respects helpful, Heidegger's Marburg colleague, Rudolf Bultmann, supposed that the distinction between spirited and soulful human was "smuggled in" from gnosticism. *Theology of the New Testament*, trans. Kendrick Grobel (New York: Charles Scribner's Sons, 1951), 1:204. In this respect, Hans Walter Wolff's *Anthropology of the Old Testament* (Philadelphia: Fortress, 1974), 10–39, is much better, showing that such a distinction and hierarchialization comports well with Hebrew usage.

17. See Krister Stendahl, "The Apostle Paul and the Introspective Conscience of the West," in *Paul Among Jews and Gentiles, and Other Essays* (Philadelphia: Fortress, 1976), 199–215.

18. In "Nietzsche and the Machine," Derrida notes that the difference between Nietzsche and Heidegger is that "everything is, for Nietzsche, interpretation." He goes on to say, "I have always admired this aspect of Nietzsche's thinking." *Negotiations*, trans. Elizabeth Rottenberg (Stanford: Stanford University Press, 2001), 245.

19. In "History of the Lie: Prolegomena," in *Without Alibi*, trans. Peggy Kamuf (Stanford: Stanford University Press, 2002), Derrida mentions again Nietzsche in relation to Paul: referring to Augustine's treatises on lying: "is always in dialogue with Saint Paul, Nietzsche's most intimate enemy and the privileged adversary of his ferocity" (29). In the same text (291, n. 18), Derrida makes mention of Paul and the question of his lying in the sense of appearing to believe what he does not, in this case with respect to circumcision. Derrida does not cite Paul's saying in 2 Corinthians 6:8 in which he links "as deceivers and (yet) true" as predicates related to his mission and ministry.

20. Citations are from Friedrich Nietzsche, *Daybreak: Thoughts on the Prejudices of Morality*, in *The Cambridge Texts in the History of Philosophy*, ed. R. J. Hollingdale (Cambridge: Cambridge University Press, 1997).

21. We have seen that Derrida may not be completely innocent of such an interpretation.

22. It is important, as we shall see, to note the way in which Paul is not merely concerned with the Jewish law, as Nietzsche seems to maintain here, but with the law in all its given instances and thus with what we will come to identify as the law "as such." This will be developed in the next chapters.

CHAPTER 2

1. In a number of ways, this complex text of Derrida's destabilizes the disjunction between "literature" and "law." What concerns us here is the relevance of certain limited aspects of this discussion as it bears on Paul's attempt to delegitimate not literature but law. This occurs, in Galatians, by way of recourse to narra-

tive, which, as Derrida makes clear, is by no means coextensive with literature. Indeed, Derrida will suggest that the very category of "literature" depends on certain developments in law that herald the dawn of modernity.

2. In *Writing and Difference*, trans. Alan Bass (Chicago: University of Chicago Press, 1978), 79–153.

3. Levinas writes, "Morality begins when freedom, instead of being justified by itself, feels itself to be arbitrary and violent." *Totality and Infinity*, trans. Alfonso Lingis (Pittsburgh: Duquesne University Press, 1969), 84. And later: "The welcoming of the Other is ipso facto the consciousness of my own injustice—the shame that freedom feels for itself" (86). See also "Philosophy and the Infinite," text and commentary in Adriaan Peperzak, *To the Other* (West Lafayette: Purdue University Press, 1993), 88–119, esp. 115–18.

4. That questioning is not the only task of thought, or is not the starting point of thought, is suggested negatively by Derrida first in his discussion of Heidegger in *Of Spirit: Heidegger and the Question*, trans. Geoffrey Bennington and Rachel Bowlby (Chicago: University of Chicago Press, 1989), esp. 129–36, n. 5, and subsequently indicated positively in the essay "There is No *One* Narcissism" (Autophotgraphies) in *Points . . . : Interviews 1974–1994*, trans. Peggy Kamuf (Stanford: Stanford University Press, 1995), 202. In these and other discussions, it becomes clear that Derrida is suggesting that a certain affirmation or even "thanking" precedes questioning as the activity of thought.

5. For example, in *A Taste for the Secret* (Cambridge, UK: Polity Press, 2001), Derrida (with Maurizio Ferraris), referring to the published form of the first half of this essay, then titled "Deconstruction and the Possibility of Justice," writes, "I said for the first time in so many words that *there is an indeconstructible*, and that justice is indeconstructible" (56). A similar reference is made in a note to *Specters of Marx: The State of the Debt, the Work of Mourning, and the New International*, trans. Peggy Kamuf (New York: Routledge, 1994), 183–84, n. 8. In "The Deconstruction of Actuality," Derrida repeats: "The undeconstructible, if there is such a thing, is justice" (*Negotiations*, 104).

6. Slavoj Žižek, although apparently often critical of a certain deconstruction, nevertheless credits Derrida with the decisive insight into what he terms the limits of deconstruction: "It is here that we encounter the limit of deconstruction: as Derrida himself has realized in the last two decades, the more radical a deconstruction is, the more it has to rely on its inherent undeconstructible condition of deconstruction, the messianic promise of justice. This promise is the true Derridean object of belief, and Derrida's ultimate ethical axiom is that this belief is irreducible, 'undeconstructible'" (*Puppet*, 139). What Žižek seems not to notice is that Derrida can identify justice with deconstruction in such a way that justice is not a limit *to* deconstruction but deconstruction's own limit or enabling impetus.

7. Without going into all that would be important to say here, it is necessary to indicate that deconstruction is always a questioning at and "about" the limit, not beyond the limit as such. Whether the question is that of justice or gift

or death, these terms function to make apparent the limits of knowledge and so to destabilize the knowledge that is constituted "inside" the limit. With respect to justice, we may say that it is that which deconstructs law or in virtue of which law may be deconstructed. Alternatively, deconstruction is the thinking activity that is incited or provoked by the claim of justice. Thus deconstruction takes place in the "interval" or on the "border" between justice and law and is not itself, as such, the "beyond" (justice). Yet it is not thinkable or doable without the beyond (justice) and the thinking of the beyond or of that which exceeds the limit (law, for example). The "problem" of limit or border is discussed at length in *Aporias*, trans. Thomas Dutoit (Stanford: Stanford University Press, 1993), esp. 1–42.

8. The relation between the universal and the singular is taken up in the discussion with Kierkegaard in Derrida's *The Gift of Death*, trans. David Wills (Chicago: University of Chicago Press, 1995), where Derrida first notes that for Kierkegaard, the singular is the break with the "ethical" form of the universal, but then goes on to demonstrate that precisely this singularity (Abraham's determination to sacrifice Isaac) is universalizable as the character of any ethical decision (64–67).

9. Geoffrey Bennington, in *Interrupting Derrida* (New York: Routledge, 2000), speaks of the quasi-transcendental in Derrida's thought. In a roundtable discussion, Derrida says, speaking of his complex relation to transcendental philosophy, "I have nothing against transcendentality." John Caputo, M. Dooley, and M. J. Scanlon, eds., *Questioning God* (Bloomington: Indiana University Press, 2001), 61.

10. Here Derrida speaks of Levinas but chooses not to engage in this reflection further. What is shared between Levinas and Derrida is the notion of the other. But one of the elements that makes this different is that Derrida wishes to speak of justice where Levinas speaks of ethics. This has to do with the multiplicity of the other(s); each and every other is wholly other, we may say. Derrida is aware that he has changed the basic terms of Levinas's discussion of ethics to emphasize justice which for Levinas, at least in *Totality and Infinity*, is secondary to ethics since justice is what is at stake when it is not only the question of the other but of "another other." What is at stake then is the adjudication of the (absolute) claims of each other and this is the question of justice, and so, as Levinas also says, of politics. Derrida pays particular attention to this question in relation to his own privileging of the question of justice (and so of politics) in "Ethics and Politics Today," in *Negotiations*, 295–314.

11. We have seen that Derrida is quite aware of the urgency of questions of justice that are not addressed by law and which perhaps cannot be; see Chapter 1.

12. It seems to me that Paul's argument about the law being taken possession of by "flesh" serves as a framework for understanding how it is that law always serves the self-interest of those who have the means to propose and enforce the law. In this case, the "particular instances" serve as examples of a general rule that applies always and everywhere that law exists as positive law. However, this sug-

gestion must be held in suspension here until it is possible to further clarify the way in which Derrida's actual argument about this is also consonant with other elements of Paul's argument.

13. Speaking of the process of the ongoing critique and transformation of the law, Derrida says, "But this process unfolds *in the name of justice*: justice requires the law. You can't simply call for justice without trying to embody justice in the law. So justice is not simply outside the law, it is something which transcends the law, but which, at the same time, requires the law." "Hospitality, Justice and Responsibility," interview in *Questioning Ethics: Contemporary Debates in Philosophy*, ed. Richard Kearney and Mark Tooley (London: Routledge, 1999), 72–73.

14. See also *Specters of Marx*, 183–84, n. 8.

15. It seems to me that Derrida regularly privileges the more commonsense view of ghosts as the presence of the dead, and nowhere more impressively that in his reflections in *Memoires for Paul de Man*, rev. ed., trans. Cecille Lindsay, Jonathan Culler, Edwardo Cadava, and Peggy Kamuf (New York: Columbia University Press, 1989), esp. 22–32. It is also true, as Peggy Kamuf has reminded me, that here in *Specters of Marx* Derrida also specifically has in mind the unborn. Moreover, as the references in *Memoires* make clear, this is also associated with the more general theme of trace. In "Marx & Sons," Derrida writes, "the effort to think the trace is inseparable, and has from the outset been literally . . . indissociable from an effort to think spectrality." *Ghostly Demarcations: A Symposium on Jacques Derrida's "Specters of Marx,"* ed. Michael Sprinkler (London: Verso, 1999), 268. For a fine analysis of the relation among the "themes" of spectrality and justice, see Peggy Kamuf, "Violence, Identity, Self-Determination, and the Question of Justice: On *Specters of Marx*," in *Violence, Identity and Self-Determination*, ed. Hent deVries and Samuel Weber (Stanford: Stanford University Press, 1997).

16. One way in which the discussion of justice that we are undertaking here entails a question of at least one ghost is the haunting, if it is that, of Derrida's discourse with or by the ghost of Paul, as already glimpsed in the earlier discussion of Derrida's "Before the Law."

17. Here it may be important to notice that Derrida's argument depends to a certain extent on the idiomatic potentialities of *droit,* which may be translated as "justice" or "law," as well as "right" in the sense of human rights. Something similar is also the case with the German *Recht.* Here as in his texts generally, Derrida is intentionally exhibiting what might be termed the idiomaticity of thought; that is, the way in which thinking is not simply universal but relies on the resources and runs up against the obstacles of the particular language (or idiom) within which and against which it works. My own essay is itself an engagement with the question of translation both in the sense of aiming at a less misleading translation of Paul's concern with justice (less misleading than talk of righteousness, unrighteousness, wickedness, and so on) and at one in which the call and claim of justice can be heard—the goal, that is, of doing "justice" both to Paul and to "justice." But it is also an attempt to translate between the "philosophical" language of Der-

rida (translated from French into English) and the "religious" language of Paul (translated from Greek into English).

18. In "Faith and Knowledge," Derrida again emphasizes this disjoining as the "condition of justice" or the thinking of justice (69, n. 15).

19. Already in *Glas*, Derrida, in his discussion with Hegel's *Spirit of Christianity*, had linked together the question of justice and the exceeding of the principle of exchange. Here, however, because he is reading Hegel, the distinction between law and justice is not brought out: "The pleroma's overabundance throws off balance the principle of equivalence, commerce, the economy of exchange that regulates *justice.*" *Glas,* trans. Jon P. Leavey Jr. and Richard Rand (Lincoln: University of Nebraska Press, 1986), 59.

20. This then provokes the question of other and of gift: "it is the experience of the other as other, the fact that I let the other be other, which presupposes a gift without restitution, without reappropriation and without jurisdiction" (*Negotiations*, 105).

21. Derrida, *Of Hospitality* (1997), trans. Rachel Bowlby (Stanford: Stanford University Press, 2000).

22. The irreducible pervertibility of law may also be connected to what Derrida also considers in relation to both science and religion as the inescapable irony of autoimmunity. See "Faith and Knowledge," 44 and 72–73, n. 27. I am indebted to Peggy Kamuf for drawing my attention to this connection. In a more recent text, "Autoimmunity: Real and Symbolic Suicides," Derrida has developed this theme of autoimmunity in relation to the so-called war on terrorism. Giovanna Borradori, *Philosophy in a Time of Terror: Dialogues with Jurgen Habermas and Jacques Derrida* (Chicago: University of Chicago Press, 2003). Here he points to "the perverse effect of the autoimmunitary itself. For we now know that repression in both its psychoanalytic and its political sense—whether it be through the police, the military, or the economy—ends up producing, reproducing, and regenerating the very thing it seeks to disarm" (99). And he gives as examples the attempt to undermine the Soviet domination of Afghanistan, which results in the arming and training of Osama bin Laden, or the "victory" of the United States over the Soviet Union, which makes nuclear terrorism possible (94–98). The general principle is formulated as follows: "As we know, an autoimmunitary process is that strange behavior where a living being, in quasi-suicidal fashion, 'itself' works to destroy its own protection. To immunize itself against its 'own' immunity" (94).

23. Note that this is dedicated to Chris Hani of South Africa, who had been recently assassinated. Although *Specters of Marx* often privileges the dead as the referent of "ghost" (as in the ghost of Hamlet's father or even the ghost of Marx himself), the term is also stretched to include, as in this citation, the call or claim of those not yet born.

24. John D. Caputo, *The Prayers and Tears of Jacques Derrida: Religion Without Religion* (Bloomington: Indiana University Press, 1997), 68, 116.

25. Of course, the question of justice, divine justice, and the indication of the priority of this question is no innovation for Romans. Not only is the question

an urgent one in Galatians, but it is present already in 2 Corinthians: Paul can speak of those who are caught up in the messianic event as becoming "the justice of God" (5:21), of bearing fruit of justice (2 Corinthians 9:10; see also Philippians 1:11), and of being instruments of justice (6:7)—that is, of that divine justice which is his primary concern. We will see at a number of points that important elements of his argument in Romans concerning the call and claim of justice, even justice "outside the law," are anticipated in Paul's earlier letters.

26. We should also note that the anteriority as exteriority to which Paul refers here in Romans is different from that to which he refers in Galatians. In the latter, we have Abrahamic faith/justice as anterior to the law of Moses (which came, as he says, 430 years after), whereas in Romans, the "before the law" appears to be before the command with respect to circumcision. This pluralization of the advent of the law and so of the "before" the law continues in a highly complex way in Romans 5, where Adam is said to be culpable of trespass (that is, contravention of express command). It is no part of Paul's intent to offer a systematic or even chronological ordering of these different situations of being "before" the law. Indeed it is by no means certain that such an ordering would be either possible or desirable for illuminating the situation with which Paul is concerned. However, the multiple situations of "before the law" (the Adamic, the Abrahamic, the Mosaic) suggest that Paul is groping toward something like law as such. The inclusion of Roman law will make this all the more unavoidable.

27. Thus Elsa Tamez, in her fine study of justification in Paul, *The Amnesty of Grace*, which is based to a considerable extent on the insights of José Porfirio Miranda that I noted in the Introduction, correctly notes that "God justifies in order that justice be done" (90) and subsequently maintains that "The purpose of justification is to transform human beings into subjects who do justice" (110).

28. Hendrikus W. Boers wonders whether Paul is oblivious to the tension in his thought here and what he was arguing only a chapter earlier—namely, that it is the doers rather than mere hearers of the law who will be made just (2:13). *The Justification of the Gentiles* (Peabody, Mass.: Hendrikson, 1994), 166; see also 107. This already suggests the basic tension in Paul's argument that I will be trying to explicate. I should indicate that although the approach taken here to Paul differs considerably from that undertaken by Boers in *Justification* in that he develops a very sophisticated semiotic and structural approach to the letter, whereas I attempt to show the significance of what was once called a poststructuralist, or more properly deconstructive, approach, there are nevertheless crucial areas of common ground. Not only do we both resist the depoliticizing tendency of translations that substitute righteousness for justice and unrighteousness or wickedness for injustice, but we are also agreed that Paul's argument does not end with chapter 4 but continues through to the end. Moreover, we are agreed that the tension in Paul's thought concerning law and obedience (or even "works") should not be one-sidedly resolved in favor of a negation of these notions in favor of faith, and that faith should not be given a one-sidedly religious as opposed to ethical significance. We are agreed, therefore, in supposing that Paul should not be imprisoned in a Protes-

tant orthodoxy and that considerable help in understanding Paul may be found by simply approaching him as a thinker, as one who thinks seriously about important issues not only for "Christians," but important for all who take seriously the imperative to think through matters of basic concern for human existence. This is not to say that we are in agreement with respect to the interpretation of Paul's argument. But I have found even points of strongest disagreement indispensable provocations to further reflection.

29. Boers correctly notes that this, however, is precisely what happens when baptism is substituted for circumcision (*Justification*, 103), and in general when the notion of a religious privilege for Christians is reintroduced by suppressing Paul's argument against any such privilege.

30. An important discussion of this topic is found in Stanley Stowers's *A Re-Reading of Romans: Justice, Jews and Gentiles* (New Haven, Conn.: Yale University Press, 1994), esp. 34–36.

31. One of the clearest attempts at explaining "deconstruction" as well as distinguishing it from destruction (or Heidegger's *Destruktion*) is in Derrida's "Letter to a Japanese Friend," in *Derrida and Difference*, ed. David Wood and Robert Bernasconi (Evanston: Northwestern University Press, 1988), 1–6.

32. In this sense, then, Žižek is correct to affirm, "This then is how we are to grasp the idea that Christianity 'accomplished/fulfilled' the Jewish Law: not by supplementing it with the dimension of love, but by fully realizing the Law itself" (*Puppet*, 117). But this could only be affirmed if we add (and modify) a further caveat proposed by Žižek: "in short, the Jewish law is not a social law like others: while other (pagan) laws regulate social exchange, the Jewish Law introduces a different dimension, that of divine justice which is radically heterogeneous with regard to the social law" (119). In order to bring this into conformity with Paul's argument, we would have to add that it is also Roman law that adverts to justice. What distinguishes these laws or polities may be that the reference to justice may more directly deconstruct law in the Israelite tradition than in the Roman one.

33. Thus Rudolf Bultmann notes, "the attitude which orients itself by 'flesh,' living out of 'flesh,' is the self-reliant attitude of the man who puts his confidence in his own strength and in that which is controllable by him" (1:240).

34. Here we may note again Derrida's reflections on autoimmunity, which corresponds fairly closely to what I have called "self-protectiveness." It is this that also perverts the law it enforces. In the case of both Derrida and of Paul, a "biological" metaphor serves to indicate this point (respectively, "autoimmune" and "flesh").

35. Derrida, *Gift of Death*, esp. 58–69.

36. These, of course, are among the texts privileged by Lacan's reading of Paul in *Ethics of Psychoanalysis*, which broaches the issue of what he calls "the attraction of transgression" (2). Subsequently he paraphrases Paul by substituting "thing" for "sin" (83) and cites Romans 7:7; later he will say that this substitution was superfluous (170). Žižek, who is of course greatly influenced by Lacan, sug-

gests that Paul's insight moves beyond the "mutual implication of Law and sin" and maintains that Christianity breaks "the very vicious cycle of prohibition that generates the desire to transgress it, the cycle described by Saint Paul in Romans 7:7" (*Fragile Absolute*, 100, 135). My own reading of Paul reverses the axiom enunciated by Julia Kristeva, who noted in *Strangers to Ourselves* that "Paul is not only a politician. He is also a psychologist" (82).

37. See, e.g., Ernst Käsemann, "On the Subject of New Testament Apocalyptic," in *New Testament Questions of Today* (Philadelphia: Fortress, 1969), 108–37.

38. J. Christiaan Beker, *Paul the Apostle: The Triumph of God in Life and Thought* (Philadelphia: Fortress, 1980).

CHAPTER 3

1. The English translation is found in *Walter Benjamin: Reflections*, ed. Peter Demetz (New York: Harcourt Brace Jovanovich, 1978), 277–300.

2. Since Derrida articulated this perspective, other continental thinkers have developed it in ways that both echo Derrida's basic insight (based on his reading of Benjamin) and develop it in alternative ways. Thus, for example, Slavoj Žižek, in *Fragile Absolute*, writes, in a way that parallels Derrida on, e.g., the American Revolution (or founding violence): "On the one hand, the Event is the impossible Real of a structure, of its synchronous symbolic order, the engendering violent gesture which brings about the legal Order that renders this very gesture retroactively 'illegal'" (92). He maintains, "the Structure can function only through the occultation of its founding event" (93). This Lacanian reading of the character of founding violence may be contrasted with a reading that is more directly dependent on a fresh reading of Benjamin together with the German political philosopher Carl Schmitt that is executed by Giorgio Agamben in *Homo Sacer: Sovereign Power and Bare Life* (Stanford: Stanford University Press, 1998) and that emphasizes the "state of exception," which, however, will be seen to overflow and overwhelm the "normal" state, thereby contaminating, in a way related to Derrida's point, the distinction between founding and preserving violence (15–67). Agamben, however, distinguishes his own reading from Derrida's (57, 65).

3. I am thinking, for example, of the students in Korea who occupied the U.S. Chamber of Commerce building in Seoul to protest the virtual declaration of war against North Korea on the part of the president of the United States (as I was first drafting these pages in 2002). The U.S. State Department labeled them terrorists and then demanded that their names be turned over to the United States, presumably to further its self-proclaimed unending war against terrorism.

4. Hegel had earlier remarked that "a great scoundrel may be admired." *The Spirit of Christianity and Its Fate*, in *Early Theological Writings*, trans. T. M. Knox (Philadelphia: University of Pennsylvania Press, 1971), 216.

5. In "Ethics and Politics Today," Derrida again returns to the question of this lawyer, Verges, whose strategy is to work within the law as a lawyer" while

radically contesting the legitimacy of this law and all its consequences," and asks, "Does he do this in the name of ethics, politics or some other law?" (*Negotiations*, 308).

6. The question of the death penalty is one that has exercised Derrida for a number of years, both as a theoretical matter, as here, and as a site of some of his most direct interventions into the political process. In *Without Alibi*, translator Peggy Kamuf notes that this goes back as far as an unpublished letter regarding the case of Caryl Chessman (286). In *Negotiations*, there is a letter to Bill and Hilary Clinton (written in 1996) regarding the case of Abu-Jamal (130–32) as well as a transcript of Derrida's remarks concerning this case before a UNESCO conference in 1995 (125–29), in which he recalls a failed attempt twenty-five years earlier to rescue George Jackson "from an infernal, juridical-prison machination" (125). Some of Derrida's most incandescent prose is unleashed in this impassioned but still carefully reasoned analysis of the U.S. prison system as "real death camps that are sometimes run by private companies in the most tranquil good conscience" (127). The passage of another seven years (even before the terrorist attacks on the World Trade Center in New York on September 11, 2001) has only made more evident the acuity of Derrida's jeremiad. That the governor mentioned there, Tom Ridge, who had run for office with the promise to kill Mumia Abu-Jamal, should then become the director of the United States office (now department) of "Homeland Security," which in concert with the "Department of Justice," seems determined to erode past recognition human rights enshrined in the Bill of Rights, is a further bitter irony. Perhaps the most sustained discussion of the death penalty comes in Derrida's essay "Psychoanalysis Searches the States of Its Soul: The Impossible Beyond of a Sovereign Cruelty," in *Without Alibi*, 238–80. See esp. 261–63, in which he relates the perpetuation of the death penalty in the United States with the insistence of the United States on maintaining undiluted state sovereignty on the world stage.

7. Unless this is what is obliquely referred to when Paul says at the beginning concerning Jesus the "Son" who is declared "son of David according to the flesh" (Romans 1:3). On such a reading, the declaration of Jesus as son of David is precisely what his execution under the sign "king of the Jews" intends. And this occurs "according to flesh" precisely in terms not only of the weakness of the messiah there displayed, but even more in terms of the anxiety of the world-political power that defends itself in this way.

8. It will be evident that I adopt the view that Paul wrote Romans after Galatians and that both were preceded by the Corinthian correspondence. This is consistent with the view taken by most of the standard discussions of the Pauline corpus.

9. If one calls the manner of detention of suspected Al Queda members or even sympathizers unjust, one may also be called an ally of Osama bin Laden; the consequence of such a liaison can readily be imagined.

10. John Milbank, in *Being Reconciled: Ontology and Pardon* (New York:

Routledge, 2003), makes a similar point, albeit without reference to Derrida, when he claims: "Accordingly one could argue that the Cross exposed the structure of arbitrary sovereign power in its ultimate exceptional yet typical instance. This is its act of discernment of the worst human violence" (93). Later, Milbank insists that "*Something* must have occurred to create a new exposure of the violence and terror latent in given social and political structures, and to give rise to a new social alternative" (95). It is precisely the perspective generated by Derrida's reflections on Benjamin, I am suggesting, that enable us to better think what it is that Paul is struggling with here.

11. In this respect, I take issue with Badiou's claim that "The historical and statist process of Jesus' putting to death . . . are of absolutely no interest to Paul" (101). In this respect, Jacob Taubes is much nearer the truth, I think, when he says, "It isn't *nomos* but rather the one who was nailed to the cross by *nomos* who is the imperator! This is incredible, and compared to this all the little revolutionaries are *nothing*" (24).

12. This is indeed one of the central concerns of *Postcard* and one that, as Derrida has insisted, always must be understood to be endemic to the situation of writing. *Postcard: From Socrates to Freud and Beyond*, trans. Alan Bass (Chicago: University of Chicago Press, 1987). Although the question of whether or not Paul knew his addressees will return in our discussion of hospitality below, I should at least emphasize at this point that Paul could not have known that his readers would include Origen, Augustine, Luther, and Calvin, let alone Derrida. That is, any reading of Romans depends on what Derrida calls the *distinerrance* of the letter, its deviation from any definite addressee. This is the condition of the readability of any text. But it is also at the same time that which makes any reading, to say the least, problematic or fraught with difficulty and even betrayal.

13. It would not be unreasonable to suppose that Paul may have satisfied himself that the rejection and execution was legitimate before enrolling himself as a persecutor of the followers of a crucified messiah. As a convinced and scrupulous Pharisee, he would, in any case, have supposed that he was well enough informed on this matter to have taken the measures he did against them.

14. We should think of that opposition that Derrida suggests in the thought of Benjamin between a force that founds law (Greek) and a force or violence that destroys law ("Jewish it seems to me," he writes). *The Force of Law: The "Mystical Foundation of Authority"* (1990), in *Acts of Religion*, ed. Gil Anidjar (New York: Routledge, 2001), 265.

15. The explication of the possibilities and limitations of the idea of exemplarity, as these are worked out by Derrida, would take me too far from my main theme here. In the final chapter, I will indicate how this and other issues may converge in an attempt to think through something like Paul's christology (or messiah-ology) as a further step in the elucidation of the way in which deconstruction may shed light on Paul's thought.

16. Through the time of Augustine, the identification of the Roman law

with the possible imposition of the death penalty served to make it impossible for Christians to accept the position of civil magistrate (similar reasons were adduced for avoiding military service). Augustine's defense of his own role of opposing the imposition of the death penalty is found in Letter 153, written to the magistrate Macedonius. The irony is that today, at least in the United States, the most ardent defenders of the death penalty are found among those who define themselves as conservative Protestant (that is, in some way, Augustinian) Christians.

17. The understanding of Paul's argument as entailing something like a general amnesty is worked out by Elsa Tamez in her *The Amnesty of Grace*, whose Spanish title is *Contra toda condena*. I will explore this issue more thoroughly in Chapter 7.

18. In the context of proposing to rethink the Aristotelian notions of potentiality and actuality, Agamben suggests, in what I take to be an exemplary formula, that "the troublemaker is precisely the one who tries to force sovereign power to translate itself into actuality" (*Homo Sacer*, 47).

19. In this connection, we may recall the suggestion of Alain Badiou that Paul's *ekklesia* should be understood as "a small group of militants" (20) and Žižek's suggestion that "Paul goes on to his true Leninist business, that of organizing the new party called the Christian community" (*Fragile Absolute*, 9). Although I believe that these descriptions better fit the Markan than the Pauline community, they do suggest at least that the Pauline movement is by no means politically innocent. Taubes can go so far as to maintain that Romans "is a political theology, a political declaration of war on the Caesar" (*Political Theology*, 16).

20. In another connection I have tried to argue that this is the very thing that is highlighted in the Gospel of Mark, written after the execution of Paul himself. *The Insurrection of the Crucified: The Gospel of Mark as Theological Manifesto* (Chicago: Exploration Press, 2003). And it was a fragment of this argument that served as my contribution to *Text and Logos* as "The Martyrdom of the Son of Man."

21. In *Negotiations*, Derrida writes: "When one says force is a weakness and that sometimes, well there is more force in weakness or that weakness is revealed to be stronger than force, at that moment one is engaged in a discourse on force that no longer has the coherence of classical logic and is no longer reliable" (35). That this goes beyond classical logic is compatible at least with Paul's linkage of the weakness that is true power with talk of "folly" that is true wisdom (1 Corinthians 1:18 ff.). Derrida comes back to this relation of the weak and the strong in "Nietzsche and the Machine," in which, speaking of spectrality and of a justice that is always unsatisfied, he notes, "This spectrality is the weakness of the powerless, who being powerless, resist the greatest strength" (*Negotiations*, 252). In another essay, "Performative Powerlessness—A Response to Simon Critchley," *Constellations* 7, no. 4 (2000), Derrida notes that the very idea or notion of performativity to which he devotes so much attention in his work may imply a certain sovereign power or mastery. However, he supposes "that there is an uncondi-

tional that is without sovereignty, an unconditional that is without power" (467–68). That justice is precisely such an unconditional without power is clear from our discussion.

22. Indeed, there is also the question of certain "Christian authorities" in Jerusalem to which Paul had also occasion to refer in Galatians 2. There also it was a question of their actual or possible "persecution" of the gentile believers, for which Paul had assumed a certain responsibility.

23. Both may be involved in the collection of taxes and duties as well. This is a situation also mirrored in the two discussions of response to taxation demands in Matthew. In one discussion, it is the tax that is "tribute to Caesar" (Matthew 22:15–22), and in the other, it is the so-called temple tax paid by Diaspora Jews to Jerusalem (Matthew 17:24–26). In both cases, we have an ironic undermining of the legitimacy of the taxers and a form of compliance with the demand that therefore cannot confuse the undermining in principle of such authorities with a mere tax revolt.

24. One of the issues to which Derrida has given the most attention in the discussion of something like ethics is the impossibility of responsibility or decision being thought of as simply the working out of the implications of a general rule and therefore the impossibility of a responsible decision, should one occur, being able to give an account of itself through appeal to such a rule or law. See, e.g., "Politics and Friendship," in *Negotiations*, 178. A particularly clear discussion is in *Aporias* (19). In the Conclusion, I will return to this issue in pointing to a possible explication of the status of Paul's own attempts to negotiate positions with respect to issues facing his communities.

25. Note that Calvin uses this text to expressly defend the death penalty. But because in Paul's overall argument the wrath of justice has been transformed into the grace or gift of justice, this defense of the death penalty is more than suspect. The abrogation of the wrath of God as the basis for any determinant human judgment has already been made evident through the elimination of judgment and condemnation, as we have already seen. In this respect, Augustine in Letter 153 is closer, and not only chronologically, to Paul.

26. We should note that the structure of this argument, taken as a whole, corresponds to the structure of prophetic annunciation relative to the alien empires as instruments of divine wrath directed against Israel's injustice while at the same time storing up wrath for themselves on account of their own injustice. This sort of prophetic annunciation is invoked explicitly by Paul in Romans 9:17–22.

CHAPTER 4

1. In "Negotiations," the lead interview in *Negotiations*, Derrida says, "I do not believe in the erasure of hierarchy. What I am opposed to is always a certain stabilizing or stabilized coding of hierarchy" (21).

2. Derrida, *Force of Law*, 291.

3. Although I am not persuaded of Robyn Horner's attempt to distinguish

Gift from gift in her reflections on Derrida's thinking of the gift, I find her depiction of the impossibility of the gift to be a reliable interpretation of Derrida's perspective otherwise. *Rethinking God as Gift: Marion, Derrida, and the Limits of Phenomenology* (New York: Fordham University Press, 2001), esp. 184–208. Among
the earlier discussions of gift, and its impossibility, that prefigure the difficulties to
which Derrida refers in *Given Time: 1. Counterfeit Money*, trans. Peggy Kamuf
(Chicago: University of Chicago Press, 1992), it is useful to consider the discussion
of this theme in *Glas*, 242–45.

4. Now one can ask of this analysis of gift and debt whether it is adequate
to simply override the distinction important also to Mauss (*The Gift*, trans. W. D.
Halls [New York: Norton, 1990], 71–83), between an economy of expropriation
and one of generosity, perhaps in the sense of Marx between one of expropriation
and one of distribution, or finally between one of circularity and one of spiraling.
Let us begin at the end. The economy of exchange, of market let us say, is a circu-
lation of existing values, but one where the division of labor made possible by market exchange ensures an increase in overall abundance. This is the classic model of,
say, Adam Smith. In the analysis of Marx, however, the division of labor is not innocent but rather produces an enforced inequality of distribution that comes from
the expropriation of labor value for the sake of market value. This surplus registers
as capital and is recorded to the account of those who possess or control capital. A
remedy is simply that the workers are appropriately compensated, which means a
redistribution of wealth and a return to the fairness of the market. In this case, expropriation is opposed to fair or equitable distribution. However, capital exploitation has taken on a life of its own in the form of finance capital, in which case
money makes money in the sense of getting for itself a surplus return. Thus we
suppose an endless spiral of augmentation of wealth. This is more than the circle.
Mauss supposes that such a spiral can be based not only on exploitation but also
on gift. That is to say, that gift or generosity is the motor of an expansion of cir-
culation of gifts/goods. Note that here we still have an economic logic, although
one that is quite different from that of exploitation. The gift and deferred return
of the gift, the alternation between payback and "pay forward," means that the
economic logic is transformed. For Derrida, this is still "economy."

For the issue to be made more acute here, we would have to ask whether an
economics of generosity would have to fall back into an economics of exploitation.
If so, then the distinction between these economies is a distinction without a(n absolute) difference. It seems clear to me that the early Christian communities did
experiment with what might be termed an economics of generosity (see Acts 2 and
4, as well as Paul on the collection for Jerusalem, and so on). Is it the case that such
an economy is sustainable only in that a fresh or continuous infusion of gratuity,
of gift, is always to be relied on (grace, spirit, and so on)? In that case, "God"
would name that gratuity, by virtue of which gift is continually infused into the
economic system, making exploitation impossible or unnecessary. But then God is
the name of the subject who is exploited. In this connection, what Derrida says

about a certain forgiveness that aims at reconciliation—that it is "a noble economy" or "strategy," even if still an economy—may be pertinent. See roundtable discussion, *Questioning God*, 57, and Chapter 7 below, on pardon.

5. Richard Beardsworth, in his fine analysis of the relation between Derrida's thinking of law and justice and that of the philosophical tradition from Kant to Hegel, and Marx and continuing to Heidegger and Levinas, has rightly maintained, "Impossibility is not the *opposite* of the possible: impossibility *releases* the possible." *Derrida and the Political* (New York: Routledge, 1996), 26. Although Derrida more often writes of the possibility of the impossible, he can also, as in the passage cited above, write of "the (impossible) possibility of the impossible," and in "As If It Were Possible," he writes of "this impossible possibility of a 'passive' decision" (*Negotiations*, 357).

6. The point is not that Barth or Bultmann mean the same thing as Derrida in speaking of impossibility, but rather that theologians who balk at talk of impossibility when applied to gift or grace have simply forgotten their own discursive tradition. For an earlier discussion of the relationship between the projects of Barth and Derrida, see Graham Ward, *Barth, Derrida and the Language of Theology* (Cambridge: Cambridge University Press, 1995).

7. Robyn Horner provides a response to what seems to be a misunderstanding at this point on the part of Milbank in her *Rethinking God as Gift*, 16–18. Although Milbank's primary interest in *Being Reconciled* is the related notion of forgiveness, it does not seem to me that he has yet quite understood the character of Derrida's reflections on gift (and so on forgiveness). Derrida maintains neither that the gift is unthinkable nor that the gift does not occur. Rather, his point is that the thinking of the gift must reckon with the aporia of gift, and that the subsuming of gift to knowledge destroys the gift as gift. In *Memoires for Paul de Man*, Derrida suggests, "And aporia evokes, rather than prohibits, more precisely, promises through its prohibition, an other thinking, an other text, the future of another promise" (133). To be sure, this talk of promise—"No path is possible without the aporia of the gift, which does not occur without the aporia of the promise" (147)—opens to another discussion that must be postponed to Chapter 8.

8. John Caputo and M. J. Scanlon, eds., *God, The Gift and Postmodernism* (Bloomington: Indiana University Press, 1999).

9. Derrida's typical way of referring to this sort of impossibility is through the term *aporia*, which we have encountered before, and will again. Speaking of this, he says, "the *aporia* or the *non-way* is the condition of walking: if there was no *aporia* we wouldn't find our way; path-breaking implies *aporia*" ("Hospitality, Justice and Responsibility," 73).

10. Throughout, I will be using Messiah for Christ and messiah-event for Christ event. This is both to insist on the basic "Jewishness" of Paul's thought and to prevent the language from automatically slipping into the familiar presuppositions of christology. At the end of this study, I will indicate some of the issues that may be dealt with in order to clarify Paul's messianic perspective with the aid of Derrida's own reflections on the messianic and related themes.

11. I noted above that Derrida claims that justice must be thought on the basis of gift. I have not yet determined how this is so for him; that question was suspended. But we are able to see that at least for Paul, the affirmation that grace is the basis of justice is quite important.

12. Already in 2 Corinthians Paul had used this metaphor to speak of his own comportment: "with the weapons of justice for the right hand and for the left" (2 Corinthians 6:7). The members here, the hands, are the way in which one deals with other people and the world, and it is this interaction that is "armed" for justice. It is this that seems to be the sense of "the power of God," to which he refers just before this metaphor, and the previous qualities (e.g., genuine love, truthful speech) are what give content to that justice with which one is armed by the "power of God." In Romans, it becomes clear that this divine power is precisely the gift of justice.

13. In the roundtable discussion "On Forgiveness" in *Questioning God* (2001), Derrida says, "So you cannot prevent me from having a bad conscience, and that is the main motivation of my ethics and my politics" (69). Although this might seem to be a hyperbolic statement, Derrida is quite consistent in his writings that a "good conscience" is, shall we say, unconscionable. Levinas had often cited the statement of Dostoyevsky: "We are all guilty of all and for all men before all. And I more than the others," cited, for example, in *Ethics and Infinity: Conversations with Philippe Nemo* (Pittsburgh: Duquesne University Press, 1985), 98. That text refers to Dostoyevsky's *Brothers Karamazov*, trans. Constance Garnett (New York: New American Library, 1957), 264. Although the importance of a bad conscience for a certain personal ethics may be attributable to a certain religious attitude, what is most important is that this is said to be the basis of politics; that is, that what is at stake here is, quite simply yet comprehensively, the question of justice—that justice that comes as or on the basis of gift. Hent deVries offers the wonderfully concise formulation: "For systematic or internal reasons, good conscience is bad faith." *Religion and Violence: Philosophical Perspectives from Kant to Derrida* (Baltimore: Johns Hopkins University Press, 2002), 386.

14. In this respect, the Jesus of Matthew's Gospel can say of one who has a good conscience that he "already has his reward" (6:2). This text, and the problem as the problem of a "good conscience," had already been referred to by Hegel in his *Spirit of Christianity*, 220. See also Derrida's *Glas*, 59.

15. This is the theme of Augustine's antipelagian polemic in his treatise *On the Grace of Christ* (Nicene and Post-Nicene Fathers First Series, 5:217–36). Although much of the argument depends on the disassociation of gift and work, it leads also to the conflation of gift and faith as the response evoked by gift. He writes of the Pelagians, "These men, however attribute faith to free will in such a way as to make it appear that grace is rendered to faith not as a gratuitous gift, but as a debt—thus ceasing to be grace any longer, because that is not grace which is not gratuitous" (chap. 34, p. 230). The careful reading of this entire treatise with Derrida's reflections on gift in mind would be an intriguing exercise.

16. The logic of "how much more" as the distinction between law and gift is already present in 2 Corinthians, where Paul writes: "if there was splendor in the service [*diakonia*] of condemnation" (referring to the law of death, verse 7 above), "the service of justice must far exceed [*pollô mallon*] it in splendor" (2 Corinthians 3:9). The idea that the service of law is accompanied by splendor or glory (*doxa*) is developed by Paul in relation to the glory that shown from Moses' face and that necessitated his wearing a veil, which in turn leads to Paul's saying that we (that is, those who serve justice) don't need a veil. This last comes in for some comment, perhaps irritable, from Derrida, in "A Silkworm of One's Own" (*Acts of Religion*, 346–47), but Derrida does not comment on the antecedent distinction between law and justice and the glory attributed (although distributed differently) to each.

17. The exuberance of Caputo's reading of Derrida provides an illustration of the relation between excess and the thought of justice. See, e.g., 168–69 in his *Prayers and Tears of Jacques Derrida*. Although an exploration of the trace of this excess in Derrida's emphasis on affirmation as prior to the questioning would take us far afield with respect to our immediate concerns, relevant consideration of the "affirmation that motivates deconstruction" is found in "Eating Well," in *Points . . .* , 286 ff. Derrida himself proposes a strong identification between deconstruction and affirmation in *Spurs Nietzsche's Styles*, trans. Barbara Harlow (Chicago: University of Chicago Press, 1979)—"deconstructive (i.e. affirmative) interpretation" (37)—and claims that "deconstruction . . . is affirmative right down to this conception of the messianic without messiansim [and] is anything but a negative movement of nostalgia and melancholy" ("Marx & Sons," 259).

18. In this connection, Robyn Horner's use of the phrase "moment of madness," derived from Derrida's reflections on the gift, is quite suggestive (186, 198–200).

19. Whether it is necessary to exceed phenomenology in order to think gift is a basic point at issue between Jean-Luc Marion and Derrida. Marion's attempt to think gift within phenomenology is best articulated in *Being Given: Toward a Phenomenology of Givenness*, trans. Jeffrey Kosky (Stanford: Stanford University Press, 2002). An excellent discussion both of Marion and of Derrida in relation to the question of the gift is provided in Horner's *Rethinking God as Gift*.

CHAPTER 5

1. Derrida's footnote here refers to *Psyche: Inventions of the Other*.

2. With respect to this discussion of duty without debt in *Aporias* as well as what we have been citing from *On the Name*, we should note that the English translation necessarily reduces the paradoxical character of Derrida's formulations in French, in which *devoir* is both "duty" and "debt." But does this mean that the English translation betrays the French? Or does it instead "complete" the original? Or both? *On the Name*, trans. David Wood et al. (Stanford: Stanford University Press, 1995). See "Des Tours de Babel," in *Acts of Religion*, esp. 121.

3. Derrida returns to this theme in his dialogue in Borradori's *Philosophy in*

a Time of Terror when he says, "we must thus be dutiful beyond duty, we must go beyond the law, tolerance, conditional hospitality, economy, and so on. But to go beyond does not mean to discredit that which we exceed" (133).

4. These remarks open up onto the complex and provocative discussions by Derrida of questions of responsibility and decision that, although highly significant for an understanding of ethics and politics in relation to deconstruction, would take us rather far afield from our attempt to reread Paul at this point. See, e.g., "Eating Well," in *Points . . .* , 272–83, 286 ff., as well as " A Madness Must Watch Over Thinking," *Points . . .* , 359.

5. This question is explored at some length in the essay "The University Without Condition," in *Without Alibi.*

6. Of course, something like love was there at the beginning for these reflections began, in "Passions," in *On the Name*, with a reflection on friendship that avoids the language of duty (7).

7. Derrida also repeatedly questions the self-evidence of such a distinction. See, e.g., "The Rhetoric of Drugs" (*Points . . .* , 247), where he disclaims belief "in the infallible pertinence of the distinction between public and private." Of course, much of *Postcard* is devoted to upsetting this distinction. In fact, Derrida suggests that *Postcard* and *Glas* are "performative problematizations of the public/private distinction." "Remarks on Deconstruction and Pragmatism," in *Deconstruction and Pragmatism: Simon Critchley, Jacques Derrida, Ernesto Laclau and Richard Rorty*, ed. Chantal Mouffe (New York: Routledge, 1996), 79.

8. It should be noted that whereas the idea of fear appears in the preceding discussion regarding the authorities, the reference to honor does not. Indeed, it takes us back to the injunction to "love one another with mutual affection," which is then clarified as, "outdo one another in showing honor." Thus Paul ties what he has been saying about fear and payment back to the question of love, to which he is now about to return.

9. Robyn Horner also asks, "What if my response to God's giving (if *that* it was God who gave remained undecidable) never returned to God, because it was converted into a gift to the Other?" (207–8).

10. The reflection on "love" that Derrida has given the most attention to is precisely a reflection on "friendship," which has the considerable merit of escaping from the monopolization in Christian discourse on love by *agape* or *caritas*. It seems to me that this is precisely the right direction to go to escape some of the limitations of the discourse on *agape*. And it may be that at those points where the discourse on friendship is found to be limited (e.g., androcentrism, numerical restriction, similarity of the friends), it may be importantly corrected by reflections that seem more compatible with parts of the Christian reflection, such as Kierkegaard's *Works of Love*, trans. Howard and Edna Hong (New York: Harper and Row, 1962). What in any case is essential is to break out of the depoliticization of the notion of love, whether as friendship or *agape*. And this is the great significance of what Derrida is up to in his reflections precisely on the *Politics of Friendship*, trans. George Collins (London: Verso, 1997). The most I can hope to do here

is to indicate that Paul's reflections on love also point toward something like the political, at least to the instantiation of justice.

11. In "A Madness Must Watch Over Thinking," in *Points . . .* , 363.

12. The same text seems to be cited in Galatians 5:14: "For the whole law is summed up in a single commandment: You shall love your neighbor as yourself." It is sometimes supposed that Paul derives this from Jesus. This is possible but by no means certain. In any case, Paul cannot be supposed to be ignorant of the fact that it is formulated in this way in Leviticus, that is, in what claims to be the Law of Moses. Nor does Paul here invoke any other authority than that law; he does not invoke the authority of Jesus here. And there is good reason to doubt that Paul was very much aware of the "teaching" of Jesus (See Galatians 1:16–17). On the other hand, in this focalizing of love of the neighbor, it cannot be maintained, as Nietzsche rather hastily did, that Paul's discourse bears no relation to or is incompatible with that of Jesus (*Anti-Christ*, trans. R. J. Hollingdale [London: Penguin Books, 1990], 162–63).

13. Jacob Taubes notes that in this Paul goes beyond (Taubes even suggests *against*) the formulation of the Jesus tradition, which links love of God to love of neighbor. Taubes writes, "This is a highly polemical text, polemical against Jesus" (*Political Theology*, 52), and he continues, "I regard this as an absolutely revolutionary act" (54). Paul reduces everything to the love of neighbor here, and this may be required by what we have noticed earlier: that the divine love toward "us" cannot be paid back if it is to remain in some way aneconomic. Thus it can only aim at the other person, including, as Taubes makes clear, the enemy of Romans 12:14.

14. The more positive content of love is suggested, for example, in Galatians 5:22–23 and, of course, 1 Corinthians 13. Žižek, in *Fragile Absolute*, proposes that it would be precisely by reading Paul in 1 Corinthians 13 that it would be possible to break out of the impasse of transgressive desire and that this might go some distance toward an appropriation of Lacan's own attempts to think of love beyond or outside the law (143, 145; see also *Puppet*, 115–16). (Several paragraphs here seem to be identical with the already cited passage in *Fragile Absolute*.)

15. Käsemann, for example, notes that the phrase "seems to point to an Egyptian penitential rite involving a forced change of mind. And that it therefore points to the remorse and humiliation of the adversary." *Commentary on Romans* (Grand Rapids, Mich.: Eerdmans, 1980), 349. That the giving of food to the enemy or persecutor interrupts the economy of payback and so may result (through the gift of food or water) in the transformation of the enemy into the one who is engaged in the infinite symmetry of "love one another" comports well with Paul's concern. It also corresponds to what we have discussed as nonviolent militancy.

16. Thus Paul can speak of bearing fruit of, or for, justice in earlier letters: 2 Corinthians 9:10 and Philippians 1:11. What is consistent is the expectation that those to whom he addresses himself will actually act justly, that is, that the claim of justice becomes effective in and through them.

17. See Emmanuel Levinas, *Of God Who Comes to Mind*, trans. Betticia

Bergo (Stanford: Stanford University Press, 1998), 15–32; and his *God, Death, and Time* (Stanford: Stanford University Press, 2000), 207–12.

CHAPTER 6

1. An assertion repeated though in different form in "The University Without Conditions," in which he speaks of deconstruction as being put to work "as justice" (*Without Alibi*, 208).

2. For Derrida's reflections on the relation of his theme of hospitality to the more Levinasian terminology of "welcome," see *Adieu to Emmanuel Levinas*, trans. Pascale-Anne Brault and Michael Naas (Stanford: Stanford University Press, 1999), 21–25.

3. See *Adieu*, 54–55, and *Of Hospitality*, 109.

4. Although Derrida does not say this so far as I can see, it seems that the situation of the arrival of the visitant is always already inscribed as a promise. That is, the coming of the visitor is the coming of the promise (which, of course, may be betrayed) of peace, shalom, *salem aleichem*, words that in every culture of hospitality open the scene of visitation. The promise to Abraham of a certain kind of well-being is but a particular specification of the promise that is already inscribed in every instance of visitation.

5. This is an important issue for Derrida, who has suggested that the carnivorous habits of the West, and of the Abrahamic traditions, betray a rather cold-blooded sacrifice of the living for the sake of one's own satisfaction. He is thus able to link carnivorous diet to the phallogocentrism of which he accuses the tradition ("Eating Well," *Points . . .*, 280–81). I expect that he would not find Paul's apparent designation of those who are vegetarians in principle as weak in faith entirely to his satisfaction, although he might find Paul's opinion here fitting, given Paul's occasional lapses into misogyny and patriarchy.

6. There were pagan groups that were opposed to both wine and the eating of meat, perhaps even influenced by ideas from India. Little evidence exists for Jewish groups with similar scruples, although it is at least imaginable that some Christians may have wanted to embody a pre-Noahcic lifestyle; Noah was the inventor of wine (Genesis 9:20) and was the one who received permission for humanity to eat meat (Genesis 9:3). On the other hand, the covenant with Noah is represented as a covenant "with every living creature of all flesh that is on the earth" (9:16), that is, as explicitly with all animals, including the human animal. The same covenantal text makes clear that the killing of a human is sacrilege against God, "for the human is the image of God," yet does so in such a way as to license, rather than abrogate, the death penalty (Genesis 9:6).

7. We should note that in 1 Corinthians as well as in Galatians, the emphasis is on the problem of receiving rather than giving hospitality. Thus in Galatians it is the question of withdrawing from the hospitality of, the sharing in meals with, those who do not observe the dietary restrictions of the sojourning Christian Jews of Jerusalem; whereas in 1 Corinthians it has to do with accepting the meal

that is set before one by the (pagan) host without worrying where the meat came from. In Romans, the issue is more inclusive of both guest and host because it is a welcoming of one another that is at stake. I will return to this below.

8. This is something it seems to me in the current situation Derrida has maintained lucidity about, which contrasts rather sharply with those who argue that certain Islamic "fundamentalists" threaten "universal human values" by their insistence on their own religious observances or opinions. Derrida asks, "Wars or military 'interventions,' led by the Judeo-Christian West in the name of the best causes (of international law, democracy, the sovereignty of peoples, of nations or of states, even of humanitarian imperatives) are they not also, from a certain side, wars of religion?" ("Faith and Knowledge," 25). What the defenders of religious tolerance seem incapable of remembering is that their view is precisely a religious view and that the war against the fundamentalists is a religious war even if, or especially when, it claims to be the opposite, that is, when it claims to represent universal human values and rights. An especially egregious example of this is the declaration "Why We Are Fighting," put forward by a group of American intellectuals to justify the war against. . . . Well, that is part of the problem, because it seems that these intellectuals seem to be arguing for a singularly open-ended war against those they accuse of intolerance. That is, the justification does not limit itself to, for example, going after a particular group of terrorists, which in any case would be a police matter rather than an international war.

9. The question of the setting aside of identity and "interest" is one to which Paul returns on several occasions. In Philippians, for example, he admonishes his readers, "Let each of you look not to your own interests, but to the interests of others" (2:4), for which the self-emptying of the messiah will serve as exemplary (2:5–8). A potentially fruitful line of inquiry would be to investigate the possible relation between Derrida's questioning of the notion of sovereignty (for both state and "subject") in connection with his more recent reflections on a democracy to come, and the various ways in which Paul suggests a renunciation of self as critical for participation in the messianic.

10. Once again, we notice that the emphasis falls upon the being welcomed, the being offered hospitality, rather than upon being the agent of hospitality or welcome. Although this situation is certainly taken into account by Levinas and Derrida, it is nonetheless striking how far the opposite emphasis is focalized, that is, an emphasis on the subject as the host rather than as the guest. And one may wonder to what extent this may be due to an unintended continuation of the western subjectivity that still thinks of itself as self-possessed plenitude even while seeking to interrogate this subjectivity. This reversal of perspective is even more striking in the Gospels, where the understudies or apprentices of the messiah are made dependent on the kindness of strangers (Mark 6:10–11). In the Gospel of Luke, Jesus' hearers are instructed in the ways of being good guests (Luke 10:5–8, 14:7–11).

11. That Paul is responsible for the notion of a universal humanity that is to

be understood both negatively (as sin) and positively (as created—Adam, and saved-Messiah) is something I also argued in "Theological Anthropology," in *Theology and the Human Spirit: Essays in Honor of Perry LeFevre*, ed. Theodore W. Jennings Jr. and Susan Brooks Thistlethwaite (Chicago: Exploration Press, 1994), 35–44. I also noted the connection to stoicism there, although I did not draw the conclusions that Derrida so helpfully does to ideas of cosmopolitanism and to the idea of crimes against humanity.

12. This genealogy of cosmopolitanism is repeated as well in the dialogue in Borradori, *Philosophy in a Time of Terror*, 130.

13. See Immanuel Kant, *Perpetual Peace and Other Essays*, trans. Ted Humphrey (Bloomington: Indiana University Press, 1993), 118–19. Derrida speaks of reading and rereading this text in *Of Hospitality* (27) and does actually read it again (70 ff).

14. The translators usually say something like "not your own doing." But there is no Greek word here that points to doing. It is a bare "not your own" that thus underlines that the gift that awakens faith is not possessed by the "recipient" at all. This is in conformity with what we have seen to be the problematic of gift above.

15. We may simply notice here the way in which Pauline conceptuality concerning Adamic humanity eerily anticipates (does it haunt?) some of the language of Heidegger concerning *Dasein*. Not only is *Dasein* of the earth, but it is also being-unto-death and subjected to guiltiness that precedes any particular deed. We may also note that Levinas suggests that humanity, at least the human confronted by the other, is not rooted in the earth but opened to history. And Derrida maintains that his own reading of Heidegger should make his readers suspicious of such Heideggerian themes as "clearing" and "path" and other terms that suggest a rootedness in the earth. See, e.g., *Of Spirit*, 109–10.

16. Badiou, whose reading of Paul is also focused on the question of cosmopolitanism figured as a universalism, proposes a link between the character of gift (*dorean*) and that of "for all" as follows: "There is for Paul an essential link between the "for all" and the without cause" (77). He asserts, "Only that which is absolutely gratuitous can be addressed to all" (77). Although I do not find Derrida making this particular connection explicit, it does seem to me to be implicit in the way in which notions of gift and hospitality are related.

17. We might also note for further discussion that Paul's language here does not separate this species of humanity from the rest of created or earthly beings. This is why he can suppose, as he does in Romans 8, that the coming of this messianic humanity is something for which all things long or groan or yearn. And it is why Paul or one of his followers can maintain that the messianic human is "the first born of all creation" and one through whom God intends to "reconcile . . . all things" (Colossians 2:15, 20). Thus, although Paul's focus is undeniably on human beings and their history and fate, he also takes this to exceed any possible border between the human and the other than human. Making the border tremble between the human and the animal, for example, is a notion with which Derrida has

long been concerned, for example in his discussion of Heidegger in *Of Spirit* as well as in important texts collected in *Negotiations*. This issue has been more recently (and provocatively) treated in "The Animal That Therefore I Am (More to Follow)," *Critical Inquiry* 28 (2002): 369–418.

18. Another indication that Paul may and must be understood as a "political" thinker comes in his use of the term *ekklesia* to indicate the character of the messianic humanity that is taking shape in the world on the basis of the messianic event. This term is not used in Romans until chapter 16 (which is often thought to be a fragment of a different Pauline letter), but it is characteristic of Paul's vocabulary in other texts. The term points to the assembly of free citizens who come together to take action for the common good. In the Greco-Roman polis, it is the political body acting both as legislative and as judicial deliberative body. In Israel, it was also the deliberative assembly that determined matters important for the life of the whole people. That Paul supposes that the people who are being drawn into the messianic event become an assembly, an *ekklesia*, is indicative of the political tone of his thought just as much as the supposition that all may be "fellow citizens" in Ephesians, which only brings out the implications of the language of *ekklesia*. This political reference is obscured in English by the use of the term "church," which is never understood to be in any sense democratically determined or charged with responsibility as such for the whole society.

19. See also *Adieu*, 71.

20. Note also that the question of a crime of hospitality has now even become the pretext of war, a war that as its proponents now claim is itself global. For what was the crime, the *causus belli*, of the Taliban? Was it not that they offered hospitality to Al Queda, a group that had, after all, been, at least in its roots, sustained and supported by the United States? No war was declared because of their atrocious attack on Buddhist statues or their treatment of women (in which they were in some respects perhaps preferable to the politics of rape of their opponents, now our new allies). No, it was that they had granted hospitality to those who had after all struggled to rid Afghanistan of Soviet troops. When the United States demanded that Al Queda be surrendered (as the sodomites, we recall, demanded the visitors be handed over to them), the Taliban actually declined (like Lot, like the Ephraimite in Judges). But even here their refusal was not absolute, for they had the temerity to demand that first they be provided with proof that al Queda was guilty of the atrocities alleged against them. They had the temerity to demand that hospitality protect those who are charged of a crime without proof. And so the crime of hospitality becomes a cause of war, a just war, several so-called American intellectuals claim, a war in which in order to apprehend bin Laden (something not yet accomplished) the whole society may be subjected to hideous war, to "rolling thunder" and "carpet bombings," all for the crime of hospitality.

21. In this connection, it is useful to recall a distinction that Derrida proposes between a politics of the state and a messianic politics. It is the former, he contends, that is the object of the suspicion that Levinas directed against politics (and law), whereas the latter is the politics with which Derrida is most especially

concerned (see *Adieu*, 74). This sort of distinction may be at work when Derrida says, "I am aware that you cannot found the politics of hospitality on the principle of unconditional hospitality, of opening the borders to any newcomer" (in Caputo and Scanlon, *God, the Gift and Postmodernism*, 132). Here he speaks of "what Kant would call the regulating idea of pure hospitality," although he supposes that it would be necessary to go "beyond Kant's own concept of hospitality as a regulating idea" (133).

22. We should also note that Paul's concern for the conditions of hospitality or welcome has a personal and urgent character in that the immediate occasion for his letter to believers in Rome was his own impending visit (Romans 1:10–15, 15:23–29). This is but a further indication of the priority in his thinking given to the situation of the (prospective) guest.

23. The political importance of the Pauline welcome to strangers and so to one another has been articulated in a related way by Julia Kristeva in *Strangers to Ourselves*, where she suggests that "Paul adopted, developing it to the highest degree, an essential feature of the spirituality characteristic of a place teeming with foreigners: hospitality" (79). And in reference to the same passage from Ephesians that we have seen Derrida cite, she claims, "The Pauline Church emerged as a community of foreigners, first from the periphery, then from the Greco-Roman citadel" (80). At this point, she seems to be suggesting that this is simply a function of the subculture within which Christianity, or at least Pauline Christianity, took shape. However, she also relates this to another theme, which she takes to be central to the Pauline message, one not explored in these terms by Derrida, for she indicates that the cosmopolitanism is to a certain extent based on a movement within an interior division between flesh and spirit: "Foreigners could recover an identity only if they recognized themselves as dependant on a same heterogeneity that divides them within themselves, on a same wandering between flesh and spirit, life and death" (82). What is of particular interest in her approach is the way that she appropriates what has all too often been taken to be merely an interior drama of flesh and spirit and proposed a way of understanding it as having fundamental political importance, thereby demonstrating the reversibility of her own assertion that "Paul is not only a politician. He is also a psychologist" (82).

CHAPTER 7

1. This point was first made by Krister Stendahl in "Paul and the Introspective Conscience of the West," in *Paul Among Jews and Gentiles*, 82.

2. In forms of what is called Protestantism, especially as derivative from Luther, "forgiveness of sins" is understood to be the meaning of justification. In Luther, this can even lead to the slogan *simul justus et peccator*, which has often meant the one is "just" in the sense of being declared so through forgiveness as well as simultaneously a sinner (that is, not just). Thus justification, through its identification with forgiveness, no longer has anything to do with actually becom-

ing (more) just. This produces the consequences to which I previously alluded, referring to Levinas.

3. Caputo and Scanlon, *Questioning God*, 49.

4. In *Memoires for Paul de Man*, Derrida writes, "It is always necessary to excuse oneself for giving, for a gift must never appear in a present, given the risk of its being annulled in thanks. . . . It is necessary to be forgiven for appearing to give" (148–49).

5. In "What Is a Relevant Translation," *Critical Inquiry* 27 (2001), Derrida, reflecting on a speech of Portia in *The Merchant of Venice*, notes that "forgiveness isn't calculated, it is foreign to calculation, to economics, to the transaction and the law, but it is good, like a gift" (192). The irony, of course is that the aneconomic character of forgiveness will lie in ruins before the play is done.

6. Hannah Arendt, in *The Human Condition* (Chicago: University of Chicago Press, 1958), had already made the idea and act of forgiveness indispensable for an understanding of human action. She writes, "The possible redemption from the predicament of irreversibility—of being unable to undo what one has done though one did not, and could not have known what he was doing—is the faculty of forgiving" (237). Quite rightly, she does not attribute this to Paul but to Jesus, or at least Jesus as represented in the Gospels: "The discoverer of the role of forgiveness in the realm of human affairs was Jesus of Nazareth. The fact that he made this discovery in a religious context and articulated it in religious language is no reason to take it any less seriously in a strictly secular sense" (238). That this may be understood in a "strictly secular sense" is what links her reflections to those that we are considering from Derrida. She does not here, however, treat of what might be termed the "unforgivable" in Derrida's sense but of what she calls "trespass," a notion that corresponds tolerably well to what I will deal with when discussing the Pauline suspension of condemnation/judgment.

Arendt maintains that forgiveness applies not to willed evil, for which the last judgment works, but "trespassing": "But trespassing is an everyday occurrence which in the very nature of action's constant establishment of new relationships within a web of relationships, and it needs forgiving, dismissing, in order for life to go on by constantly releasing men from what they have done unknowingly" (240). It seems that this is also the sense in which we should understand the position of Julia Kristeva, who has devoted considerable study to Arendt but who also makes use of the notion of forgiveness in relation to the psychoanalytic situation. Kristeva points again to a secular sense of the religious or Christian notion of forgiveness: "analytical interpretation emerges as a secular version of forgiveness, in which I see not just a suspension of judgment but a giving of meaning, beyond judgment, within transference/countertransference." *Intimate Revolt: The Powers and Limits of Psychoanalysis*, trans. Jeanine Herman (New York: Columbia University Press, 2002), 2:12.

The importance of transference/countertransference for Kristeva's view is that "it is impossible without the forgiving and interpretation-free listening it implies on the part of the analyst, who identifies with the other's ill-being in order to make better sense of it" (19). The way this works, she explains, is that "the language of forgiveness, beyond judgment, is an interpretation (and here I allude to psychoanalysis) that restores the meaning of the suffering. This interpretation suspends the time of punishment and debt, provided it comes from love" (16). Although this interpretation focuses on the analytic situation, as Kristeva has said, it nonetheless is pertinent for our discussion insofar as it further underscores the relation to questions of debt and, by way of the idea of punishment, to law. Moreover, "forgiveness is the luminous phase of the somber unconscious atemporality, the phase during which the latter changes laws and adopts the attachment to love as a principle of renewal of the other and the self" (20). In Kristeva's view, then, it is forgiveness that serves as the opening to love, and we shall see something similar in our Derridean interpretation of the role of forgiveness as operating on the past in such a way as to open the way to a duty beyond debt, whose name, as we have seen, is love.

7. In "What Is a Relevant Translation?," he offers as his translation of the phrase "when mercy seasons justice": "when mercy elevates and interiorizes, thereby preserving and negating, justice (or the law)" (195). In this discussion, he is constantly referring to his proposed translation of Hegel's *Aufhebung* by *relever*, something developed at some length in his reading of Hegel in *Glas*. What is more important for my immediate purpose, however, is the relation between forgiveness or mercy and justice, or law. Thus, earlier in his essay, he wrote of forgiveness, according to Portia: "It rises above the law or above what in justice is only law" (188).

8. It seems to me that there may be a systematic confusion in the way in which John Milbank interprets Derrida in relation to notions of forgiveness, duty, and gift in that he seems not to notice that Derrida regularly insists on *both* heterogeneity and indissociability. When these are conflated, as it seems to me sometimes happens with Milbank, then we can get incautious formulations like "Forgiveness, therefore, perfects gift-exchange as fusion" (*Being Reconciled*, 70; see also 72). He can even suggest that "the ethical is only genuinely imaginable as a mutual and unending gift exchange, construed as an absolute surrender to moral luck or absolute faith in the arrival of the divine gift, which is grace" (154). It is not the last idea, of "surrender" to grace or the gift (or perhaps the impossible—otherwise, why speak here of surrender?), that is so problematic, but the way in which he seems to economize the aneconomic. When he writes that "only utter exposure constitutes the ethical" (148), this seems to me to be correct. What seems to happen, however, is that in the place of utter exposure, he sometimes is disposed to have a gift and a forgiveness one can count on. When he criticizes Derrida, it is often because he seems to hear only the "heterogeneity" in Derrida and not the "indissociability." But he seeks to "correct" this by replacing heterogeneity with indissociability and thus to enter into exchange without reserve, an exchange that is able to be described as "fusion."

9. One way of trying to clarify the tension between the unconditionality of forgiveness (it does not depend on confession/repentance/worthiness) and its con-

ditionality (you will be forgiven, as you forgive) would be to say that it is in our forgiving of one another that it becomes clear whether the unconditional divine forgiveness has arrived in us or at us. Insofar as it has arrived, it produces forgivingness in or through us. Insofar as it does not produce or effect this activity of forgiving of the other, it will not have arrived. It will have arrived precisely insofar as it opens up the closedness of the past (e.g., debt, retribution) to the repetition of the new (a forgiveness then that keeps replicating itself as this forgivingness). But where there is no such opening or no such repetition of opening, then forgiveness will not have arrived, will have disappeared without a trace into the endless repetition of the past, of debt, of the economy of retribution.

10. For a remarkable discussion of the French case, see "History of the Lie: Prolegomenon," in *Without Alibi,* 45–52.

11. See also *Negotiations,* 381–84, where the relevant discussion seems to be but a different draft of much of the argument found in the quoted passage.

12. In speaking of Truth and Reconciliation Commissions, he writes, "if the aim is reconciliation then it is an economy: It is perhaps a very useful, a very noble strategy, but it is not forgiveness. If I forgive, or ask to be forgiven, in order to be redeemed, that is a noble and worthy calculation" ("To Forgive," in *Questioning God,* 57) but it is not yet pure forgiveness. This is however, not simply opposed to the purity of forgiveness as such, for we recall concerning unconditional forgiveness that it still must "bend toward conditionality," must enter into history and so be contaminated by conditionality if it is not to remain abstract or ineffective. That is, as Derrida will maintain in other connections, it is imperative to negotiate the nonnegotiable. I will return to this briefly in the next chapter.

13. As this was first being written, the United States was threatening a veto of the U.N. peacekeeping mission in Bosnia unless its personnel be granted immunity from any war crime prosecution. Because no peacekeeping personnel have ever been so charged, it is evident that the reason for this utter recalcitrance (which is not shared by any other nation involved in U.N. peacekeeping operations) must have a different agenda. It appears that it is an attempt to prevent any possibility of charges of war crimes or of crimes against humanity ever being brought against U.S. citizens. When it is recalled that the U.S. ambassador to the U.N., John Negroponte, was the point man for U.S. policy and operations in Central America during the Reagan administration and thus in charge of Iran-Contra as well as U.S. collaboration with death squads in El Salvador and Honduras, one can begin to imagine why there is so much concern over any possible precedent for the prosecution of any war crime or crime against humanity on the part of an administration that is composed of persons heavily involved in policies that were illegal not only from the standpoint of international law, but also U.S. law. "Today" the United States advances deeper into Iraq in contravention of the U.N. charter. And in a subsequent "today," as I revised this footnote, the evidence of U.S. contravention of the Geneva Convention with respect to prisoners of war had become an international cause célèbre. At the same time, the aforementioned John Negroponte

had been named ambassador (or proconsul, as news reports do not hesitate to affirm) to Iraq.

14. Such distinction between a crime against a human and crimes against humanity as such seems essential for the current development of international law, but it is perhaps impossible to sustain with rigor. Is a crime against humanity a question of number, for example? Certainly the idea seems to begin in the shadow of the Holocaust, under the heading of genocide. But if it is a question of the violation of the sacred in humanity, and if any other is wholly other, then the violation of the other, any other, is a violation of the sacred in humanity and so is a crime against humanity—that humanity which is instantiated in each and every human. If, however, we seek to make the distinction on the basis not of the victim but the status of the victimizer, where the latter is a state, we may at first seem to be on firmer ground. But the ground shifts, for example, in Rwanda, where those arraigned are not simply officers of a state or members of a party. A similar difficulty arises with what is called terrorism, especially where it is not in any meaningful sense state-sponsored. Even if the grounds are shifted to the question of motive, as in the South African Truth and Reconciliation Commission, where the crimes to be dealt with had to have a demonstrable political motive, we are still left in perplexity about how and when to say that an atrocity has or had a political motive. For example, in the cases of chattel slavery or of genocidal conquest, how do we distinguish among political, economic, and religious motives? Similar perplexities may arise with respect to the former Yugoslavia. This is only to suggest that the questions here touched on are immense and have as yet unforeseeable consequences.

15. Oddly, Derrida does not invoke this principle at this point, even though it is one of his most characteristic formulations. See *Gift of Death*, 82 ff.

16. It is tempting to launch here a discussion of the idea of authorship, as this is greatly troubled by Derrida. The whole question of Pauline authorship offers itself to a deconstructive reading. After all, what does "Paul" mean? To whom or what does this name refer?

17. This is the term that was used in Romans 4:7 and that occurs throughout the Gospels, especially in Matthew, with the sense of "forgive." It also occurs often in the New Testament with the general sense of "leave (behind)" or "separate" and in this sense occurs in 1 Corinthians 7:11, where husbands are exhorted not to abandon their wives.

18. There is another point here that calls for some comment in Paul's use of the verb form of *charis*, translated in 2 Corinthians as "forgive." It is the odd phrase "if I have forgiven anything." Of course, this oddity may be explained as Paul's way of deferring to the congregation's act so that he will act as they act and so submerge his will in theirs. But certainly one who has read Derrida cannot help but be reminded of Derrida's repeated warnings that it would be indecent to use the phrases "I forgive" or "I forgave," for this would entail a kind of arrogance of the sovereign subject that is out of place in any conceivable—at least, interhu-

man—scene of forgiveness. The oddity of Paul's locution here exactly anticipates what Derrida seems to suggest about the event of forgiveness, if there is any.

19. Nor is this view of Paul's alien to the Greco-Roman world that he indicts, for notorious injustice is regularly understood as impiety, whether or not a specific law for the occasion exists.

20. The idea of divine wrath is one of the constants of Pauline theology (e.g., 1 Thessalonians 5:9), but it does not have the highly individualized sense that much later comes to be associated with it. Instead, it is the sense of the inevitability of global catastrophe that is the ineluctable and foreseeable consequence of global injustice. If it is not individual but corporate injustice that is the correlative of "wrath," then corporate justice is also the means of averting the fate of catastrophe. Here, however, we focus on the question of justice itself rather than the eschatological horizon, connected to the messianic event, consideration of which must be postponed to a different study. This will be briefly clarified in the last chapter.

21. In *Archive Fever*, Derrida says, "I shall no doubt be unjust out of concern for justice." *Archive Fever*, ed. Eric Prenowitz (Chicago: University of Chicago Press, 1996), 63.

22. See Augustine, *City of God*, book 14, chap. 16.

23. Here we should at least point to what Derrida has maintained about the iterability of the singularity of the event—in this case, the event of something like forgiveness. But again this must be postponed to a point where more detailed attention can be given to the messianic as event in the reading of Derrida and the thinking of what Paul is up to in Romans.

24. As should be quite evident by now, I do not suppose this restriction to be in any way "religious" but rather "ethical."

25. "So forgiveness, if there is such a thing, should be devoid of any attempt to heal or reconcile, or even to save or redeem." At least, this is Derrida's perspective (*Questioning God*, 57). But on this I will have to reserve judgment.

CHAPTER 8

1. The full title is "Deconstruction in America: An Interview with Jacques Derrida," conducted by James Creech, Peggy Kamuf, and Jane Todd, *Critical Exchange* 17 (1985): 1–33.

2. For Heidegger's early attempt to understand Paul and for the way this prefigures his later "method," see the fascinating study by Hent deVries, *Philosophy and the Turn to Religion* (Baltimore: Johns Hopkins University Press, 1999), esp. 181–232, where there are important discussions of Heidegger's early reading of 1 and 2 Thessalonians and of Galatians.

3. When this interview was conducted and published (with the engagement of two of my friends), I was far removed from the academic scene, teaching would-be evangelical pastors in Mexico, where, as it happens, I first had the op-

portunity, rare on this continent for a theologian (given the division of labor so characteristic of a certain theological-academic institution), to actually teach a seminar on Romans. That I only now discover the interview as I conclude this study of Derrida and Romans is certainly an irony.

4. I do not thereby mean to clear deconstruction of the accusation mentioned by Derrida on the same page of the interview that I have been citing, of "corrupting academic morals," a charge with an all too anti-Socratic ring to it. Some morals desperately need corrupting (not excepting morals "in the most sexual sense of the term")—in the name of justice, of course.

5. "Negotiations," in *Negotiations*, 11–40; "Ethics and Politics Today," in *Negotiations*, 304; "On the Priceless," in *Negotiations*, 325 ff.

6. The strife between the Abrahamic faiths seems never far from Derrida's thought: see, e.g., *Specters of Marx*, 58.

7. On Paul's ambivalence concerning circumcision, see "A Silkworm of One's Own," in *Acts of Religion*, 344–46; and *Without Alibi*, 291.

8. See Neil Elliot, *Liberating Paul* (Maryknoll, N.Y.: Orbis, 1994), 3–51.

9. "A Silkworm of One's Own," in *Acts of Religion*, 345–47.

10. See, e.g., *Specters of Marx*, whose subtitle refers to "the new international" a reference given specificity in these terms: "a link of affinity, suffering, and hope . . . without coordination, without party, . . . without co-citizenship, without common belonging to a class" (85).

11. This is the question we have already encountered when Derrida warns, "the religions for which the Messiah has arrived, where the messianic vocation has already been accomplished, always run the risk of lacking this transcendence of justice and the to-come with respect to totality" (*Taste for the Secret*, 22).

12. See, e.g., "Faith and Knowledge," 16, and *Archive Fever*, 80.

13. "Passions," in *On the Name*, 140–41, n. 10.

14. In my *Insurrection of the Crucified*.

15. Genesis 23:1–20. This piece of land becomes Abraham's burial place as well (Genesis 25:10).

16. Regarding "hauntology," see *Specters of Marx*, 51; regarding the dead, see *Specters of Marx*, xix. Something like the postponement of the eschatological horizon in Derrida compared with Paul is indicated by the way "ghosts" in Derrida refers not only to the already dead but also to the yet not born. This last is not something that comes into view for Paul, given his more immediate horizon of expectation.

17. See, e.g., "Eating Well," in *Points . . .*, esp. 277 ff.

18. See "Faith and Knowledge," 17.

19. *Specters of Marx*, 56 ff.

20. Thus, in "Eating Well," in *Points . . .*, 266.

21. Jacob Taubes avers, "Now I of course am a Paulinist, not a Christian, but a Paulinist" (*Political Theology*, 88).

22. In a certain way, Derrida has flirted with this question even more explicitly, while somewhat deflecting it as well. In an interview, he says, "I am and am not Jewish, and I am and am not Christian," and adds, "because I live in a Christian culture no doubt" (45). "Following Theory," in *life. after. theory*, ed. Michael Payne and John Schad (New York: Continuum, 2003).

23. Although it may be recalled that I have suggested at one or two points that Derrida's reading of Paul may have been too much influenced by Augustine (or even Nietzsche), especially in references to Romans 7.

24. Indeed, it was this book that incited me to undertake even more urgently a more extensive reading of Derrida.

25. Hent deVries has suggested that the promise of deconstruction could be that of a discourse that doubles (shadows and haunts) as much as it respects the formal structure of a traditionally dogmatic, negative, affirmative, hyperbolic, or mystical theology (*Religion and Violence*, 289).

26. Curiously, Derrida pluralizes "Christianities" and "Islams" but not Judaism. *On Cosmopolitanism and Forgiveness*, trans. Mark Dooley and Michael Hughes (New York: Routledge, 2001), 28.

27. See *Negotiations*, 337.

Bibliography

Agamben, Giorgio. *Homo Sacer: Sovereign Power and Bare Life.* Stanford: Stanford University Press, 1998.

———. *Il tempo che resta: Un commento alla Lettera ai Romani.* Toreino: Bollat Boringhieri, 2000.

Arendt, Hannah. *The Human Condition.* Chicago: University of Chicago Press, 1958.

Augustine. *City of God.*

———. Letter 153, written to the magistrate Macedonius. In *From Irenaeus to Grotius,* edited by Oliver O'Donovan and Joan Lockwood O'Donovan. Grand Rapids, Mich.: Eerdmans, 1999.

———. *On the Grace of Christ.* Nicene and Post-Nicene Fathers First Series, Vol. 5.

Badiou, Alain. *Saint Paul: The Foundation of Universalism.* Stanford: Stanford University Press, 2003.

Beardsworth, Richard. *Derrida and the Political.* New York: Routledge, 1996.

Beker, J. Christiaan. *Paul the Apostle: The Triumph of God in Life and Thought.* Philadelphia: Fortress, 1980.

Benjamin, Walter. *Walter Benjamin: Reflections.* Edited by Peter Demetz. New York: Harcourt Brace Jovanovich, 1978.

Bennington, Geoffrey. *Interrupting Derrida.* New York: Routledge, 2000.

Boers, Hendrikus W. *The Justification of the Gentiles.* Peabody, Mass.: Hendrikson, 1994.

———. *Theology out of the Ghetto: A New Testament Exegetical Study Concerning Religious Exclusiveness.* Leiden: E. J. Brill, 1971.

Borradori, Giovanna. *Philosophy in a Time of Terror: Dialogues with Jurgen Habermas and Jacques Derrida.* Chicago: University of Chicago Press, 2003.

Bultmann, Rudolf. *Theology of the New Testament.* Vol. 1. Translated by Kendrick Grobel. New York: Charles Scribner's Sons, 1951.

Calvin, John. *Institutes of the Christian Religion.* Edited by John T. McNeill. Philadelphia: Westminster Press, 1960.

Caputo, John. *The Prayers and Tears of Jacques Derrida: Religion Without Religion.* Bloomington: Indiana University Press, 1997.

Caputo, John, M. Dooley, and M. J. Scanlon, eds. *Questioning God.* Bloomington: Indiana University Press, 2001.

Caputo, John, and M. J. Scanlon, eds. *God, the Gift and Postmodernism.* Bloomington: Indiana University Press, 1999.

Cornell, Druscilla. *The Philosophy of the Limit.* New York: Routledge, 1992.

Derrida, Jacques. *Acts of Literature.* Edited by Derek Attridge. New York: Routledge, 1992.

———. *Acts of Religion.* Edited by Gil Anidjar. New York: Routledge, 2001.

———. *Adieu to Emmanuel Levinas.* Translated by Pascale-Anne Brault and Michael Naas. Stanford: Stanford University Press, 1999.

———. "The Animal That Therefore I Am (More to Follow)." *Critical Inquiry* 28 (2002): 369–418.

———. *Aporias.* Translated by Thomas Dutoit. Stanford: Stanford University Press, 1993.

———. *Archive Fever: A Freudian Impression.* Translated by Eric Prenowitz. Chicago: University of Chicago Press, 1996.

———. *Circumfession: Fifty-nine Periods and Periphrases. Jacques Derrida.* Edited by Geoffrey Bennington and Jacques Derrida. Chicago: University of Chicago Press, 1993.

———. "Deconstruction in America: An Interview with Jacques Derrida." Conducted by James Creech, Peggy Kamuf, and Jane Todd. *Critical Exchange* 17 (1985): 1–33.

———. "Faith and Knowledge: The Two Sources of 'Religion' at the Limits of Reason Alone." In *Religion,* edited by Jacques Derrida and Gianni Vattimo. Stanford: Stanford University Press, 1998.

———. "Following Theory." In *life. after. theory,* edited by Michael Payne and John Schad. New York: Continuum, 2003.

———. *The Force of Law: The "Mystical Foundation of Authority."* 1990. In *Acts of Religion,* edited by Gil Anidjar. New York: Routledge, 2001.

———. *The Gift of Death.* Translated by David Wills. Chicago: University of Chicago Press, 1995.

———. *Given Time: 1. Counterfeit Money.* Translated by Peggy Kamuf. Chicago: University of Chicago Press, 1992.

———. *Glas.* Translated by Jon P. Leavey Jr. and Richard Rand. Lincoln: University of Nebraska Press, 1986.

———. "Hospitality, Justice and Responsibility." Interview. In *Questioning Ethics: Contemporary Debates in Philosophy,* edited by Richard Kearney and Mark Tooley. London: Routledge, 1999.

———. "Letter to a Japanese Friend." In *Derrida and Difference*, edited by David Wood and Robert Bernasconi. Evanston: Northwestern University Press, 1988.

———. "Marx & Sons." In *Ghostly Demarcations: A Symposium on Jacques Derrida's "Specters of Marx,"* edited by Michael Sprinkler. Verso, London, 1999.

———. *Memoires for Paul de Man.* Rev. ed. Translated by Cecile Lindsay, Jonathan Culler, Edwardo Cadava, and Peggy Kamuf. New York: Columbia University Press, 1989.

———. *Monolingualism of the Other.* Translated by Patrick Mensah. Stanford: Stanford University Press, 1998.

———. *Negotiations.* Translated by Elizabeth Rottenberg. Stanford: Stanford University Press, 2001.

———. *Of Hospitality.* 1997. Translated by Rachel Bowlby. Stanford: Stanford University Press, 2000.

———. *Of Spirit: Heidegger and the Question.* Translated by Geoffrey Bennington and Rachel Bowlby. Chicago: University of Chicago Press, 1989.

———. *On Cosmopolitanism and Forgiveness.* Translated by Mark Dooley and Michael Hughes. New York: Routledge, 2001.

———. *On the Name.* Translated by David Wood et al. Stanford: Stanford University Press, 1995.

———. *The Other Heading: Reflections on Today's Europe.* Translated by Michael B. Naas and Pascale-Anne Brault. Bloomington: Indiana University Press, 1992.

———. "Performative Powerlessness—A Response to Simon Critchley." *Constellations* 7, no. 4 (2000): 466–68.

———. *Points . . . : Interviews 1974–1994.* Translated by Peggy Kamuf. Stanford: Stanford University Press, 1995.

———. *Politics of Friendship.* Translated by George Collins. London: Verso, 1997.

———. *Postcard: From Socrates to Freud and Beyond.* Translated by Alan Bass. Chicago: University of Chicago Press, 1987.

———. "Remarks on Deconstruction and Pragmatism." In *Deconstruction and Pragmatism: Simon Critchley, Jacques Derrida, Ernesto Laclau and Richard Rorty*, edited by Chantal Mouffe. New York: Routledge, 1996.

———. "A Silkworm of One's Own." In *Acts of Religion*, edited by Gil Anidjar. New York: Routledge, 2001.

———. *Specters of Marx: The State of the Debt, the Work of Mourning, and the New International.* Translated by Peggy Kamuf. New York: Routledge, 1994.

———. *Spurs Nietzsche's Styles.* Translated by Barbara Harlow. Chicago: University of Chicago Press, 1979.

———. "To Forgive." In *Questioning God*, edited by John Caputo, M. Dooley, and M. J. Scalon. Bloomington: Indiana University Press, 2001.

———. "What Is a Relevant Translation?" *Critical Inquiry* 27 (2001): 174–200.

———. *Without Alibi*. Translated by Peggy Kamuf. Stanford: Stanford University Press, 2002.

———. *Writing and Difference*. Translated by Alan Bass. Chicago: University of Chicago Press, 1978.

Derrida, Jacques, and Maurizio Ferraris. *A Taste for the Secret*. Translated by Giacomo Donis. Cambridge, UK: Polity Press, 2001.

Derrida, Jacques, and Elisabeth Roudinescu. *For What Tomorrow . . . : A Dialogue*. Translated by Jeff Fort. Stanford: Stanford University Press, 2004.

deVries, Hent. *Philosophy and the Turn to Religion*. Baltimore: Johns Hopkins University Press, 1999.

———. *Religion and Violence: Philosophical Perspectives from Kant to Derrida*. Baltimore: Johns Hopkins University Press, 2002.

Elliot, Neil. *Liberating Paul*. Maryknoll, N.Y.: Orbis, 1994.

Georgi, Dieter. *Theocracy in Paul's Praxis and Theology*. 1987. Minneapolis, Minn.: Augsburg Fortress, 1991. Originally appeared in *Theokratie*, edited by Jacob Taubes. Paderborn: Ferdinand Schöningh, 1987.

Hegel, G. W. F. *The Spirit of Christianity and Its Fate*. In *Early Theological Writings*. Translated by T. M. Knox. Philadelphia: University of Pennsylvania Press, 1971.

Horner, Robyn. *Rethinking God as Gift: Marion, Derrida, and the Limits of Phenomenology*. New York: Fordham University Press, 2001.

Horsley, Richard A., ed. *Paul and Empire: Religion and Power in Roman Imperial Society*. Harrisburg: Trinity Press, 1997.

———. *Paul and Politics*. Harrisburg: Trinity International Press, 2000.

Jennings, Theodore W. *Beyond Theism*. Oxford: Oxford University Press, 1985.

———. *The Insurrection of the Crucified: The Gospel of Mark as Theological Manifesto*. Chicago: Exploration Press, 2003.

———, ed. *Text and Logos: The Humanistic Interpretation of the New Testament*. Atlanta: Scholars Press, 1990.

———. "Theological Anthropology." In *Theology and the Human Spirit: Essays in Honor of Perry LeFevre*, edited by Theodore W. Jennings Jr. and Susan Brooks Thistlethwaite. Chicago: Exploration Press, 1994.

Kamuf, Peggy. "Violence, Identity, Self-Determination, and the Question of Justice: On *Specters of Marx*." In *Violence, Identity and Self-Determination*, edited by Hent deVries and Samuel Weber. Stanford: Stanford University Press, 1997.

Kant, Immanuel. *Perpetual Peace and Other Essays*. Translated by Ted Humphrey. Indianapolis: Hackett Publishing, 1993.

Käsemann, Ernst. *Commentary on Romans*. Grand Rapids, Mich.: Eerdmans, 1980.

———. *New Testament Questions of Today.* Philadelphia: Fortress, 1969.

Kierkegaard, Søren. *Works of Love.* Translated by Howard and Edna Hong. New York: Harper and Row, 1962.

Kristeva, Julia. *Intimate Revolt: The Powers and Limits of Psychoanalysis.* Vol. 2. Translated by Jeanine Herman. New York: Columbia University Press, 2002.

———. *Strangers to Ourselves.* Translated by Leon S. Roudiez. New York: Columbia University Press, 1991.

Lacan, Jacques. *Ethics of Psychoanalysis.* Translated by Dennis Porter. New York: Norton, 1992.

Levinas, Emmanuel. *Difficult Freedom: Essays on Judaism.* Translated by Sean Hand. Baltimore: Johns Hopkins University Press, 1990.

———. *Ethics and Infinity.* Pittsburgh: Duquesne University Press, 1985.

———. *God, Death, and Time.* Stanford: Stanford University Press, 2000.

———. *Of God Who Comes to Mind.* Translated by Betticia Bergo. Stanford: Stanford University Press, 1998.

———. *Otherwise than Being, or Beyond Essence.* Translated by Alphonso Lingis. Pittsburgh: Duquesne University Press, 1981.

———. "Philosophy and the Infinite." Text and commentary. In *To the Other*, by Adriaan Peperzak. West Lafayette, Ind.: Purdue University Press, 1993.

———. *Totality and Infinity.* Translated by Alfonso Lingis. Pittsburgh: Duquesne University Press, 1969.

Lyotard, Jean-Françoise, and Eberhard Gruber. *The Hyphen: Between Judaism and Christianity.* Translated by Pascale-Anne Brault and Michael Naas. New York: Humanity Books, 1998.

Marion, Jean-Luc. *Being Given: Toward a Phenomenology of Givenness.* Translated by Jeffrey Kosky. Stanford: Stanford University Press, 2002.

Milbank, John. *Being Reconciled: Ontology and Pardon.* New York: Routledge, 2003.

Miranda, José Porfirio. *Marx and the Bible: A Critique of the Philosophy of Oppression.* Maryknoll, N.Y.: Orbis, 1974.

Mauss, Marcel. *The Gift.* Translated by W. D. Halls. New York: Norton, 1990.

Nanos, Mark. *The Mystery of Romans.* Minneapolis: Augsburg Fortress, 1996.

Nietzsche, Friedrich. *Daybreak: Thoughts on the Prejudices of Morality.* In *The Cambridge Texts in the History of Philosophy*, edited by R. J. Hollingdale. Cambridge: Cambridge, 1997.

———. *Twilight of the Gods and The Antichrist.* Translated by R. J. Hollingdale. London: Penguin Books, 1990.

Stendahl, Krister. "The Apostle Paul and the Introspective Conscience of the West." In *Paul Among Jews and Gentiles, and Other Essays.* Philadelphia: Fortress, 1976.

Stowers, Stanley. *A Re-Reading of Romans: Justice, Jews and Gentiles.* New Haven, Conn.: Yale University Press, 1994.

Tamez, Elsa. *The Amnesty of Grace: Justification by Faith from a Latin American Perspective.* Translated by Sharon H. Ringe. Nashville: Abingdon, 1993.

Taubes, Jacob. *The Political Theology of Paul.* Translated by Dana Hollander. Edited by Aleida Assmann and Jan Assmann. Stanford: Stanford University Press, 2004. Translation of *Die Politische Theologie des Paulus.* Edited by Aleida Assmann and Jan Assmann. Munich: Wilhelm Fink Verlag, 1993.

Ward, Graham. *Barth, Derrida and the Language of Theology.* Cambridge: Cambridge University Press, 1995.

Wolff, Hans Walter. *Anthropology of the Old Testament.* Philadelphia: Fortress, 1974.

Žižek, Slavoj. *The Fragile Absolute, or, Why Is the Christian Legacy Worth Fighting For?* New York: Verso, 2000.

———. *The Puppet and the Dwarf: The Perverse Core of Christianity.* Cambridge: MIT Press, 2003.

Index

Cultural Memory in the Present

Timothy J. Reiss, *Against Autonomy: Global Dialectics of Cultural Exchange*

Hent de Vries and Samuel Weber, eds., *Religion and Media*

Niklas Luhmann, *Theories of Distinction: Redescribing the Descriptions of Modernity*, ed. and introd. William Rasch

Johannes Fabian, *Anthropology with an Attitude: Critical Essays*

Michel Henry, *I Am the Truth: Toward a Philosophy of Christianity*

Gil Anidjar, *"Our Place in Al-Andalus": Kabbalah, Philosophy, Literature in Arab-Jewish Letters*

Hélène Cixous and Jacques Derrida, *Veils*

F. R. Ankersmit, *Historical Representation*

F. R. Ankersmit, *Political Representation*

Elissa Marder, *Dead Time: Temporal Disorders in the Wake of Modernity (Baudelaire and Flaubert)*

Reinhart Koselleck, *The Practice of Conceptual History: Timing History, Spacing Concepts*

Niklas Luhmann, *The Reality of the Mass Media*

Hubert Damisch, *A Childhood Memory by Piero della Francesca*

Hubert Damisch, *A Theory of /Cloud/: Toward a History of Painting*

Jean-Luc Nancy, *The Speculative Remark (One of Hegel's Bons Mots)*

Jean-François Lyotard, *Soundproof Room: Malraux's Anti-Aesthetics*

Jan Patočka, *Plato and Europe*

Hubert Damisch, *Skyline: The Narcissistic City*

Isabel Hoving, *In Praise of New Travelers: Reading Caribbean Migrant Women Writers*

Richard Rand, ed., *Futures: Of Derrida*

William Rasch, *Niklas Luhmann's Modernity: The Paradox of System Differentiation*

Jacques Derrida and Anne Dufourmantelle, *Of Hospitality*

Jean-François Lyotard, *The Confession of Augustine*

Kaja Silverman, *World Spectators*

Samuel Weber, *Institution and Interpretation: Expanded Edition*

Jeffrey S. Librett, *The Rhetoric of Cultural Dialogue: Jews and Germans in the Epoch of Emancipation*

Ulrich Baer, *Remnants of Song: Trauma and the Experience of Modernity in Charles Baudelaire and Paul Celan*

Samuel C. Wheeler III, *Deconstruction as Analytic Philosophy*

David S. Ferris, *Silent Urns: Romanticism, Hellenism, Modernity*

Rodolphe Gasché, *Of Minimal Things: Studies on the Notion of Relation*